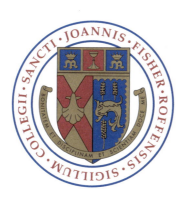

Courting
the
Media

Courting the Media

Public Relations for the Accused and the Accuser

Margaret A. Mackenzie

Westport, Connecticut
London

Library of Congress Cataloging-in-Publication Data

Mackenzie, Margaret A., 1951–
    Courting the media : public relations for the accused and the accuser / Margaret A. Mackenzie.
        p.   cm.
    Includes bibliographical references and index.
    ISBN 0–275–99125–3 (alk. paper)
    1. Public relations and law—United States.   I. Title.
    KF390.5.P8M33   2007
    343.7309′98–dc22   2006025920

British Library Cataloguing in Publication Data is available.

Library of Congress Catalog Card Number: 2006025920
ISBN: 0–275–99125–3

First published in 2007

Praeger Publishers, 88 Post Road West, Westport, CT 06881
An imprint of Greenwood Publishing Group, Inc.
www.praeger.com

Printed in the United States of America

The paper used in this book complies with the
Permanent Paper Standard issued by the National
Information Standards Organization (Z39.48–1984).

10 9 8 7 6 5 4 3 2 1

This book is dedicated to the lawyers who believed in my media relations skills and strategies. I was and am privileged to work with them and their clients. Several of them and the clients we represented are part of this book. I acknowledge and thank Richard Ancowitz, Patricia Cashman, Johnnie L. Cochran Jr. (1937–2005), Roy B. "Skip" Dalton Jr., Philip Damashek (1940–2006), Dennis Donnelly, Joseph DuRocher (Orange County, Florida, Public Defender 1980–2000), Don Lykkebak, Cheney Mason, Michael Maher (President ATLA, 1992–1994), Mark O'Mara, Will Techmeier and Harvey Weitz.

I am also especially grateful to George Diaz, Alice Mackenzie, Jim Cypher, Alice Peck and Hilary Claggett for supporting me and making the publication of this book possible.

Contents

Introduction

I am not a lawyer. I advise lawyers and their clients on how to conduct effective public relations to defend themselves in the press and to reach their public through the media. After nearly twenty years as a public relations professional, I am convinced that in certain cases lawyers must represent their clients in the court of public opinion as well as in a court of law. In fact, what happens before an accused person's first courtroom appearance may be equally important to obtaining the most successful outcome possible for the accused or the accusers.

Since 1987, I have provided public relations direction and advice to lawyers. I've also developed and carried out media campaigns to help clients represented by criminal defense and civil trial lawyers. Throughout this book, I will write about lawyers, not attorneys. The difference was once defined by Joseph D. Jamail Jr., a Texas trial lawyer who in 1985 won a $10.53 billion judgment from Pennzoil, a company that had caused a devastating oil spill in Alaska. Mr. Jamail insisted on being called a lawyer. The difference, he said, was, "I think that the lawyer is somebody that would bleed for his client; an attorney is someone [who . . . sits] on his fat ass and collects fees."[1]

The field of public relations for the accused and the accuser is very different from the public relations arena of representing corporations, companies or individuals who are involved in purely civil litigation. The difference between researching and consulting on media bias for a lawsuit defending Major League Baseball (which I did in 1990) or advising an international corporation in a legal dispute with a large city over the performance of a desalination plant (which I did in 2004) and representing men, women and teenagers accused of crimes is the level of personal involvement with people in crisis.

Another significant characteristic of media relations for the accused and the accusers is budgetary. The majority of people arrested for crimes in the United States do not have the resources to pay both an experienced and expensive criminal defense lawyer and a media relations expert, even though media relations may become critical to the outcome of their defense. In the area of civil trial law, the client is not paying a fee to the lawyer for anything, least of all media relations. Therefore, in most cases, it is up to the lawyer to see the value of media relations and budget for that expense just as he would for the expert services of a forensic expert or an engineer.

A question of ethics arises here. Are there cases where the importance of media relations is so great that it is unethical for the lawyer not to employ media relations services for the benefit of her client? In Chapter 5, "The Face of a Murder Suspect," I argue that media relations can save a client's life. A legal system that gives media relations expertise to law enforcement and to the state prosecutors but not to the accused is unfair and unethical. I hope that this book will open the minds of lawyers and charge them with the responsibility to change this aspect of our nation's justice system.

When the accused or the accuser uses media relations, it is always a reactive campaign, usually a response to a situation that was not desired, often unexpected, and one that the private individual wishes he or she did not have to undertake or fund. Conducting media relations for the accused and the accusers is always highly personal. To succeed in this specialized profession, a publicist must be willing to work closely with people who are often in the worst situation of their lives. Whether they are accused of a crime with a life-changing penalty or they have been seriously injured, these clients (and those around them) are usually suffering. To effectively represent these people and their families, the media specialist must earn their trust.

I spend time with the families of the accused in their homes. I visit and correspond with the accused in jail. I delve into the personal lives of the accused and the injured. They invite me to their weddings and funerals, and they continue to send Christmas cards twenty years after their case has closed. A good lawyer recognizes the situation whereby a client requires and will benefit from media relations expertise.

Johnnie L. Cochran Jr. was one of these lawyers. He was one of the best-known and most successful lawyers in America. Even before his defense of O.J. Simpson became the "Trial of the Century," Johnnie Cochran represented injured people who were both victims and accusers, including several people who were beaten by the police in Los Angeles.

There is an exclusive organization of lawyers in America, known as the Inner Circle of Advocates. Their 100 members are among the most successful trial lawyers in the world. They have handled personal injury, wrongful death and other civil lawsuits against local and state governments and some of America's largest corporations that resulted in multimillion and multibillion dollars in damages for their clients.

Mr. Cochran was invited to join the Inner Circle, not because of his success in defending the accused, but because of his success in winning civil lawsuits. When I first met him in 1999, I instantly felt the charisma that I first saw on television when he represented Mr. Simpson in 1995. We first worked together to publicize a $2.55-million settlement in a high-profile civil case resolved in Buffalo, New York, *The Estate of Cynthia Wiggins v. Pyramid Co., et al.* In this case, a young woman was forced to cross a busy highway on a snowy winter day because buses from her poor minority neighborhood were not allowed to enter the parking lot of an upscale mall. She was hit and died from her injuries.

After spending some time with Johnnie Cochran on marketing projects for his national firm and the New York office of The Cochran Firm, I recognized that his success in the courtroom was rooted in the genuine warmth and love he had for people and his unwavering commitment to justice. He also knew that his representation of both the celebrity and the common man was most effective when he defended them in the legal *and* public arenas. When I asked him to write a foreword for this book, he generously agreed. Even when he was dying of a brain tumor in late 2004, he was caring enough to provide me with his thoughts that he asked me to incorporate into an introduction. He wrote the following:

> The power of the media in our society cannot be overemphasized or under-estimated. As the power of the media grows, the need for media relations specialists in high-profile cases grows as well. As public interest in court cases grows, so too does media involvement and coverage. A smart lawyer recognizes that the media play a significant role in swaying public opinion in high-profile cases and, accordingly, looks to an expert like Marti Mackenzie to shape perceptions in a manner consistent with his or her view of the case. Without experts like her to assist them, lawyers in high-profile cases do their clients a tremendous and often irreparable disservice.[2]

Media relations are not just for the rich and powerful. This book introduces the men, women and families who garnered headlines for the real crimes they committed or who were victims of untruths and unwarranted prosecution. Each chapter recalls unique media relations challenges. With the help of a media relations expert, the accused and their lawyers fought the often one-sided and biased portraits that police and prosecutors tried to create.

A skillful media relations outreach also gets results in civil lawsuits. A $100-million verdict can be reported in one New York City newspaper, or it can be in five newspapers, on seven television stations that night, and a radio talk show the next morning, enhancing the lawyer's reputation tenfold and educating the public about the negligence or wrongdoing of the defendant, who can be successfully sued and judged by the injured people.

There are many public relations professionals who represent defendants in corporate litigation and those who advise wealthy clients whose court proceedings make headlines. Rarely do the criminally accused or their criminal defense lawyers recognize the critical need for media relations expertise in defending their clients. More common are personal injury lawyers who employ an expert to handle the media when they file a high-profile lawsuit accusing an individual, a government entity or a corporation of harming their client. When they do, the work of a media specialist can have a significant impact on the outcome of the case or influence the long-term effect of the result through media coverage.

Media attention can be intense and intrusive. The sole practitioner lawyer who is court-appointed to represent an indigent client in a high-profile case often prevents the client from giving any interviews. This lawyer is accepting a limited fee and has a limited budget for defending the indigent client accused of a heinous crime. In some cases, the lawyer—to the detriment of the accused—may ask for a gag order because he is overwhelmed by media interest.

I first became aware of the power of the press when I served as Executive Director of the American Civil Liberties Union of Mississippi in 1979. The ACLU is aggressive both in responding to the media and proactively drawing attention to the civil liberties issues that are the heart of the organization's work. When the ALCU of Mississippi filed a lawsuit on behalf of people whose civil liberties had been violated, the standard procedure was to hold a press conference to announce the lawsuit and to address the issues.

ACLU activities and lawsuits regularly made the front page of the local newspapers and the nightly television news. When we represented Iranian students expelled for demonstrating during the 1980 hostage crisis, the national media came to cover the story. During the press conferences I called, the staff lawyer and cooperating legal counsel made statements and answered questions. As executive director, I made opening remarks and also answered questions.

The news broadcasts and print media often limited their coverage to my statements. I realized that the lawyers were usually too verbose and legalistic in their statements. For this reason, the media preferred my plain talk and the explanations of the ACLU position that I provided; I was more quotable than the lawyers.

Following my ACLU work, I became a fundraiser for the Orlando, Florida, PBS and NPR affiliate. Producing promotional spots for major donors further honed my skills in copywriting and the on-air delivery of a message. Six years later, in 1987, I founded my public relations firm with the purpose of providing ethical and effective alternatives to lawyers who refused to advertise their services but who were losing business to lawyers who advertised.

In 1987, lawyer marketing and advertising had been in existence for only ten years. The U.S. Supreme Court ruling that opened the doors for lawyers and other professionals to advertise their services was handed down June 27, 1977. In 1976, John Bates and Van O'Steen, who owned a legal clinic in Phoenix, placed a newspaper ad promoting their affordable legal services and were punished by the state bar. They lost the first round of their lawsuit challenging the Arizona Supreme Court's disciplinary rule prohibiting lawyers from advertising. However, their appeal to the U.S. Supreme Court, arguing that lawyers had a First Amendment right to advertise their services, was successful.[3]

Many trial lawyers handling personal injury and wrongful death cases used this ruling as a springboard to aggressive advertising campaigns. There were also lawyers who felt that advertising was detrimental to their professional image. One lawyer in South Florida ran a television ad in which he rode around on a tricycle, fell over and then delivered the message, "If you are injured, call us, and we'll get you monetary damages."

When I founded my firm, Professional Profiles, my first client was a successful trial lawyer who abhorred advertising, but wanted to compete for clients who had been injured. I also began to represent criminal defense lawyers. My media relations work for these lawyers was highly effective in raising their profiles, both within the legal community that referred cases to them and among the general population who hired lawyers.

For the first two years, my media relations assistance was proactive, promoting a lawyer's expertise or announcing significant verdicts or settlements. I sent out releases about new law firm partnerships and identified issues and opportunities for lawyers to speak about those issues. One of my first clients was an Orlando, Florida, criminal defense lawyer, Donald Lykkebak. Although he made a good living defending people arrested for use of illegal drugs, he also embraced the issue of legalizing marijuana and decriminalizing other drugs. I developed a public relations campaign for him on these issues. He was interviewed by newspapers, wrote essays and spoke to organizations and clubs.

In 1987, when I recruited my first law firm client, a firm that included Mel Martinez, former HUD Secretary, a cabinet member under President George W. Bush, and now a U.S. Senator from Florida, lawyers were rarely proactive with the media regarding their clients. By the mid-1990s I no longer limited my public relations services to creating an ethical alternative to advertising; I simply produced advertising campaigns that were ethical. My firm regularly published newsletters for personal injury law firms; created other marketing tools, including brochures, direct mailings and print ads; and also produced television campaigns in the form of public service announcements. I also became an expert in high-profile case management.

After working with the Humphrey family, a case that is detailed in Chapter 5, "The Face of a Murder Suspect," I became widely recognized for my expertise in public relations work for the accused.[4] I also continued to use my skills helping civil trial lawyers gain media coverage for the lawsuits they filed accusing companies of injuring their clients and the outstanding verdicts and settlements they obtained on behalf of injured people. I knew that there were far too many below-average lawyers who took on personal injury matters and did not invest the time and funds required to investigate fully and litigate on behalf of their injured clients. I told my clients that they had an ethical obligation to let the public know who the best lawyer was to handle a case.

Lawyers who hire public relations firms that may have a wealth of experience in representing corporations, small businesses or other professionals (like doctors) may find their clients misrepresented. A public relations generalist may conduct inappropriate media relations and the campaign may backfire, as it did for a Wisconsin firm who once obtained a $25 million settlement from a power company for a badly injured boy.[5]

Providing public relations for the accused and the accusers is specialized work. The demands of representing lawyers and their clients cannot be overestimated. The stakes are high, and knowledge of the legal system is essential. In criminal cases, the accused may face life in prison or even the death penalty. Inappropriate media relations may result in coverage that harms the accused or the accuser's image and demonizes his willingness to go public with a story. For this reason, many lawyers choose to do nothing—they don't respond to the media or allow media access to their clients. In this way, the lawyer gives the media power to the prosecution and police, who are always willing to discuss a case with the press.

After working with small law firms and individual lawyers who wanted to conduct media relations, I realized that just knowing the tactics is not enough. Until a lawyer has worked with the media on several high-profile cases and gained the experience needed for a successful media relations campaign, there are numerous ways the lawyer can mishandle and overlook media opportunities.

When a lawyer files an unusual case, or defends or prosecutes a high-profile client, the media will cover it and the public will follow it. The media reach the same people who will sit on the jury or even on the bench. This book is written for those who are the subjects in high-profile cases, the lawyers who work on those cases, and the people who follow them.

One

The Power of the Press

The field of public relations for the accused and the accusers is very different from the public relations arena of representing corporations, companies or individuals who are involved in purely civil litigation. When the accused uses media relations, it is always a reactive campaign, usually a response to a situation that was not desired, often unexpected and one that the private individual wishes he or she did not have to undertake or fund.

When people entangled in lawsuits or criminal trials speak for themselves or their families, the media coverage may well influence their community and the nation. The depiction of a suspect or defendant by *CNN*, the nightly news, *The New York Times* or the local home town paper—the court of public opinion—even before a trial or a conviction, will frequently influence what happens in front of a judge or jury. Private industry and corporations, as well as prosecutors, have long used media consultants.

Most district attorneys and many police departments have public information officers. To level the playing field in today's judicial system, all lawyers need to be ready to advise and represent their clients before the media as well as the judge and jury. Not only can this be done ethically, but given what defendants are up against today, I believe it is unethical to ignore the media when the other side is using every possible media contact and opportunity to taint the image of the accused or the victim. This does not mean that the lawyer must respond directly to the media. In some cases, it is far more important for the accused to respond personally with the guidance of the lawyer and the expertise of a media specialist who works in tandem with the lawyer.

Professor Stephen Gillers, who is the author of *Regulations of Lawyers: Problems of Law and Ethics* and one of the leading experts on lawyer ethics,[1] stops short of using the ethical argument, but says, "The lawyer has an obligation to consider the usefulness of public relations and to give his client advice. He may certainly advise whether the client is legally permitted to do something by way of publicity even if the lawyer cannot be an active participant to it."[2]

Public relations in the legal arena became a recognized field after the U.S. Supreme Court opened the door for lawyers to advertise with the *Bates* decision in 1977.[3] Fourteen years later, in 1991, the Supreme Court's decision in *Gentile v. State Bar of Nevada* specifically addressed media relations on behalf of the accused. The majority opinion was written by Justice Anthony and challenges lawyers to recognize the court of public opinion.[4]

Dominic Gentile, a Nevada criminal defense lawyer, had been sanctioned by the state bar from holding a press conference in 1988 after his client was charged with owning a company whose vaults were used in an illegal drug operation.

Gentile was reacting to the adverse publicity that police had generated about his client, who was completely innocent and being used as a scapegoat. Six months later, Gentile's client was found not-guilty. However, regarding the press conference, Gentile appealed the Nevada Bar Association's disciplinary action against him and its Rule 177 that prohibited a lawyer from making extrajudicial statements to the press. He appealed to the Nevada Supreme Court. When that court rejected his argument that Rule 177 prevented him from exercising his right of free speech, he appealed to the U.S. Supreme Court.

Since the time Dominic Gentile appeared before the Supreme Court, he has met four of the Justices who ruled in the case. "The last one I met was Justice Kennedy. He thanked me for standing up and making a contribution, for helping to change the prevailing attitude."[5]

The decision in *Gentile v. Nevada State Bar* cleared the way for lawyers to defend their clients in the court of public opinion through media relations. Justice Anthony Kennedy wrote in his majority opinion that "an attorney's duties do not begin inside the courtroom door. He or she cannot ignore the practical implications of a legal proceeding for the client.... A defense attorney may pursue lawful strategies to obtain dismissal of an indictment or reduction of charges, including an attempt to demonstrate in the court of public opinion that the client does not deserve to be tried."[6]

However, even before Gentile, there were lawyers who saw the importance of leveling the playing field when district attorneys began to use every available means, including the media, to prosecute accused people.[7]

During a seminar for lawyers at The Florida Bar Association Convention in 1989, several lawyers commented on their stance on media relations in high-profile cases. One of them was a criminal defense lawyer from Miami, Albert J. Krieger, who is a founding member and former president of the National

Association of Criminal Defense Lawyers (NACDL) and past-chair of the American Bar Association's Criminal Justice Section. Krieger has successfully defended those accused of white-collar crimes and handled numerous high-profile cases for notorious clients, including accused drug smugglers, accused mobsters John Gotti and Sr. Joseph Bonnano, as well as fellow lawyers. While he was in Tampa defending a lawyer accused of perjury, the *St. Petersburg Times* described Krieger as someone "considered by many [to be] the dean of the nation's defense lawyers."[8]

At the 1989 seminar, Krieger "agreed that defenders have to try to balance an inherent media advantage enjoyed by prosecutors."[9]

> I can remember when major criminal indictments were one page.... The indictments that come out today are novels, designed to poison jury pools by getting prosecutors' views into the public record. But if that's the game, I'll play.... There's lots I can say that is not a clear and present danger to the fairness of the trial. To stick your head in the sand and not say anything is an abdication of your responsibility to the client.[10]

Fifteen years later, Krieger is eighty-two years old and still actively trying cases. He believes that prosecutors use the media by preparing "speaking indictments." He says of his comments in 1989, "I don't want to play the game anymore. I want the government and the police restricted in reasonable fashions."[11]

However, he readily admits that "since I made that statement, the situation has gotten worse, not better. The government has perfected its technique of creating an indictment that is its final argument to the jury. As a result, it contains matters that are much different from the simple statements of alleged facts and law that puts the defendant on notice of the charges. This gives the government a literal summation for the jury to take back to the jury room. Most judges direct defense lawyers to give the jury a 'theory of the case' and routinely restrict it to one paragraph."[12]

Krieger acknowledges that "most lawyers neglect or ignore the damaging effect of publicity." Albert Krieger was a legal pioneer in media relations for the accused; unlike a majority of lawyers, he was media savvy and capable of ensuring that the pretrial publicity about his client was balanced. Today, he proposes that lawyers regularly file motions to strike "surplusage" and rein in the current loose standards of due process that permit such "speaking indictments" (see Chapter 12).[13]

Because lawyers usually want as much control possible over their defense of an accused person, the majority who engage in media relations do it themselves. Lawyers who recognize the value of an expert may hire a public relations professional. However, there are few in the publicity field who specialize in criminal defense or personal injury law. When lawyers use a publicist who lacks experience and knowledge of the legal process, the media relations campaign may backfire.

There are lawyers who have developed the expertise to handle public relations for their clients as effectively as they represent them in the courtroom. However, these lawyers are few and far between.

A lawyer may sometimes employ effective campaigns and handle media opportunities in his client's best interests. However, media relations work can be labor-intensive and time-consuming. Few lawyers can both do their job in the legal arena and handle the media in a high-profile case. Many lawyers will ignore the media because they do not have the time or they do not use their resources or their client's. Lawyers need to understand the power of the press, how to handle media interest and how to assist the accused and the accusers in developing and executing a media strategy to ensure that they are represented as fairly and as soon as possible after they become the suspect or the accused.

There is always an ethical response that a lawyer representing an accused person can make to a media inquiry. Although most bar associations no longer have blanket restrictions about speaking to the media on behalf of a client, there are high-profile cases when judges may impose a gag order. Yet, by the time such an order is in place, police and prosecutors have likely already had their say in the local press. The defense lawyer must be prepared to make a public statement on behalf of his client before a gag order or to use the open courtroom to raise questions about the accusations against his client, as I show in Chapter 8, when I discuss what the lawyer for basketball star Kobe Bryant did when he was charged with the rape of a hotel clerk.

To understand clearly how a media relations campaign affects public opinion, it is critical to recognize how our government has used the media to promote its agenda. In 1917, President Woodrow Wilson created the Committee on Public Information, headed by a former journalist, George Creel. Its purpose was to convince the American public to support our entry in World War I. Also on that committee was Edward Bernays, known as "the father of pubic relations." Their work was overwhelmingly successful, involving media relations, advertising and short speeches written to promote the war and delivered by "Four Minute Men," who traveled the country tailoring their appearances to different communities. A similar office was established prior to World War II, called the Office of War Information.[14]

This bit of public relations history was included in an article published in *Newsday*, a few months after 9/11.[15] The author, John Hanc, compared the World War I propaganda campaign to the efforts by President George W. Bush's administration to justify a war against Iraq.

According to *USA Today*, on November 30, 2005, the *Los Angeles Times* published an article revealing that the U.S. military paid $6 million to the Lincoln Group, a public relations firm, to plant favorable articles about the American military occupation of Iraq.[16] Granted, these payments were made to Iraqi journalists and ran in Iraqi newspapers. However, a *USA Today/CNN/*Gallup Poll in mid-December 2005 showed that almost three-quarters of Americans think that this secret government public relations effort is wrong.[17]

Government funding of media relations expertise is a budget item in police departments and district attorneys' offices in this country. Media relations experts also play a significant role in marketing products and services of corporations. When a corporation is the target of a lawsuit, it employs media relations professionals to disseminate its position and defend its business profile.

When the police arrest someone in a high-profile case or when the district attorney charges, indicts and prosecutes someone in a newsworthy case, they issue media releases and hold press conferences. They work behind the scenes to cultivate relations with the press that are useful when it's time to announce an arrest, release inflammatory records of evidence, and keep the public aware of the charges against the accused.

What about the accused? Every person criminally prosecuted in America is guaranteed a lawyer: "If you cannot afford a lawyer, one will be appointed for you." Police and prosecutors create and use media opportunities to sway public opinion from the time a person is arrested until a sentence is handed down from the judge. When someone is publicly accused in a press conference and then often persecuted and crucified by the media, there is no guaranteed representation to refute the public allegations by lawyers defending the accused.

State and district attorney offices have public information officers on staff to advise their lawyers and handle the media. Public defenders do not. There is a difference between these government prosecutors and other government agencies that use media relations to promote their agendas. Prosecutors are lawyers first and government employees second. There are professional codes of ethics and regulations that govern lawyers in addressing media relations and the release of any information about their investigation and prosecution. However, the police and other law enforcement agencies will have already worked with the media when an arrest is made, and much of their media relations may be "off the record."

Although it is still an exception, not the norm, criminal defense lawyers in the private sector increasingly use the help of a media specialist when the client can afford to pay. I have been privileged to work with some of the best lawyers in America. There are also lawyers who have a better grasp of media relations than the majority of their peers, and are by their nature more skilled in media relations. In some cases, the accused will be his own best spokesperson—especially if he is counseled appropriately by a media expert working under the supervision of the defense lawyer.

The best criminal defense lawyers know when to hire a media expert to ensure the best possible result for the accused. At a minimum, criminal defense lawyers need to become better informed, more educated and trained to practice effective media relations on behalf of their clients. All lawyers need to be ready to represent clients in the court of public opinion.

Before the advent of television, newspapers and radio were the medium for coverage of high-profile crimes. An early example of widespread media coverage in a particular region occurred in the1920s, when there were eleven New York daily newspapers and four additional papers in Brooklyn. The news business was becoming increasingly competitive, especially with the growing market for radio. Then, as now, reporting crimes, investigations and prosecutions helped to sell newspapers. In 1924, readers followed news reports of robberies carried out by a woman, Celia Cooney. Although her stickups were relatively small crimes, her gender made big news. She was eventually caught and served seven years in prison.[18]

On a national level, the kidnapping of the Lindbergh baby in 1932 captivated the country, and the media coverage was intense throughout the investigation, when the ransom money used was traced, leading to the arrest of Bruno Hauptmann. During 1934, the media reported on the trial and evidence from the crude ladder and handwriting samples taken from the accused. Finally, after several unsuccessful appeals, the media covered the execution of Hauptmann in 1936.[19]

In the 1950s, courtroom dramas were a fixture on television. I grew up wanting to be a lawyer after watching *Perry Mason*. Shows about law enforcement and even white-collar crime have been popular since the same era. For more than three generations of jurors, practical information about police actions and the investigation and prosecution of people and their defense have entertained the general public and sold newspapers. An early reality show was *Cops*, that showed the arrests of real people; *CSI* details the science of investigations. Among the dozens of courtroom dramas, there's the long-running *Law & Order* and a new show in 2006 called *Justice* that pits the media strategies of the prosecution against the media skills of a high-profile criminal defense firm.

In June 1980, *CNN* began broadcasting and gave the public the ability to watch live court proceedings.[20] In 1991, I was watching *CNN* on television while working out on a stair master at my fitness center and saw the jury announce a not guilty verdict in the rape trial of William Kennedy Smith (see Chapter 11 regarding the use of a publicist by the Kennedy family).

On October 3, 1995, viewers could tune into the O.J. Simpson trial and watch as the jury returned with a not guilty decision on either *CNN* or *CourtTV*, which went on air in 1994. Each year, millions of viewers follow a wide array of high-profile trials, from a teacher's sex with her student, the Andrea Yates murder trial, to many of the other cases reviewed in this book.

A good lawyer recognizes the case and the client who needs and will benefit from media relations expertise. If the media don't call, lawyers may need to be proactive and draw attention to the client's case. Lawyers who respect and understand media relations represent their clients in every venue and prepare them for interviews.

I have always maintained that public relations results in a high-profile case have an effect both internally and externally, both on the accused and in the court of public opinion. Dominic Gentile agrees.[21]

> When someone is accused of a crime for the first time, there is an immediate loss of support, of what I call emotional capital. Particularly in a white-collar case, an accused person needs his lawyer to shore up his spirit. People who slapped you on the back before you were accused; their arms suddenly grow too long to reach out to you. A lawyer absolutely must be willing to do something so that the defendant knows they have support. That is a PR effort.[22]

Unlike corporations, lawyers do not carry out their professional responsibilities under the largely unwritten rules of business; they are ethically and legally required to consider how the consequences of media relations affect their clients. However, when accused people present their side of the story in a succinct and positive way as soon as possible after they are associated with a crime, it affects them on every level, from self-esteem in the courtroom, increased confidence in legal proceedings, preservation and rehabilitation of their reputation, to a more effective defense. It's not just about telling the truth; it's about how you tell it.

Two
The Problem with Celebrities

The difference between fame and celebrity is continuity. A person can be famous for the Warholian fifteen minutes by winning the lottery or having seven children at once. Celebrities are widely known for long periods of time—once a celebrity, always a celebrity. They may drop out of the spotlight for years, but there's nothing like a criminal accusation and arrest to awaken the sleeping media beast. The press will sink its teeth into a celebrity story and—without intervention—shake it to death.

Celebrities are people known because they are entertainers, movie stars, high-profile politicians or leaders in their professions. Someone who is familiar because of his accomplishments, wealth or status may be a local celebrity in a more limited region. People accused of particularly heinous crimes may become infamous, but they are not celebrated; instead, they become notorious. The common denominator with all these people emerges that when they commit a crime, they attract the media like bees to honeysuckle . . . or flies to garbage.

This poses a challenge to the lawyers who defend the famous or represent them in any kind of lawsuit. Most celebrities have a team of publicists who are focused on their clients' careers, not their sudden criminal notoriety and starring role in the hard news of the legal arena. In many ways, it is easier to work with a client who has never experienced the media spotlight. On the one hand, celebrities already have a degree of universal appeal and immediate access to millions of viewers; on the other hand, they now must respond about criminal accusations to that large established audience. The lawyer who represents a celebrity must accept the media factor and the responsibility of dealing with the celebrity's team and the celebrities themselves.

During two decades working with lawyers who represent the accused and lawyers who file lawsuits against those accused of injuring someone, I have successfully managed the media for several professionals who were well known in their communities, like the mayor of a small town in Florida and a prominent surgeon in a small Florida city. My clients have also included several people who became notorious because of the crimes police suspected or accused them of committing. Edward Humphrey, who was an unknown nineteen-year-old attending the University of Florida became a serial murder suspect, and his notoriety followed him for over a decade.

The challenge for defense lawyers who represent celebrities accused of any kind of criminal behavior is complicated by the immediate, overwhelming and relentless media attention on the accused client. This is also the case for lawyers representing the alleged victim or victim's family. How the alleged victims react to media attention influences public perception of the accusers and the accused. Examples of pertinent cases are numerous: Michael Jackson, O.J. Simpson and Robert Blake, to name but a few. Jackson was twice accused of molesting young children. O.J. Simpson and Robert Blake were both tried for the murder of their wives. In all of these cases, the victims' characters were scrutinized with as much intensity as the characters of the accused.

In the months and years leading up to the trial of a celebrity, media coverage will saturate a community. The influence on the potential jury pool is indisputable. A media specialist working with a lawyer may find that their primary responsibility is simply to manage the volume of media inquiries and issue written statements. The lawyer without a media consultant or trained staff will not have the time to respond to the media. A lawyer in this situation may elect to issue a blanket refusal to talk about the client and instruct the client to say nothing. This is not always in the best interest of the accused celebrity.

After following the media coverage of celebrities accused of crimes with a critical eye, I concluded that celebrities fall into two classes. Either they have excellent instincts and are more capable than anyone else at defending themselves in the media, or they are their own worst enemies when discussing their alleged criminal behavior and should never say anything in public.

Lawyers representing celebrities face unique challenges from both the accused and their team of advisors. According to Eric Franz, a New York City lawyer who experienced an onslaught of media attention when he represented both a celebrity accused and the accuser of a celebrity, "Any lawyer who represents a celebrity must also deal with a variety of people trying to influence decisions about media coverage. It is the lawyer's job to run the case successfully, to defend the client on all fronts including the media when strategically appropriate."[1] In the summer of 2005, Franz defended actor Christian Slater from criminal charges and also represented the hotel clerk who was hit by a telephone thrown by actor Russell Crowe. I followed both cases closely, because I knew Franz through a mutual friend.

Russell Crowe threw a telephone at hotel clerk Nestor Estrada on June 6, 2005. After weeklong media speculation about who Estrada was going to hire to sue Mr. Crowe, *The New York Daily News* reported that Eric Franz was the chosen lawyer. This was a shot heard round the world. The South African Press Association (SAPA) was only one of dozens of news wire services that reported a lawsuit against Russell Crowe would seek "unspecified punitive and compensatory damages."[2] The SAPA news story also included, "Estrada's lawyer Eric Franz told the paper: 'I'll do my talking through the legal process.'"[3] In actuality, Franz never filed a lawsuit. He strategically made periodic statements and apparently issued only one press release. He also put up an impenetrable shield around his client, Nestor Estrada.

Eric Franz is relatively young. He is a 1993 honors graduate of Fordham Law School with the good sense of a seasoned and successful trial lawyer. He says that he views media attention as taking place on a "chessboard" with the plaintiff's lawyer on one side and the defendant's on the other.[4] Between the Crowe matter and the Slater arrest, Franz demonstrated that he's on his way to becoming a chess master. For many lawyers, that much attention paid to his client's case might have gone to his head. Franz had some experience with media coverage, having represented a defendant in a Georgia federal racketeering trial involving professional athletes and a high-class strip club, but nothing prepared him for the media coverage of Russell Crowe's temper tantrum and telephone attack.

Like many criminal defense lawyers, Franz has specialized both in representing those accused of committing a crime (criminal defense) and those who sue someone for crimes committed against them (civil litigation). The skills required for success in these legal processes and the media relations skills needed when the case becomes high-profile are very similar.

In a high-profile case, the lawyer may become a celebrity in her own right. Never has this been truer than in the 1992 O.J. Simpson case. Although the lawyers who prosecuted Simpson also experienced recognition and developed high profiles during and after the trial, ask anyone on the street today who the lawyer involved in the O.J. Simpson trial was and the answer will be "Johnnie Cochran."

Before the Simpson trial, Johnnie L. Cochran Jr. was a successful personal injury lawyer based in California who had handled a number of multimillion-dollar cases suing the Los Angeles Police Department in misconduct cases. After the jury acquitted his celebrity client, O.J. Simpson, Cochran became the best-known lawyer in the world.

Eric Franz may never rise to the level of fame and fortune that Cochran achieved, but they share a media savvy that benefits their clients. Unlike Franz, and unlike just about any lawyer in America, Cochran was a celebrity himself, representing other celebrities. This made him uniquely qualified to speak on behalf of his clients. Lawyers without his stature can also develop the skills to represent a client effectively in the media arena even if they themselves never specifically address the media. However, the best defense of the accused is accomplished by a lawyer who is trained and comfortable in both the courtroom and in front of the media.

When lawyers appear in courtrooms on behalf of their high-profile clients, they are also, in effect, addressing the media. The statements they make can be stuffy legalistic jargon or creatively worded to be more quotable on the nightly news or in the next day's newspapers. In the Kobe Bryant trial in 2003 (see Chapter 8), his lawyer demonstrated her media savvy to her client's benefit.

The major celebrity in the Crowe-Estrada civil process was Russell Crowe, who hired lawyer Gerald Lefcourt to defend him from the criminal charges and represent him in the civil process. Lefcourt maintained a relatively low profile, but Crowe's celebrity necessitated a media response after the telephone attack and his arrest. I found Lefcourt's defense and media awareness personally interesting. In 1996, the *Orlando Sentinel* wrote a story about the public defender in central Florida hiring me, a publicist, and paying me with county money. The *Sentinel* printed this quotation from an interview with Lefcourt: "'The prosecutors always have press conferences, and they're always spinning the press,' said Gerald Lefcourt, First Vice President of the National Association of Criminal Defense Lawyers."[5]

The initial press release from Crowe was issued by his publicist, Robin Baum of PMK/HBH. Whether Lefcourt saw it first or not (and he certainly should have), the press release was damaging because it was a blatant attempt to deflect responsibility for the incident and was inaccurate. Baum or Lefcourt or both were either unaware or ignored the fact that the hotel lobby was videotaped by security cameras. The release was reprinted and ridiculed on the Web site www.defamer.com on June 6, 2005. It read:

> Frustrated by a clerk's unwillingness to help him put through a phone call to his family in Australia; Russell Crowe was involved in a minor altercation at the Mercer Hotel earlier this morning. After asking the front desk several times to replace a fault phone in his room and getting only attitude from the clerk on duty, Crowe brought the phone down to the front desk in an effort to address the situation in person. Words were exchanged and Crowe wound up throwing the phone against a wall. He regrets that he lost his temper, but at no time did he assault anyone or touch any hotel employee.[6]

In his first court appearance, Lefcourt was less specific and said, "This arose because he was trying to get his wife on the telephone on Australia. He was in his room. He couldn't get a line and there was a disagreement." A few days later, Crowe appeared on David Letterman's show, the choice of platforms for celebrity *mea culpas* since Hugh Grant used the late night forum after his arrest for solicitation of a prostitute in 1995. While Crowe apologized and actually gave his victim a name, using Estrada's first name "Nestor," he also inappropriately took the telephone that Letterman had jokingly hidden, and pretended to "bludgeon" the show's bandleader Paul Shaffer for playing "Mr. Telephone Man" when Crowe walked on stage.[7]

Since Crowe's arrest occurred while he was promoting his starring role in the biopic about a boxer during the depression, *Cinderella Man,* there was also periodic press coverage about the negative effect on movie ticket sales of his telephone tantrum and injury to Nestor Estrada, a simple hotel clerk. This speculation was fodder for several exchanges on late-night television.

At this point Crowe was batting zero in the media relations game. His publicist released a statement that misrepresented the incident and underplayed his actions to the point of lying. By June 14, Crowe and his lawyer faced the legal skills and instinctive media know-how of Eric Franz. His opening pitch was quoted in the *Daily News*: "Mr. Estrada has been traumatized by the incident. We ask that his privacy be respected. He wants to return to his previous life."[8]

This simple statement established several believable facts. First, the reference to being "traumatized." Franz does not overstate physical injuries. Second, he says that Estrada wants his privacy "respected," indicating that the last thing he wants is to discuss the Crowe attack publicly; and finally, he says that the non-celebrity hotel clerk wants to "return to his previous life." These dignified comments contain no reference to a lawsuit or mention of Russell Crowe.

The Crowe–Estrada matter was covered in every major newspaper, magazine and all the entertainment publications, broadcasts and online sites. *Radar* magazine, a bimonthly entertainment magazine had frequent updates on its Web site. On June 24, 2005, *Radar Online* published damning speculation about the way Crowe's lawyer Gerald Lefcourt and his publicist handled the case, writing that it "could have been settled with a simple handshake, we hear, if it wasn't for the star's hothead lawyer. . . . When Estrada and his lawyer Eric Franz again suggested the pair shake hands, 'Lefcourt went crazy,' says our source. 'He just about told Nestor to go screw himself. It made no sense.'"[9]

Although this report is from an unnamed source, if true, it still does not address a settlement figure. My extensive experience with personal injury lawyers and settlement negotiations makes me quite sure that any offer from Eric Franz to arrange a public handshake with Russell Crowe also included a large payment to Estrada. However, when he was asked about the handshake offer, Franz was quoted in the *Radar* report as saying, "There's been no resolution to the matter and I'm in the process of filing a complaint. I'm curious to see what Crowe says on the witness stand when his publicist isn't scripting comments for him."[10]

On June 28, 2005, the media were full of additional details about Crowe's behavior the night of the telephone attack, and the details were incriminating. That night on the MSNBC program *Scarborough Country*, the host introduced Pulitzer Prize–winner William Sherman of the *Daily News*. Sherman reported, "Well, June sixth, about four-twenty a.m., Crowe was trying to make a long-distance call to Australia to his wife, Danielle. And he was unable to get through. And he called the desk clerk repeatedly. And, in one of several profanity-laced tirades, he asked the desk clerk his name. And the desk clerk said, 'Joshua.' Crowe said, 'I am coming downstairs,' came downstairs with the phone and asked, 'Are you Joshua?' Joshua said yes. Crowe picked up the phone with two hands, as I have been told and the videotape shows, from three feet away, threw it at Estrada and hit Estrada."[11]

When the host of the program asked for clarification, Sherman affirmed that Crowe threw the telephone from only three feet away from Estrada, "Right. That is what Estrada's attorney, Eric Franz, maintains." Sherman then related, "Well, Estrada was knocked to the floor, he maintains and I guess he was—suffered a one-inch gash in his right cheek."[12]

"And then Crowe apparently picked up a ceramic bowl and hurled that at Estrada, who was at that point lying on the floor. The ball [sic, bowl] shattered near Estrada's face, but did not injure him. Estrada then sort of scurried out a door, called nine-one-one. In the meantime, Crowe bowed to two other hotel employees who were sort of standing there, mouths agape, if you will, and took this deep bow, and assumed a karate stance and then left."[13]

This interview is one of the rare references to Franz's having a dialogue, as opposed to releasing a set statement, with anyone in the media. In the ten weeks between his hiring by Nestor Estrada and the settlement announcement from Crowe's publicist on August 24, it appears that Franz calculated the media factor as a critical bargaining chip in the settlement negotiation process. Sherman's comments indicate a rare on-the-record discussion in a media relations plan that contained limited written statements when he was besieged for comments.

A few days later, *Radar* quoted from a written statement released by Franz: "Crowe is a man whose violent history demonstrates that he first responds to his rage and then responds to his ratings," and went on to state that Franz was going to file a formal complaint against Crowe. In this same article, *Radar* made a "dig" at Franz, probably in frustration that the only comments from him were in a written statement, released to any media requesting information about the case and called Eric Franz "Estrada's headline-loving lawyer."[14]

Along with the rest of the media, *Radar*'s writers and editors must have been chafing at the bit because Nestor Estrada was never available for comment. Franz obviously made it quite clear to his client that a media appearance was his strongest negotiating tool and not to be used until all other avenues were exhausted.

By July 5, media reports were filled with a pending lawsuit; in fact, the *Daily News* reported that the lawsuit was imminent.[15] Instead of filing a lawsuit, Franz tried his civil lawsuit behind closed doors by letting the media speculate. Through his judicious, controlled and limited comments to the media and his strategic shielding of Nestor Estrada from a very hungry media, Franz rarely issued comments. When he did, they were widely reported and weighted with restraint. Interestingly, and in direct opposition to the comment on *Radar*, his media restraint was reported by Cindy Adams in her *New York Post* gossip column on June 20: "Mr. Franz is not into PR. Not into giving interviews. Not making tabloid deals.... Russell's lawyers will have to deal with Mr. Franz soon."[16]

The media coverage of the Crowe case—both the criminal proceedings against Crowe and the pending civil suit by Nestor (Joshua) Estrada—was intense and worldwide. From the coverage I observed, Franz handled the media flawlessly. In August, there was a flurry of articles in the local New York newspapers as well as the international media, speculating that a settlement for Estrada was in the works.

As is typical, the British tabloids were the most outrageous in their coverage. The *Daily Mail* announced on August 13 an expected settlement of six million pounds sterling (more than ten million dollars).[17] The next day the *Age.com* reported that Russell Crowe "is preparing to pay $14 million."[18] On August 15, Lefcourt and Franz were both quoted in the *Daily News* and denied any settlement. Lefcourt stated, "It's doesn't exist."[19]

Franz added, "It's preposterous and bewildering as to why anyone would put out a story like that."[20] My personal conjecture is, "Methinks he doth protest too much." There is no downside to a report of a multimillion-dollar settlement no matter how absurd it appears. It allows ample room for Russell Crowe and his lawyer to come up with a reasonable yet substantial amount much lower than what the media reported.

This was the last statement I ever saw or heard about the settlement until August 25, when *Entertainment Tonight* quoted Russell Crowe's publicist Robin Baum as saying, "Russell Crowe and Nestor Estrada announced that they have reached a settlement of Estrada's claims stemming from an incident in June at the Mercer Hotel.... Both sides expressed satisfaction at the resolution."[21]

It was obvious that a confidential settlement and a confidentiality agreement had been negotiated. The *Daily News* reported as much on the same day.

> Apparently everyone is close to being happy. Sources said there are only two small holdups: Crowe wanted to find out whether he'd have to pay a settlement himself or whether it would be covered by insurance. There was also some disagreement about keeping the settlement terms secret.

According to sources, Estrada, 28, was willing, but Crowe, 41, was reluctant to put into writing that he would hold his tongue. Both sides are now said to have agreed to strict language that penalizes anyone who talks.[22]

I never spoke to Franz about the Crowe–Estrada matter. The media coverage, however, was readily available. Franz's published comments and his limited responses to media inquiries protected his client, the accuser, and this position led him to leverage media access in his settlement negotiations. The media relations conducted by Franz on behalf of Estrada resulted in a textbook case of what to do and what not to do when representing a person accusing a celebrity in a civil lawsuit. On the other hand, the media relations from the Crowe camp, his lawyer, his publicist, and Russell Crowe himself were damaging to Crowe's celebrity and, more than likely, his pocketbook.

In the Christian Slater case, the actor was charged with sexual assault. He hired Eric Franz to defend him. Like the Russell Crowe case, Franz's representation of Slater when he was accused of grabbing a woman's buttocks outside a New York City restaurant was also widely covered, but the outcome was not confidential, and Franz spoke to me about his media experiences in defending a celebrity from criminal charges.

During his representation of Slater, Franz acknowledged that there were a number of people with a stake in the outcome of the criminal charges against Slater. However, he was also aware that the prosecution takes a special interest, "Because it's a celebrity involved, the charges are more difficult to refute and it's harder to negotiate an early resolution. Prosecutors are always wary of appearing to favor a celebrity."[23]

When representing a celebrity, the lawyer may also have to answer to agents, publicists, managers, and even film studios and distributors, who have a vested interest in the image of the accused. The key to success for the lawyer is to keep his focus on defense and control over media relations—control that the client is used to paying publicists to handle. The Slater matter was in itself minor, yet when factoring in his bad-boy image and previous arrests, there was a real need to resolve the accusations with as little fanfare as possible.

The media was ready to jump into the fray. In addition to reporting Slater's arrest on May 31, 2005, several newspapers reminisced about earlier criminal charges and convictions. *CNN's* report on his arrest included the information "Slater has had previous trouble with the law. In 1997, he was charged with three counts of assault and one count of battery after he assaulted a girlfriend while intoxicated. He served fifty-nine days of a three-month sentence."[24]

Likewise, *Newsday* reported on previous criminal charges, stating that "in 1996, he was convicted of assaulting an ex-girlfriend and trying to grab the gun of an officer . . . In 1994, he reportedly was busted at Kennedy Airport for carrying a gun and in 1989 he served 10 days for driving while intoxicated."[25]

The next flurry of news coverage occurred in July, during Slater's first appearance in court. (Russell Crowe probably helped lower the media radar on Slater's case when he threw that telephone on June 6.) The media converged on the Manhattan Supreme Court building in downtown New York.

Eric Franz handled the media through his open court statement when he rejected a plea offer of three day's community service. He stated, "We believe this case warrants dismissal." These six words were broadcast and printed repeatedly because there was nothing else to report. This is a perfect example of stating one thing and one thing only—the statement you want to dominate the news and that's all. In one report, the statement was shortened to "The case warrants dismissal."[26]

Regardless, Slater's past behavior was still part of the story. When *CourtTV* reported his turning down the plea deal, it also reported details of the 1996 incident and called it a "cocaine and booze-driven melee."[27] The media continued to refer to earlier problems with the law. Because Slater was scheduled to take part in the British production of the play "Sweet Bird of Youth," the London *Times* also reported his arrest and noted that he had served fifty-nine days in prison after "reportedly biting a man in the stomach and throwing a police officer against a wall during a party in Los Angeles."[28]

Resurrecting these earlier criminal matters might not have been as much a concern for Slater and his publicists when the actor was younger. In 2005, he was thirty-five years old and focused more on performing on stage in classic plays; the bad-boy image didn't work well. Although, ideally, Slater might have prepared and delivered a statement himself, Franz recognized that Slater was better off saying nothing to the media, because even when he apologized for not being able to answer a question, he looked bad.

An obviously restrained Christian Slater was besieged by the media when he and Franz exited the Manhattan courthouse after his court appearance. According to a *CourtTV* reporter, he apologized to the media, saying, "I'm really sorry" and "I can't say anything."[29] However, she also characterized Slater's tone as "sardonic." Sarcastic and disdainful is exactly the opposite of how Slater needed to be portrayed while his lawyer was taking a strong position on his innocence and more than likely negotiating with prosecutors to drop the charges.

Although I recognize that Franz likely refused to speak to the media because he was intent on getting the cases dismissed, a goal he achieved for Slater, there was a way to avoid the media frenzy. My standard procedure before any court appearance in high-profile cases is to notify the media the day before that the lawyer will make a statement at a designated place after the hearing is concluded.

In this way, the media can be set up and ready. Naturally, there will be a desire for a Q&A session following the statement. The answers to any question can reiterate the statement—a statement that may simply reword exactly what the lawyer said in court. There is no difference between "This case warrants dismissal" and "Christian Slater is innocent of these charges," and "I'm confident that the truth will come out."

By Slater's next court appearance on September 19, the prosecutor announced that the charges against Slater were dropped with the caveat that he stay out of trouble for six months. Thus Franz achieved the best possible result for his celebrity client in the legal arena. While both were far from murder cases, during his representation of Christian Slater and the hotel clerk made famous by the Russell Crowe telephone attack, Eric Franz gained extensive experience in handling media relations for the accused and the accusers in the summer of 2005 that will certainly prove invaluable in his next celebrity case.

Of all the celebrity cases since the seminal trial of O.J. Simpson in 1995, the award for best media relations goes to actor Robert Blake. I followed the media coverage of his wife's murder, his arrest nearly a year later, and his decision-making process regarding media relations. I watched his interview with Barbara Walters while still in jail awaiting the trial, and his second interview in the weeks after he was found not guilty. I was in awe of his effective responses.

Between May 6, 2001 (the date his wife was murdered outside a restaurant where they had just had dinner), and March 16, 2005, Blake handled his own media relations with dramatic results. I do not mean dramatic in the sense of acting, although he was an actor for most of his life, beginning with the "Our Gang" character he played as a child in the 1940s. He also appeared in 161 films, according to his promotional Web site.[30] His results were dramatic because during the nearly four years he was on trial for his wife's murder, he consistently adhered to his instinctive belief that if he proclaimed his innocence and lamented his unjust persecution to the public through the media, he would be found not guilty. And he was.

The jury that ultimately set him free was drawn from Los Angeles County, California. This jury was made up of men and women who had to be aware of Blake's character. They were also people who had lived through earlier celebrity trials. Blake was absolutely correct when he decided that after his wife-with-the-checkered-past was murdered, the rest of his life depended upon media relations. He was so convinced of the rightness of his decision that he was willing to have three lawyers resign from his case because they did not agree with his conviction that media relations were imperative.

Eleven months after Bonnie Bakley was killed, on April 18, 2002, the police arrested Blake, who was had already hired lawyer Harold Braun. The police and prosecutors in the Robert Blake murder cases were adamant about his guilt, and the media reported their accusations:

> "Robert Blake shot Bonnie Bakley," said LAPD Police Captain Jim Tatreau.[31]

> "Based on the evidence in this case, it can be proved beyond a reasonable doubt that this defendant, Robert Blake, killed Bonnie Lee Bakley," said Los Angeles County Deputy District Attorney Shelley Samuels. [32]

Up to this point, Blake had kept a low profile. After his arrest, he was held without bail in solitary confinement for six months and then denied bail once again. Then, he began actively seeking to tell his story on national television. The first interview he agreed to do was with ABC's Diane Sawyer, who also interviewed Bonnie's brother. His decision was in direct opposition to his lawyer, Harold Braun. Blake refused to follow his lawyer's advice and allowed him to resign. Braun told the media, "I think it's insane for a person charged with a crime to go on camera to answer questions about the case. No lawyer in the country would allow a defendant to do this."[33]

Braun may have been trying to protect his client, but he was wrong to say that no lawyer would allow his accused client to give an interview. Some lawyers do; I have worked with them. However, the key to protecting the client is to prepare them carefully for the interview and avoid any possibility of compromising their innocence plea. Whether or not the accused is a celebrity, preparation for the interview must be taken very seriously. A media relations expert in high-profile cases may be the key to working closely with both the lawyer and the client. Both need to be on hand before and during the interview.

A month after Braun's resignation, Blake hired two new lawyers: Thomas Mesereau Jr. and Jennifer Keller. He obviously remained open to requests for media interviews; as a result, Keller soon resigned from the case. The interview with Diane Sawyer never occurred because ABC did not receive permission from the jail to bring in a camera crew and conduct an interview. However, after *20/20*'s Barbara Walters successfully argued with the LA County Sheriff Lee Baca that she had previously conducted interviews in the jail; Robert Blake finally got his chance to tell people he is innocent on national television.

The interview that aired February 26, 2003, is unforgettable. Blake was adamant when asked if he was innocent, "Of course. Of course." When asked if he'd killed his wife, he replied "Of course not." Walters posed the question, "Will you be found innocent?" To which Blake replied, "They took away my reputation, my entire past, my entire future. What are they gonna take, my testicles and make earrings of them!" What he really cared about, he told Walters, was that "people are laughing at this," referring to a segment on *The Tonight Show with Jay Leno*.[34]

Robert Blake's statement of his innocence is one of the most memorable I've ever heard. Who can ever forget "testicles for earrings"?

The televised interview with Walters was also included in the closing statements of the trial by both the prosecution and the defense. The state showed one portion of the interview, and the defense played a longer version in an attempt to provide jurors with a balanced context for Blake's statements. In the interview, Blake admits to Walters that, at first, he tried to find a way to keep his daughter, Rosie, while having Bakley stay in Arkansas, but eventually decided to marry her in November 2000 because "There was no downside for me."

He explained that Bakley was going to live in his guesthouse and the two would get to know each other. He also said that on the night of her murder, they had a lot to talk about, including plans about their future, and his desire for Bakley not to conduct her mail-order porn business on his property.

"What did I have to lose? You tell me!" Blake shouted at Walters in the clip, adding that having his daughter, Rosie, was "God's gift of a century . . . I wasn't going to mess it up by being selfish," Blake said.[35]

Although Blake never took the witness stand, a decision his lawyer probably made for him, he used media relations to proclaim his innocence. The jury heard the evidence. It deliberated nine days before finding him not guilty. The district attorney, Steve Cooley, completely lost his cool after the verdict and told the media that Blake was "guilty as sin," and a "miserable human being" and that the jury was "incredibly stupid."[36]

Jurors who spoke to *CourtTV* reporters after the trial ended commented on both the evidence and the impressions they had of witnesses. The jury foreman called the case against Blake "flimsy" and "disjointed." He also called one of the prosecution's chief witnesses, a former stunt man who claimed Blake asked him to kill Bonnie Bakley, "a prolific liar." Another juror said of the prosecution, "Their case was built around witnesses who weren't truthful."[37]

If the jurors were reacting to their impressions of whether witnesses were truthful or not, it is likely that they also developed an impression of Blake in the televised interview they were shown during closing arguments. In the face of losing his lawyer, Blake believed strongly enough in the power of the media to go forward with an interview that allowed him to tell viewers he was innocent and to tell them emphatically and memorably. He made a serious and persuasive impression in the interview that he was being truthful.

While reviewing Blake's media image after he was accused of murder, it is appropriate to reference the civil lawsuit Bonnie Lee Bakley's family filed against Blake before he was even charged with the murder. On April 3, 2002, two weeks before he was arrested, Bakley's family sued to recover monetary damages for her murder.[38]

The outcome of the civil suit against Blake mirrors the outcome of the civil suit filed by the family of O.J. Simpson's murdered wife. Unlike in criminal trials, where jury decisions must be unanimous, juries in civil trials may render split decisions. There is also a very different attitude in a courtroom when the argument is about money, not about a person's life.

Even though two different juries found Simpson and Blake each liable for more than $30 million in the murders of their wives, laws generally protect the homes owned by defendants, as well as pension and retirement accounts, from these kinds of judgments. Although a jury awarded Bonnie Lee Bakley's family $36 million, Blake has his freedom and a life where he can be with his family, notably his daughter with Bakley, who is being raised in the home of Blake's oldest daughter. Simpson also has his freedom and regained custody of his two children by his murdered wife, both children had been in the custody of her parents. Perhaps the real irony in these two civil judgments is that a significant portion is awarded to the surviving children who remain in the custody of the formerly accused person or his family.

During the two years Robert Blake was out on bail before his criminal trial, his friends and family rallied around him and offered significant support. One friend moved her elderly mother out of an oceanfront condo so that Blake would have a comfortable place to live. There's little doubt that he will continue to live out the rest of his life in more comfort than the majority of Americans regardless of the civil trial judgment.

Celebrities who are accused of committing crimes are in a class by themselves. The lawyers who represent them must have the good sense to understand and make decisions about media responses that are in the best interests of their clients. In some cases, the lawyer needs to prepare for the media onslaught and make statements on his client's behalf. When the celebrity has excellent instincts about how to respond, the lawyer and client must be on the same page and work closely together on every media decision, perhaps excluding the team of publicists who managed media inquiries before the celebrity was ever charged with a crime.

Three

Accusations in Custody Disputes

When the rich and famous go to domestic court—people like former New York Mayor Rudolph Giuliani or cosmetic magnate Ronald Perelman—the battles that dominate the news are over their children and, of course, their money. There may also be a prenuptial agreement. Every state has different laws regarding spousal and child support, and most states have strong incentives to get the marital parties to settle. Acrimonious divorce and custody disputes are harmful to the children involved. The longer the matter drags on, the more expensive the lawyer fees.

If a husband and wife cannot reach an out-of-court settlement, then chances are they may be accusing each other of serious falsehoods, deceptions and misconduct. It's also possible that one party feels like the victim and wants to see the other perceived wrongdoer suffer in a public arena. In the cases of Giuliani and Perelman, powerful and successful men, their previous experiences with the media may not have served them well in a custody battle. As the media followed every court filing and appearance, the public relations skills of their lawyers were tested.

Yet public relations for the single mother without resources can be just as critical and the stakes so much higher. If the government is involved, the task of mounting a defense can seem almost insurmountable. Florida has one of the most reviled foster care systems in the country. When a government agency like Health and Human Resources becomes involved in a custody dispute, the private citizen who's parenting skills and lifestyle come under scrutiny may well lose custody of her child.

I worked on one of the most unusual custody matters in history in 1992 when a Florida judge granted a teenage boy's request to "divorce" his mother. In 2003, I again become embroiled in a media relations campaign to help a foster care mother regain custody of her own disabled child, who was unjustly removed from her home because of criminal allegations against her son—allegations that were later dropped.

In these two struggles, neither mother had any financial resources or experience with the media. Both were extremely reluctant to speak to reporters. Their initial refusal to respond fueled the public perception that they were ashamed and had something to hide. In the custody wars waged by New York's sitting mayor and the city's wealthiest business tycoon, each had access to legal and media expertise. One man lost his custody fight; the other won.

During his divorce proceedings and custody battle, Rudolph Giuliani emerged as a cheating lothario who made Gracie Mansion a battleground and showed complete disrespect for the mother of his two children. When Ron Perelman fought the mother of his child, his lawyers successfully discredited his ex-wife. Both were represented by good attorneys and had media relations professionals ready to help.

Giuliani's high-profile divorce and custody battle with Donna Hanover, his second wife and the mother of his two children, began in May of 2000. The legal and public relations fight spanned the year that he was praised for his compassionate and strong leadership during and after the 9/11 terrorist attacks on New York City. Giuliani and Hanover finally reached a settlement in July 2002. As the mayor of the country's most newsworthy city, Rudy Giuliani, like many of his predecessors, had an extremely colorful and loud personality. The media constantly covered his professional and personal controversies, and he was well aware of his high profile. However, when it came to domestic matters, he failed to recognize the backlash that can arise when a father is insensitive to his children's mother. The media scrutiny of the Giuliani case was fueled not only by his political office (the mayor was also the former federal prosecutor who ultimately got mobster John Gotti convicted) but by his wife's own headline-grabbing abilities—the journalist-turned actor appeared in *The Vagina Monologues* during the proceedings.[1]

Instead of choosing an attorney who might have tempered the nastiness of the divorce trial and custody battle, the mayor choose Raoul Felder, an aggressive lawyer, whose insulting remarks were widely quoted and frequently repeated throughout the media. His comments about Hanover reflected poorly on the mayor, who chose not to minimize the ugliness of the legal fight over the children, even when he had been openly engaging in an extramarital relationship. At the crux of the Giuliani divorce were his well-known affairs with other women—the first with his staff publicist and the second, an ongoing relationship with one Judith Nathan.[2] The *New York Post* reported extensively on the mayor's relationships, including a series of stories about his "love-nest" at the St. Regis Hotel and references to a *People Magazine* cover story, "The Mayor, The Wife, The Mistress."[3]

Rudy Giuliani had aspirations to other elected offices; at one time, he considered running against Hillary Clinton for the New York senate seat in 2000. There was also widespread speculation that President Bush might appoint him to his cabinet. While there were certainly other factors, notably Giuliani's fight with prostate cancer, his callous behavior before the media about the very private matter of divorce certainly worked against his consideration for higher office.

In the June 6, 2001, issue of *New York Magazine*, Michael Wolff, who wrote extensively about Mayor Giuliani, observed that the mayor's behavior surrounding his affairs, his divorce and custody matters would set "a new litmus test for how a politician deals with his family. If you can't control your spouse's discretion, loyalty, finances, mood swings, then why should we think that you deserve the public trust?" In speculating about the Mayor's future, Wolff writes that, "it seems certain the present contretemps will mean no Bush appointment."[4]

The Mayor's poor judgment in how he addressed the media concerning the divorce is revealed in a long tirade he delivered at a press conference after the judge rejected his lawyer's second request for a gag order. On May 23, 2001, *CNN* covered Giuliani's litany of complaints accusing the news media of a voracious pursuit of new angles in his drawn-out divorce saga, going on to say, "You're relentless. People jump out of cars. Virtually, people can't go to the bathroom without being covered."[5]

If Giuliani really wanted the press to back off, I would have advised him to stop yelling and ask for compassion and respect. He also allowed his lawyer to attack the mother of their two children. At one point, Fedler called Hanover "an uncaring mother" who was "howling like a stuck pig." His denigration of her reflected the Mayor's own nastiness.[6] After all, a lawyer is not called a "mouthpiece" without reason. He speaks for the client in the court and to the media. The lawyers people rely upon to speak for them in the courtroom must be prepared to see their every statement broadcast to the public.

Despite the positive image of the mayor that dominated the national news after terrorists felled the World Trade Center towers on September 11, 2001, the Giuliani divorce and custody battle continued to reflect poorly on him. Owing to term limits, Giuliani was forced to leave office at the end of 2001. At the same time, he was battling prostate cancer, certainly a potential sympathy factor.

Giuliani's domestic disputes were finally resolved in July of 2002 with a multi-million dollar settlement to his former wife, who also got primary custody of their children. His heightened national profile fueled speculation that he might run for national office. The image problems he developed during the custody and divorce proceedings may have ultimately contributed to the decision that he not run on the Republican presidential ticket in 2003 or for senator of New York.

Rudy Giuliani could have had the best public relations advice available during his divorce proceedings. However, neither he nor his lawyer demonstrated any knowledge in taking the high road and promoting the image of a good father while still aggressively litigating a fair divorce settlement. Of course, the desire to put forth a positive image and to listen to expert advice on media relations in this type of case must be there in the first place.

In the child custody case of Revlon billionaire Ronald Perelman versus Democratic fundraiser Patricia Duff, the battle raged over child support, custody and visitation. In addition to lawyers, both sides employed public relations professionals. The difference in the media relations management was that Ron Perelman relied on his experts throughout the litigation. Patricia Duff hired a media expert but failed to use his services throughout her fight.

When representing the extremely wealthy client in domestic cases, a media specialist must be able to understand, simplify and communicate requests by either party that become public. In divorce and custody cases, some of the disputes can seem ludicrous to the general public. In the Giuliani case, the request by Hanover for canine support—$1,140 per month for their Labrador retriever—was widely reported and ridiculed. Yet, to live in New York and be a busy professional with an elderly dog often means employing a dog walker several times a day, vet and medicine expenses, grooming fees and the expensive special pet food. In this light, $1,140 doesn't seem so extreme.[7]

I briefly worked on a case during the 1990s, when a Palm Beach socialite sought child support that included $25,000 each year for their child's birthday party. Initially, the amount looked outrageous, yet when she itemized the normal expenditures for such a party in their social circle, it actually made sense. It was standard to have the party catered for the children and the parents and nannies, perhaps twenty children and forty adults. There were also professional entertainers like magicians and live animal acts or perhaps pony rides. There were expensive goody bags *de rigueur* as well. Add it all up and the $25,000 seemed reasonable.

In the *Perelman v. Duff* dispute, the media expert who advised Duff was able to justify many of her requests for support from New York's billionaire husband and father through astute media relations management. Jim Haggerty, a lawyer and media advisor, chronicles this case in his book *In the Court of Public Opinion*. Haggerty met several media challenges for Duff and reportedly fueled the story about Perelman's saying he could feed his four-year-old daughter on $3 per day since all she ate were chicken fingers, hot dogs and ice cream. However, in the end Duff lost custody and was forced to accept considerably less than the support payments she might have gained after the Perelman legal team demonstrated that she was not appropriately celebrating Jewish holidays with their daughter.[8]

When advising clients embroiled in any type of litigation, the media relations specialists and the lawyers must be on the same team and for the most part on the same page when it comes to media management. The more powerful and successful the clients have been in their lifetimes, the more controlling they may want to be in litigation as personal as divorce and custody cases and the more headlines they are likely to garner.

When a low-income, usually single-parent, family becomes entangled in the court system, and the case makes headlines, the legal process and outcome can be devastating. In 1992, a young mother placed two of her three children in foster care. The oldest boy was taken in by a Mormon family in rural Florida. In my opinion, they emotionally manipulated him before initiating proceedings to sever his family ties by "divorcing" his mother. Her court-appointed lawyers tried to work the media, but without a media strategy early in the case, the local newspaper hammered away at incriminating and damning facts about the boy's birth mother. When I eventually became involved, I worked with the mother and her lawyers to shed a new light on her story.

In cases involving minor children and a state agency, judges and the media usually protect the names of the parties. In this case, the foster family for the boy who sued to divorce his mother by asking the court to sever her parental rights was creative and aggressive with the media, and it paid off. Because they agreed to interviews on nationally televised programs, the mother's lawyer eventually appeared in an interview with Barbara Walters. The judge used this exposure as an excuse to allow the names to become public and opened the trial of twelve-year-old Gregory Kingsley versus Rachel (and Gregory Sr.) Kingsley to a media frenzy.

To understand this case fully, it is necessary to know something of the basic tenets of the Mormon faith and the Church of Latter Day Saints in America. Mormons do not believe in birth control and typically have very large families. The Book of Mormon describes three separate heavens; the top echelon of the three is reserved for those who accept the Mormon faith. Mormons are dedicated proselytizers; most young people give two years of their life serving as missionaries in countries around the world trying to convert people to their faith.

When Rachel Kingsley, the thirty-year-old mother of three moved from St. Louis, Missouri, to Orlando, Florida, to start a new life, she was finally reunited with her oldest son, Gregory. During this time, she was a waitress and could not cover child care expenses. She made a difficult choice and placed her two older children in foster care. When she was able to get on her feet, she brought them back home in 1990. After a few months, she returned the two oldest boys to foster care, and Gregory was taken to the Florida Boys Ranch, a residential facility outside of Ocala, Florida, a small conservative city north of Orlando.

Rachel Kingsley wanted her sons back, and while she was in Missouri getting family support from her father, she also completed a case plan for the government agency in charge of foster care, Health and Rehabilitative Services (HRS), that included parenting classes and getting a job. She continued to call the boys, although it was often difficult to get them on the telephone.

By this time, her oldest son, Gregory, was no longer staying at the ranch; he had been invited to stay at the home of George Russ, a lawyer, a board member of the Boys Ranch, and the head of a large Mormon family. He had Gregory over to his home on several weekends and then successfully sought to make him a foster child. However, it soon became apparent that the family had more complicated motives. Because Russ was on the Ranch's board, he apparently (and inappropriately) obtained access to Gregory's history and began directly contacting his mother, Rachel Kingsley, to tell her he wanted to adopt Gregory. She became alarmed at the Russes' influence over her son. Kingsley then returned to Florida to regain custody. HRS advised her that she needed a lawyer and recommend she see Jane Carey. Carey agreed to represent her; as an indigent client, Orange County paid Rachel Kingsley's legal fees.[9]

When George Russ learned that Carey was representing Kinsley, he called her at her office. Fifteen years later, Carey says she still remembers his tone when he demanded why she hadn't encouraged Rachel Kingsley to sign the adoption papers. She was shocked to receive such a call. He actually ordered her to have Kingsley sign the adoption consent. Carey, a strong black woman and a lawyer protective of her clients, says, "He talked about Rachel like she was trailer trash and had no right to her own child."[10] Carey assured him that Kingsley intended to regain custody of her children.

The very next day after Russ' telephone call, Carey saw one of the several newspaper headlines, with the phrase "Boy Sues for Divorce."[11] The fact that at least three newspapers in Central Florida carried the story strongly suggests that George Russ had a PR campaign in place before the lawsuit was filed.[12] Russ had come up with a novel way to prevent Rachel Kingsley from exercising her parental rights. With the help of another Ocala, Florida, lawyer, Jerri Blair—described in the *Orlando Sentinel* as "a children's crusader after working for HRS on child custody cases in the late 1980s"—Russ filed a lawsuit in rural Lake County, Florida, on April 8, 1992, for the minor child to sever parental rights, to "divorce" his mother.[13]

The Russ family already included eight children. Neither Jane Carey nor the news media were aware of the religious influences in this lawsuit. In an unfortunate case of timing, the story was too far developed to introduce this element effectively when I began to work with them. There were a number of facts in Kingsley's defense that were overlooked when the lawsuit was filed. Once the window of opportunity for introducing these factors was lost, it was never opened again. For example, in one of the earliest articles on the case that appeared in the *Orlando Sentinel*, a sidebar in the article summarized events in Gregory Kingsley's life, including the fact that soon after his mother was awarded custody during a divorce in 1994, the father kidnapped their oldest boy for five years. This horrific event was indisputable but largely never reported again.[14]

The Russ family was active in their local Mormon temple; it is likely that this family also believed in the Mormon practice of enlarging their family through adoption. By the time the Kingsley child began to enjoy the comfort of the family's home and the security that every child craves, he was also attending church with them. It probably helped that the Russ family got $700 per month for Gregory from the HRS. They later made an undisclosed amount of money for selling the rights to Gregory's story for two TV movies.

This "divorce" terminology phrase catapulted the Kingsley matter into the national media spotlight. It was a brilliant public relations strategy. The lawsuit was soon moved to Orange County Juvenile Court as Kingsley lived in Orlando. At this point, an experienced court reporter, Bob Levenson, of the *Orlando Sentinel*, was assigned to the story.[15]

Today Levenson is also a lawyer, the regional trial counsel for the Southeast Region of the Securities and Exchange Commission. When I contacted him about his coverage of the *Kingsley* case, he remembered George Russ as "someone who seemed to want publicity to promote his own agenda."[16] According to Levenson, after the lawsuit was filed, Russ kept twelve-year-old Gregory Kingsley under wraps until he allowed him into the exciting world of national television—the boy was ultimately interviewed on ABC's *20/20* by Barbara Walters herself.[17]

Meanwhile, Carey did her best on the case. Levenson described her in the *Orlando Sentinel* as a lawyer with "extensive experience in juvenile court representing abused children and parents whose children have been taken by HRS."[18] Levenson recalls that Carey initially "seemed overwhelmed by the publicity; she was trying to litigate a normal parental law case, and it turned into a media portrayal."[19]

Harry Morall, Carey's husband and also a lawyer, worked on the *Kingsley* case as well. Nothing in their careers had prepared them for the media onslaught. When I read about the case in June, I recognized that the coverage was seriously slanted in favor of the young accuser. He was being allowed to manifest every child's fantasy of getting back at parents who had hurt him.

There's no question that a child placed in foster care suffers feelings of neglect and abandonment. As a mother of four children, I cannot imagine ever placing one of them in foster care. I also know the terrible trauma children suffer when they go through their parents' divorce. There was something very wrong with this case, and Rachel Kingsley did not deserve, within legal or moral standards, to lose her parental rights. Yet that's the way it was looking in the media circus that Russ and his lawyer created. The courts did not have a legal right to enable the twelve-year-old to sue his mother—this is evidenced by the later decision to overturn the adoption and other courts' refusals to allow such actions to be filed by minors.[20]

Rachel Kingsley was never charged with being an unfit mother. Although she was accused repeatedly in the media of unfitting behavior, she was never investigated for abuse or neglect of her children until the Russ lawsuit and media campaign pulled out all the stops. The very fact that she retained custody of both her other sons, one of whom suffered from Tourette's syndrome, proves that she deserved the same parental rights as every other mother who makes the difficult choice to put one or more children in foster care.

Although the judge assigned to the *Kingsley* case, Judge Thomas Kirk, died in 1995, I suspect that he too was taken in by the media excitement. In fact, although it was quite inappropriate of him, after his decision, he actually participated in national news programs and talked publicly about the case after his decision. Levenson, who covered the police and courts for eight of his thirteen years as a reporter, says the judge's ruling to allow the case to become public was unusual. From his perspective then and his legal experience today, Levenson says he is "not convinced that he [Judge Kirk] looked at the legal factors of the case or made his decisions based on legal standards."[21] This observation is supported by the fact that Judge Kirk's decision was overturned by Florida's 5th District Court of Appeals less than a year later. However, before the *Kingsley* "divorce" trial began, the Russ family kept busy fueling the press, negotiating movie rights and, in my opinion, poisoning the mind of Gregory Kingsley against his mother.

When I first read about the Gregory Kingsley case in the *Sentinel*, I saw the villains as the Russ family. The media response by Carey needed to be more proactive and aggressive. I contacted her office and was hired to help with the case. Carey paid me from her personal funds. I now believe that this was a perfect case for petitioning the county to pay for a media expert in a high-profile domestic lawsuit. Two years later, the Orange County Public Defender did ask the county to pay for a publicist and his request was approved (see Chapter 6).

Prior to my involvement to assist Carey in media strategy, she had been overly protective and allowed Kingsley to give only one interview, through a series of written answers to questions posed by Levenson. This attempt to control what is printed usually fails and is something acceptable only when the client is imprisoned and not allowed to give interviews directly. Even then, the best way to handle it is to set up a telephone interview that can perhaps be recorded. Whenever possible, the character and personality of the accused need to be injected into any interview given to a reporter; the accused needs to feel, hurt and breathe in the interview.

Because Carey's legal experience was largely working with children, nearly all her cases were protected from media scrutiny. Her natural mistrust of the media and the numerous articles and interviews that attacked Kingsley made her extremely defensive. I sat with Carey and her client and convinced them to allow Kingsley to do as many interviews as possible to publicize her plight and her heartache.

Levenson agreed that after I became involved, "Rachel became a much more sympathetic and accessible figure."[22] I also arranged a number of television interviews, but by this time, the maverick rulings by Judge Kirk did not bode well for a positive decision for Rachel Kingsley. We were also hindered by the distance factor; Kingsley had returned to St. Louis with her two other sons to be closer to her family for emotional and practical support.

There were facts in the Kingsley matter that needed to be stressed and repeated from the time the case was first filed. Gregory had been taken from his mother and siblings for five years. Rachel never hurt her children. She was poor, and the Russ family was much wealthier and had many more resources.

By the time the trial began on September 21, 1992, Carey felt that the law would prevail and that Judge Kirk would not permit the Russ lawsuit to terminate Kingsley's parental rights. However, his rulings throughout the trial and the testimony he allowed, much of which was hearsay about Kingsley's lifestyle, seemed to foretell a bad decision. Carey had gone before Judge Kirk on numerous occasions. She says, "I think that Judge Kirk was a good man who wanted what he thought was best for children. But he made a bad decision in Rachel's case, and I believe that he suffered because he looked back and saw that he did wrong."[23]

One of the critical decisions we made at the trial was that Rachel Kingsley was not to be in the courtroom when the verdict was rendered. Judge Kirk had already shown his hand repeatedly through the process with one bad ruling after the other. Instead, I focused on setting up a press conference at Carey's office with Rachel and her two children. I wanted to do everything possible to balance to some degree the overwhelming attention that was going to be focused on the Russ family.

For Rachel Kingsley, the chance to sit with her other two sons and speak of her loss and what she was suffering was therapeutic. Her father also attended the press conference. She needed to believe in herself again. By giving her the media spotlight, we gave her the reassurance that her feelings were just as important as Gregory's. She needed what Dominic Gentile calls "emotional capital."[24]

People Magazine covered the trial. I usually sat next to the writer, Meg Grant, and, when appropriate, pointed out the Russ family and referenced their Mormon motives. The day after the trial ended, with Judge Kirk terminating Kingsley's parental rights and allowing the Russ family to adopt him, there was a telephone call from Grant requesting a photo of Rachel with her other two children. Carey and Kingsley had made a mistake that occurs all too often in high-profile cases. They had given all available photos to the national news media and had none available when another story opportunity arose. I found out that the Kingsleys were leaving from the Orlando airport that afternoon. Carey's office assured me that she would call before she got on the airplane. This was in the early years of mobile telephones, and Kingsley did not have one. I asked them to tell her I was on the way to the airport to photograph her and her two sons for *People Magazine*.

I arrived to find them waiting outside the Delta terminal, and I took a dozen shots of the three of them. (Thus, I earned my first and only photo credit from *People Magazine*, which insisted on paying me $125.00 for the right to use the photo. I deducted the $125 from the remainder of my fee due from Carey & Morall).

The *People Magazine* story was extremely balanced.[25] The photo of Rachel and the two boys was poignant and spoke volumes. Today, Rachel Kingsley lives in St. Louis, where she raises her two younger sons. According to Carey, she heard from her oldest child, Gregory, when he sent her a high school graduation announcement.

When the ruling was overturned by the Florida 5th District Court of Appeals, I contacted the *Orlando Sentinel*. Bob Levenson had left a few weeks before, and no other reporter was as familiar with the case. I reminded the editor in charge that the *Sentinel* had given plenty of publicity to Judge's Kirk's decision, and I appealed to journalistic ethics that they give some prominent space to reporting the decision overturning his ruling. The article appeared on the front page of the August 19, 1993, edition.[26]

However, even though the appellate court ruled that the decision was wrong, it also said it was in the best interest for Gregory to stay with the Russ family because so much time had passed. Jane Carey tried to go to the Florida Supreme Court, and she was turned down.

Carey says, "If this happened today, I would use everything I've learned about media relations. This was a time when the media aggression about all kinds of cases was dramatically increasing."[27]

I learned something from the *Kingsley* case that I have never forgotten. Persuading the accused to speak to the media and giving them the training and courage to be themselves, their good selves, before strangers who have been reporting all the terrible accusations about them that their accusers have made, is valuable in itself as well as healing. Even if the outcome of their personal trials and/or actual trial is not what they wanted, they must go on with their lives. Balancing the negative image projected in the media gives them (and their families) a better start on life after the media onslaught ends.

Losing children or access to children in a custody fight or because of criminal charges is one of the most terrifying and overwhelming matters in a battle between accusers and the accused.

On March 22, 2002, I received a call about the case of a foster care mother whose own eighteen-year-old son had been arrested for allegedly abusing some young foster care children in his mother's home. This criminal matter became even more devastating and newsworthy because the fifteen-year-old biological daughter of the mother had also been removed from the home by Department of Children & Families (DCF) after police arrested her brother. To make matters even worse, the girl was wheelchair-bound and suffered from cerebral palsy. What made this telephone call most unusual was that it came from a journalist, Rene Stutzman, the reporter for the *Orlando Sentinel* who covered the Seminole County, Florida, legal beat. She was someone with whom I had worked on another case (see Chapter 7) and who understood exactly what I did as a high-profile case expert working with lawyers. The challenge was that there was no lawyer involved.

Stutzman was very clear up front that she was "just a selfish reporter who wanted a story."[28] But it was also apparent to me that that she was a reporter who really cared about people and reacted to injustice. She wanted an interview with Marie Jasmin, the fifty-five-year-old mother who had been arrested and charged with not reporting the alleged abuse that her son had inflicted on the foster children in her home. On the day that Stutzman called me, Jasmin was in the office of Dr. Clyde Climer.

The doctor and Jasmin were from different worlds. She was black, and her only income was from foster care. He was a white Ob/Gyn. What they shared was a strong faith and membership in the same community church, the Church of Christ in Altamonte Springs. Dr. and Mrs. Climer were trying to help her by giving limited statements to the media, but like most people, they were wary and uncertain about the media and whether going public might help her get her child back.

I was intrigued, not just by the circumstances of the case, but because the reporter had called me to ask for my help in facilitating an interview with Jasmin. To make the right decision, Jasmin needed a media consultant who specialized in high-profile criminal matters. I realized up front that there was little or no money in this job. I had never worked pro bono on such a case. I decided that I'd consider helping Jasmin if, after meeting her, I believed in her innocence.

I checked online to see what had been written so far. The first few articles (March 9, 10, 13 and 14) all focused on the arrests and allegations by children—these stories were all fed to the newspaper by the police.[29] On March 17, Stutzman reported that DCF records indicated that Marie Jasmin had cared for sixty-nine foster kids and quoted social workers as calling her "nurturing" and dedicated to children.[30] According to these articles, in records released by DCF, Jasmin was praised as "wonderful" and "strong and caring." A few days later, another story quoted an HRS report and claimed that Jasmin "hid a pattern of abuse," and that some social workers "feared for the safety of children" in her care.[31]

The time for the accused—Jasmin—to respond had arrived. She needed to present her side before the DCF continued to try and to cover its ass by casting aspersions on the foster parent it had once praised. Stutzman gave me the name and telephone number of Dr. Climer, and I called his office. Because Stutzman had advised them that they needed someone to help them with the media, they were expecting my call. I got through in a very short time, considering it was a doctor's office. It turned out that Marie Jasmin and her other adult child were in the office when I phoned; Stutzman was also in the building. On the telephone, I did my best shorthand description of what it is that I do, dropped a few names, and told Dr. Climer that I was willing to come and speak to the mother. If I felt that she really was a victim and that her disabled daughter had been unfairly removed from her home because of the accusations against her son, I might help facilitate an interview. I told him that the power of the press cannot be disregarded.

Timing is so critical is these matters. To the uninitiated, and this means 99 percent of all accused people, media relations strategy is a complete mystery. They have never heard of someone like me, and I have to cut through their preoccupation with the frightening and unfamiliar experience of being arrested or shot or attacked in the news and convince them that I can help. If they don't get it and get it the first time, the opportunity to proclaim their innocence in media that have been publicizing the accusations against them may be lost.

Within an hour, I was at the medical center and sitting down with Dr. Climer, his wife, Jasmin, and her daughter. I asked Jasmin to be perfectly honest with me, and I would do what I could to help her. I also asked her to give me a dollar so that we had a fiduciary relationship. Anything she said would be protected by client confidentiality. Although this may seem to be a showy exercise in establishing a relationship with a client, it accomplishes two things: it breaks the ice and by giving me the dollar the client actually establishes professional confidentiality. (I've have also used this tactic with lawyers and sources concerned about confidentiality.)

In any civil or criminal matter, confidentiality must be established from the first conversation. This is also why, whenever possible, any fees paid to the media consultant should come directly from the lawyer's office. As an expert hired by the lawyer, even if the lawyer bills the client for the expenses of a media expert, the expert is protected from being subpoenaed by the prosecution for the defense. I learned the lesson while representing a topless dancer whose family paid my fee directly (see Chapter 9).

I asked Marie Jasmin a series of questions, and I made my judgment immediately. Having some familiarity with the deficiencies of HRS, I had no doubt that her daughter was in far more danger while in HRS custody than she might be at home. Since her older brother had been arrested and was sitting in the county jail, there was no chance of contact between them. I also had my doubts about the children's accusations against the older boy once Jasmin explained the circumstances to me.

Two children who had been placed in foster care with Jasmin because of a drug-abusing mom had recently been released into the family of their aunt. The aunt was angry that she had not been able to get custody of them from the start. If fact, there had been words between Jasmin and the children's relatives over the years about the appropriateness of their visitation. Within a week of the aunt's gaining custody, she had elicited an accusation about the older boy from the children and called the police. Based upon this accusation, the police arrived at the Jasmin home and arrested the young man and his mother. Jasmin was taken to jail because she was accused of standing by while her son abused the children. HRS summarily removed all foster care children from the Jasmin home, as well as her disabled teenager.

When the actual allegations were eventually revealed, I was even more convinced that the children were lying.[32] First of all, two of the four were girls under ten who claimed they were raped. This charge is the easiest to prove or disprove with a medical exam. The other two were boys aged four and six, one of whom was allegedly fondled and the other allegedly saw nasty photos on the computer screen of the accused, Jacques Jasmin. While I thought there might be some truth in the computer photo, I suspected that the six-year-old had invaded the privacy of the eighteen-year-old and there was no crime there.

My years of experience and knowledge about criminal matters make me suspicious of police who act solely on reports by children about their caretakers. Police are notorious for being suggestive and leading in their questioning of children if they have received a report that child abuse has occurred. The line of questioning of children under the age of ten often leads to untrue allegations and initiates a nightmare for the adults, who are eventually arrested and charged with abuse. The series of devastating events that occur in the lives of the accused never ends, even if the charges are shown to be unfounded and then dropped.

With Stutzman waiting in the hallway, I went over a number of statements that I thought were the key to make in attacking HRS and demonstrating that Jasmin was a caring and considerate foster parent. She frequently took many more children than most foster families. HRS was willing to exceed the placement limits because there was such a shortage of foster care homes in Central Florida.

Preparation for an interview is critical. Even if there is only a twenty-minute window to prepare a client, I go through an intense rehearsal. During the preparation of Ms. Jasmin we reviewed likely questions, wrote down answers, reworded answers for effective delivery and rehearsed the answers. This process makes the difference between a chance at a positive portrayal and a sloppy, confused-sounding interview where the client looks defensive and unwilling to tell the whole truth.

The most important statement the accused makes is to deny the allegations and to do so emphatically. When someone is innocent, I ask him to give an immediate response to these questions: *Are you innocent? Are these accusations true?* I write down the answers. Usually, the first response is the most honest and explicit. If the client rambles through the answer, I help them edit it down to the crux of the matter. The natural tendency of the untrained interviewee is to keep talking after answering the question. Reporters will ask a question and then look quizzically at the interviewee and take notes on everything said. This is one of the first rules I set when preparing the accused for an interview. Answer the question with the answer you've prepared. Then stop talking. Wait for the next question, and think about it. If you haven't prepared an answer to that question, ask the reporter to repeat the question. If there's not prepared answer, respond 'I can't answer that, but I can say....'" Then, repeat a different statement, one already prepared.

As I told Jasmin, all the questions should relate to the topic at hand: the accusations, the alleged crimes, her innocence. The best-case scenario is one in which the answers are reflected in the article headline. The next day, while waiting to board a plane to New York, I opened the newspaper to this headline, "Foster Mom Calls Allegations Against Her Son 'False'; Marie Jasmin Asked to Care for Her Disabled Daughter Who Was Taken from Her When She Was Charged."[33]

I read over the article with some pride. I felt good about the profile of Marie Jasmin and her articulate protestations of innocence, "The allegations against [me] and [my] son 'are false, false in every way, in every word.... That never happened in my house or anywhere else.'" Finally, in her plea for the return of her daughter, she is quoted as saying, "I want my baby back."[34]

I knew that the article would make a difference in how people in her church and community would view her and raised awareness that HRS had unfairly and overzealously removed her disabled daughter from the only home she had ever known and where she received the best care available.

Then I stopped feeling so self-satisfied for a minute and decided that there was something far more important that I might do. Help her get a lawyer for the same price she paid me—$1. I wanted a pro bono lawyer, someone who disliked the foster care system and HRS as much as I did and who understood the power of the press. I called Don Lykkebak before the plane took off and asked him to read the story and talk to Jasmin. If he felt the same way I did, I asked him to be on the same team with me and work to get her daughter home to her as soon as possible.

By the time I landed in New York, I had an answer. I called Jasmin and told her to make an appointment with Lykkebak, stressing that this was not going to be representation for her son, still sitting in the county jail. By the end of the day, she had what extremely few, if any, families, people accused of being unfit foster parents, have: a great lawyer and a legal-savvy publicist.

It took two court hearings, an ongoing media campaign, and just over a month before Marie Jasmin had her "baby" home. Today, Jasmin works as a seamstress in a small crafts company. With the help of her fellow church members, she was able to keep her home. Son Jacques, who was working on an associate's degree in criminal justice when he was falsely accused, works as a loan officer in a mortgage office and lives at home with his mother and sister.

Rene Stutzman went on to write a series of articles on the deficiencies at DCF and its shortcomings and internal investigations and is still covering courts for the *Orlando Sentinel*. [35]

I asked Marie Jasmin why she decided to give the interview that day, and she said, "I talked to the media because of your support—by telling me what to expect and listening to me tell my story first. I felt that you believed me, and that helped me make my decision to talk to the media whenever you were there."[36]

The *Kingsley* case took place in 1992, when media coverage of trials was burgeoning. *CourtTV* went on the air the year before, in 1991, with four million viewers. On its current Web site, the network boasts demographics of more than 86 million homes.[37] Lawyers must ask themselves, "How many of these viewers will serve on a jury that decides the fates of their clients?"

In November 2005, the chairman of *CourtTV* Networks, Henry Schleiff, testified before the United States Senate Committee on the Judiciary and reported that, "Court TV has covered more than 900 U.S. trials and legal proceedings, providing more than 30,000 hours of courtroom coverage."[38]

Cameras were once rare in courtrooms. By 2005, forty-three states permit cameras in their civil trial courts—and, of those, thirty-nine states permit cameras in their criminal trial courts. In the twenty-first century, everyone involved in the justice system—lawyers, judges, the public in general—knows the media is watching in the high-profile cases. For the accused or accusers, those who have a lawyer and a media specialist on their team have a much better chance of seeing justice served.[39]

Four

Matters of Life and Death

Media relations efforts on behalf of someone accused of a capital crime can literally make the difference between life and death. In all but twelve states in America and in the District of Columbia, the deathy penalty is allowed as a sentence for a convicted person. Before such a sentence is imposed, the defense has many months of opportunity to make public any extenuating circumstances related to the commission of a crime and to publicize the background of the accused.

There are several reasons why a lawyer has an ethical obligation to do everything possible, including implementing media relations, to ensure that his or her client does not receive the death penalty. These include the existence of a flawed judicial system that wrongfully convicts; the possibility that new evidence, perhaps DNA testing, may eventually exonerate a convicted person; that a reformed person may one day receive clemency; or even a belief that capital punishment is immoral. In no other criminal defense case are the stakes higher than when a person is charged with a capital crime and the prosecution decides to seek the death penalty. As long as the accused person is alive, his avenue of legal appeals remains open.

The earlier a lawyer can begin to defend his client in the arena of public opinion, the more powerful the message becomes. Media relations are the only way a lawyer can balance the information already put out to the public by police and prosecutors. As a conduit to the population from which the jury pool will come, the media are the links for the lawyer and the defendant to the public.

In some instances, a defendant may have already done himself irreparable harm by talking to the media during an investigation. This is especially true during investigations of a missing spouse or child. When the family member ultimately becomes the accused and is arrested as the one responsible for the death or disappearance, the media profile developed during the investigation must be addressed by the defense.

If the lawyer does not handle the media effectively, everything that the accused has said and done prior to his arrest "may be used against him." In Scott Peterson's case, this image was severely damaged because of his behavior before and after his pregnant wife, Laci, disappeared. The Peterson case is a textbook example of police effectively working to convict a suspect through media relations.

Laci Peterson was reported missing on Christmas Eve 2002. In January 2003, police held a press conference and announced that Scott Peterson had been having an affair prior to Laci's disappearance.[1] Ongoing coverage of the affair included stories of Peterson's continued contact with the "other woman" and taped conversations of him lying to her about what was happening during the investigation. Persistent police communication with the media was so damaging that it was lethal to any effective defense in a public forum.

In addition to his extramarital affair, Peterson's alleged intention to sell his house, his purchase of a new vehicle, and the relatively modest $250,000 life insurance policy were all hung out before the media like dirty laundry.

At the time of Peterson's arrest, his parents gave an interview with *Time* magazine and logically refuted the way these facts had been tainted: there were two life insurance policies, one for Laci and one for Scott; the couple had looked at new cars together; Scott wasn't trying to sell the house but considered doing so after his community turned on him. Peterson's parents also addressed the police tactics used to convince Laci's parents that her husband was responsible.[2]

Although the comments of Peterson's parents in this national interview were excellent responses, there would have had to have been an ongoing media campaign in Modesto that rivaled the police media relations campaign to sway public opinion. Like almost every family in America, the Petersons had no experience dealing with the media. During the month before Scott's arrest, the police systematically released damning information about their prime suspect.

By the time the jury was selected in Scott Peterson's murder trial, he was one of the most vilified men in America. Although there was a change of venue that moved the case from Modesto to Redwood City, California, this accomplished little. To ensure an objective trial, his case would have to have been tried on the moon and a jury selected from a crew in a space station without access to news.

Peterson had a good lawyer in Mark Geragos, yet by the time there was a gag order in the case, his accused client had been profiled as his pregnant wife's brutal killer. There's no doubt that Peterson was a philandering, insensitive husband whose behavior after his wife vanished was self-centered and counter to the grief-stricken image that the general public wanted.

Scott Peterson was convicted on purely circumstantial evidence. MSNBC broadcast details of an Associated Press report, November 13, 2004: "The circumstantial evidence proved persuasive. Prosecutors presented one hundred seventy-four witnesses and hundreds of pieces of [circumstantial] evidence, from wiretapped phone calls to videotaped police interrogations, depicting Peterson as a liar and a philanderer who sweet-talked his massage therapist girlfriend . . . while publicly pining for his missing wife."[3]

Like so many Americans, I followed the Peterson case, ad nauseam, and from my professional perspective observed such egregious behavior by the man that I found him guilty of being a repulsive, stupid and unfaithful jerk. What if this is as far as his immoral behavior went? Is he waiting out his appeal on death row innocent of murdering his wife?

One thing is unquestionable: the police and prosecutors were able to build a highly convincing case against Peterson before he sat in front of a jury and continued to exhibit his insensitive and unrepentant behavior. *The Modesto Bee*, the Peterson's hometown newspaper, provided comprehensive coverage from day one.

After the conviction, two articles published in *The Modesto Bee* on November 6, 2005, address key points. In "Tales from a Trial," written by Garth Stapley, he noted that the prosecutorial players "racked up four major awards celebrating prosecutorial excellence. All have traveled to share their stories with law and order groups."[4]

In the same issue, another reporter, Jeff Jardine, wrote, "Initial public sympathy toward Peterson as the worried husband of a beautiful and pregnant woman eroded after . . . photos captured him chatting on the phone and laughing while so many truly caring people prayed for Laci's safe return. It ended when Amber Frey emerged as the other woman—duped by a duplicitous lover. From that point, Scott Peterson rose to fame as the prime suspect, the villain and the man who couldn't keep his lies straight. He hired Geragos—a celebrity by virtue of being a celebrity lawyer and TV talking head—and that upped the exposure."

It is important to emphasize that the Modesto police investigators were building a case against Peterson in the court of public opinion by releasing these photos and videos to the media. Jardine continued, "The media's coverage created a chicken and egg debate. Did they cover it because it was a major event or did they make it a major event because they covered it?"[5]

Clearly, it was the latter. The year after the verdict, in 2005, members of the prosecution team attended a national judicial conference in Reno. The focus was dealing with the media in high-profile cases. The name of the seminar was "O.J. to Martha to Michael." And Scott Peterson was a big topic, reported Jardine.[6]

The jurors selected in Peterson's case, like all jurors in death penalty cases, were asked if they could render a death sentence in a life-or-death case. Prosecutors always try to weed out those who are opposed to the death penalty. The potential jurors are also asked what they know about the defendant of the alleged crime. But the answers of potential jurors are always tainted by their personal desire to serve or not serve on the jury.

In 1976, after a twelve-year hiatus, the death penalty was again declared constitutional by the U.S. Supreme Court. States increasingly opted to reinstate the death penalty as a punishment for certain crimes. Although there are nearly 4,000 people on death row, over 230 condemned men and women have received clemency. If they had been executed, the evidence and circumstances that eventually resulted in clemency would have been meaningless.

Clemency does not necessarily mean a pardon or release from prison. However, the difference between serving a sentence on death row and a life term in the general population of a prison is vast. With few exceptions, the nearly 4,000 people in so-called death houses in prisons suffer restrictions that those in a general prison population do not.

In the East Block of San Quentin prison, where Scott Peterson avoids mingling with the other condemned men, he does not take part in any work or educational programs and is strip-searched every time he leaves his cell. At this prison, officials installed metal screens to block a view of the San Francisco Bay that was "considered too beautiful for inmates."[7] Yet, even for those who live on death row, the opportunity to make a positive contribution to society and to influence positively the lives of others is very real.

On December 14, 2005, Stanley "Tookie" Williams was executed in California, but during his more than twenty-five years as a condemned prisoner, he used his notoriety and experiences as the leader of a violent Los Angeles gang, the Crips, to educate young people about the dangers of gang life by writing a series of children's books, including one addressed to African American teenagers warning them about prison. Williams was nominated for the Nobel Peace Prize for his efforts to promote peaceful actions by gang members, denounce gang violence and set up an international Internet program for peer mentoring among gang members. Williams was even awarded the Presidential Call to Service Award by George W. Bush. Williams' life after a death sentence serves as a perfect example of a prisoner reformed regardless of whether he was responsible for two robberies that resulted in the murders of four people in 1979.[8]

Williams, like the majority of people convicted of capital crimes in this country, did not have the money to hire a criminal defense lawyer, let alone a publicist. His good works in prison heightened his profile and were a significant factor in his lengthy appeals process. However, the usual time to employ public relations is before the accused is sentenced.

The process for indicting and charging a person with a capital crime differs from state to state. Before creating a media relations strategy for the accused, the publicist must research the legal procedures. There will always be junctures when mitigating factors about the alleged crimes need to be publicized. Most people accused of a capital crime will not understand the appropriate timing for media interviews, nor will they receive any professional advice. Without trained counsel, the suspect may give an inappropriate or damaging interview. A reporter may contact the suspect in jail, perhaps with the help of a cooperative jail employee.

The rare wealthy and well-educated suspect who is charged with a capital crime may hire a defense lawyer knowledgeable and experienced in handling the media or even a public relations specialist. This is certainly the exception.

Once the lawyer can become a spokesperson for the client, he needs to contact the media and defend the client. He may categorically deny his client's guilt, or he may allude to soon-to-be revealed circumstances and evidence. At some point, the lawyer may refer to mitigating circumstances in the commission of the crime. The public who reads and hears about the crime during the initial press coverage of the suspect's arrest will then be exposed not only to the police and prosecutor's reports on the arrest, but also to the defense lawyer's explanation of why the accused is innocent as charged.

Most people accused of a capital crime do not hire a lawyer; one is appointed for them. This means that taxpayer dollars fund both the prosecutor and the defender. However, the state or district attorney and the public defender are allocated different budgets and both offices are run by elected officials. One of the non-legal professionals at the state attorney's office will probably be a public information officer. Often this individual will be a former news reporter and someone who has honed his skills in disseminating information that advances the prosecution of people charged with committing high-profile crimes. A corresponding position does not exist in public defender offices.

Murder cases are always big news in a community. Particularly heinous or unusual high-profile capital crimes—such as those involving children or multiple deaths—will garner statewide and national attention.

If the accused is assigned a public defender, he will not meet his lawyer until well after the initial reports of the crime have occurred. The release of information to the media about the crime will have come from either the police or the prosecution. In some cases, family members of the accused, neighbors, or friends may be identified by the media and asked to comment. These comments are harder to elicit and not as widely covered in the media as the comments of those close to the victim. In most cases, a particularly sharp reporter striving to be an investigative journalist will seek out someone connected to the accused willing to grant an interview. Once this person is quoted on the news or in the newspaper, the lazier reporters will also go to this loquacious individual and get a statement. This is often disadvantageous to the accused.

Dominic Gentile says that when he was before the Supreme Court in 1991, Justice Anthony Scalia asked the amicus lawyer representing the Department of Justice a question about public relations. Scalia used an example; if an employee in a lawyer's office, for example, Perry Mason's assistant, Della, put out some good press for their client, was that allowed under the existing rules? The lawyer, arguing that Gentile's press conference was not allowed under the rules, said no. However, when Scalia asked him if it was allowable for the law firm to hire a public relations firm, the lawyer said he did not think it violated the rules.[9]

Gentile says that it occurred to him then that the financial ability to employ public relations professionals may raise the issue of "effective assistance of counsel." For example, if the prosecution has the resources to use media relations to inject its case "into the public mix" and the defense does not, that is, when the accused is represented by a public defender, then it may be possible to raise the issue of effective assistance of counsel.[10]

Without a media plan for the defense, the only reports are those usually generated by the police or prosecutors, which are designed to be potentially inflammatory. Although most people related to the accused will shy away from the media intrusion into their once-private lives, there are exceptions. In particularly high-profile crimes, there always seem to be people who will come forward to comment about their purported knowledge of the accused. These people often just want to be part of the media parade, and when their derogatory opinions of the accused are publicized, they help to build a better case for convicting the accused in the court of public opinion.

During a case I worked on in 1994, a nineteen-year-old from a small ocean-side city on the east coast of Florida became the primary suspect in the serial killings of five students at the University of Florida. Most of his surfing buddies refused to talk to the media. One, considered a good friend by the suspect, decided to speak to reporters and, instead of defending his friend, commented that he did have a "crazy side." Years after he was completely exonerated, the innocent suspect, Edward Humphrey (see Chapter 5), remained hurt and confused by his friend's remarks.

In America, in the past decade, a majority of those convicted of a capital crime and sentenced to death were represented by the office of a public defender. When there is a conflict because multiple defendants are represented by the public defender, a lawyer, paid a reduced fee will be appointed by the courts. The public defender or court-appointed lawyers will rarely employ a media relations specialist and will almost always have far more limited resources for investigation than the prosecution.

Just how unusual it is for an indigent accused to have access to media relations advice became apparent in 1996 when the long-time public defender in Orange County, Florida, Joseph DuRocher, decided to test the waters for leveling the media relations in a capital murder case and hired me.

DuRocher was a popular public defender, evidenced by his having been elected to five four-year terms. He is an outspoken anti–death penalty advocate and included a Major Crimes Division, headed by Patricia Cashman, within his office. In 1995, she and another experienced public defender, Bill McClellan, were preparing for the murder trial of a professional boxer who had killed his former manager. They had received inquiries and requests for interviews with their client from media outlets and publications around the world.

In 1995, Timothy "Doc" Anderson, a thirty-seven-year-old former professional light-heavyweight boxer set up a meeting with his manager at an Orlando motel under the pretense of interviewing him for a book. After a brief discussion, Anderson pulled out a small-caliber pistol and shot thirty-nine-year-old Rick "Elvis" Parker six times. Anderson then reloaded the weapon and fired again, perhaps to be sure that Parker, who weighed over three hundred pounds, was dead.

The media began reporting at the crime scene, where Anderson calmly turned himself over to police. He qualified for a public defender because he could not afford to hire a lawyer. He had not worked in several years due to illness and chronic lethargy, a result, he claimed, of his former manager's poisoning his water during a professional fight.

After indicting Anderson for first-degree murder in May 1995, the state attorney's office announced that it was seeking the death penalty. Cashman and McClellan had each interacted with the media in other high-profile trials and handled numerous capital murder cases. They respected the potential influence of media coverage on public sentiment.

Since Tim Anderson had been a professional athlete, his prosecution was drawing media inquiries from beyond the local area. The fact that he reloaded his gun and that he was white—unlike the majority of indigent clients represented by public defenders—increased the drama quotient of an already dramatic case.

Along with DuRocher, Cashman and McClellan decided to request a media specialist to work with the Anderson defense team. DuRocher says he was going to "try to save Tim Anderson's life and get the best possible legal result."[11] The state attorney's office was represented by a lawyer familiar with the local media and was fully capable of handling all inquiries and opportunities. Furthermore, its full-time public information officer served as a liaison with the local media and assisted attorneys in publicizing high-profile arrests, prosecutions and trials.

DuRocher knew that "the state always wanted the benefit of a climate favorable to the outcome of a case" and wanted Tim Anderson to gain more control of this climate. He agreed with Cashman that Anderson's case was a good one to test the waters for using a media relations expert. DuRocher's office had been fielding calls by sports writers and reporters as well as the local media, who wanted interviews with Anderson.[12]

Although Cashman had an article sent to her about Anderson published in a German boxing magazine—one of many sports publications that contacted the public defender's office—it was not likely to be read by anyone living in Orlando. Yet, local media coverage had great potential to affect public sentiment.

In November 1995, DuRocher called to discuss hiring me as a media relations expert in the Anderson case. I had known Joe DuRocher since the year I opened my firm and developed a media-training seminar for lawyers. In addition to having a professional relationship, DuRocher and I share the belief that the death penalty is morally wrong. DuRocher commented, "We always treated first-degree murder as a potential death penalty case. Our goal from the start is to save the client's life. In cases like Tim Anderson's, when there are aggravating circumstances, we do everything possible so that the state attorney will come off the death penalty."[13]

Because the state of Florida sought the death penalty, even without meeting Anderson, I was interested in contributing to a media campaign to prevent his execution. I learned that although there was no question that he killed Rick Parker, there was also a long history of abuse in their professional relationship, as well as other contributing factors that made a quest for a lesser conviction realistic.

After an initial meeting with Cashman and McClellan, I agreed to prepare a proposal for Orange County to hire me as a media relations expert to assist the public defender's office in Tim Anderson's case. Our strategy was to include references in the proposal to the use of media relations specialists by the state attorney's office. The public defender agreed that if my proposal was rejected, the public defender would litigate the issue and file a lawsuit arguing for equal protection under the law.

It's important to note that the availability of media relations experts in high-profile trials frees up the lawyers to focus on trial preparation without ignoring the media opportunities. Public defenders are already overworked, often representing dozens of their indigent clients at any given time.

I requested a fee of $3,000—$2,000 less than the minimum retainer I ask from a private lawyer and his or her client. Lawyers who do public defender work are paid on a lower fee scale than lawyers in the private sector command. Since I believed we were setting an important precedent, I wanted to meet the county halfway. My proposal was submitted to the Orange County assistant county attorney and accepted without delay.[14]

Before I turned my full attention to the Anderson case, I knew from media reactions to my involvement in an earlier high-profile case that we needed to address the issue of why the county hired a publicist to assist the lawyers defending an indigent client against first-degree murder charges. I advised DuRocher to prepare for the element of controversy in my hiring. Although he knew that we were setting a precedent, he was not as prepared as I was for the kind of media coverage that I anticipated. My strategy was to get the story about my hiring over and done with before I began representing Tim Anderson. This approach is similar to "feeding the beast" when reporters swarm over a high-profile incident. Once they are given something to report, they are more likely to move on to another story.

I compare this tactic to the advice experts give on what to do if a dog or bear attacks you. Never try to run away; they will catch you and tear you to pieces. In an animal attack, curl up in a ball, stay small and still. When the media is involved, secure yourself behind a table or podium; speak thoughtfully and assuredly until you can walk away calmly.

Several reporters had already asked public defender Cashman to allow Anderson to be interviewed. I contacted Gerard Shields, then a reporter at the *Orlando Sentinel*, to discuss both my role in the case and the possibility of an interview with Anderson. At that time, Shields was one of the *Sentinel*'s golden boys, a respected reporter valued and liked by the editors, who gave him the latitude he wanted to work on stories that interested him.

As soon as I mentioned to Shields that I was calling about the Anderson case, his interest was piqued. I embargoed the explanation I was going to give him, asking him to research the use of media experts by criminal defense lawyers and discuss my hiring with DuRocher before he completed his story. He wanted to write an article about the media relations role I had been hired to do as an expert requested by the public defender's office and paid for by the county.

Two days before Shields' article announcing my hiring was scheduled to be printed, Kathi Belich, a local television reporter with WFTV, Channel 9, the Orlando ABC affiliate, who had petitioned Cashman for an interview with Anderson, contacted her office once again. This time, she was told to call me regarding any interview requests.

On January 10, Belich called me and asked why I was the person setting up interviews with Anderson. I asked her to go off the record for a moment to discuss the Anderson case. "Off the record" is a media relations tactic that I teach. There is case law to support a verbal contract established with a reporter that protects off-the-record information (see Chapter 11).

I did not simply ask to go off-the-record and then start talking. I did what I counsel lawyers to do: established a verbal contract with the reporter and listened for a response. I asked her if she agreed to go off-the-record, and she said yes. I told her about my contract with the county and said that after the *Sentinel* article ran, I would discuss her interest in interviewing Tim Anderson.[15] She agreed to call me then. However, after we hung up the telephone, she proceeded to violate the off-the-record agreement and, within an hour, appeared with a cameraman at the public defender's office to ambush Joe DuRocher for a "whistleblower" story.

When DuRocher called me, he had already given a statement. I first called Belich's assignment editor, Linda Page, to protest. Then, I followed up with a letter copied to the news director and station manager. In the end, Belich denied having the off-the-record discussion, and her editor told me that she believed her.

This is the only time in seventeen years that a reporter violated an off-the-record agreement with me. I declined to be interviewed for the whistleblower story. The news segment that aired raised the question, "Was this public money being appropriately spent?" Needless to say, I never gave this reporter access to interview Anderson. I pegged her as unethical and untrustworthy.

The *Orlando Sentinel* article by Gerry Shields appeared the next day.[16] It was a balanced look at the reasons for my hiring. A few days later, an *Orlando Sentinel* editorial criticized DuRocher's decision to hire a publicist. In his twenty years as public defender, this was only the second time he had been criticized by the local newspaper.[17]

Once the story about my hiring had been addressed and become old news, I began to focus my media relations expertise on introducing Tim Anderson to Central Florida through the media. Unprecedented was that the accused was poor and taxpayer dollars were used to pay the expert's fee. As *Florida Trend* magazine characterized the hiring a few months later, this was "indigent P.R."[18] What the article did not note was that the hiring was a calculated move to level the playing field in the strategic game of media relations in a death penalty case.

I first met Tim Anderson at the Orange County Jail in a small room near the front entrance, the usual place for lawyer–client conferences. Trish Cashman, Bill McClellan and I waited while Anderson was brought down from his cellblock. He was handcuffed and wore leg shackles when he arrived, but he also wore a smile. After he was led into the room, the guard removed his handcuffs and left, and we were locked into the room with Anderson. We discussed my role in the case, and then Anderson began to tell me his story.

At thirty-seven, Tim Anderson was a washed-up, punch-drunk, ex-pugilist. He was unemployed and broke, but in his glory days, he had been enough of a force to have gone up against the likes of George Foreman and Larry Holmes. The cause of his fall from grace, he claimed, was Rick "Elvis" Parker, the flamboyant former cleaning products salesman who became Anderson's manager. They teamed up in 1985, when Parker decided to get into the fight game and promised Anderson that he would turn him into a "great white hope" and make them both rich men.

Instead, Anderson told me, Parker slipped deeper and deeper into cocaine abuse and unscrupulous business practices, eventually coming under investigation by the FBI. He held back $148,000 that he owed Anderson.[19] He wanted Anderson to fix fights, including taking a fall in a highly publicized 1992 bout with former New York Jets football-star-turned-boxer Mark Gastineau. Anderson refused and beat Gastineau badly. Parker arranged a rematch six months later, and Anderson told me that during the fight, Parker instructed a corner man to give Anderson poisoned water. While hospital records do not confirm Anderson's claim that he was poisoned, Gastineau won the fight, and Anderson was found unconscious in his locker room. Anderson hired a lawyer, "legendary Miami attorney Ellis Rubin, who filed suit against Parker for the back money and the alleged poisoning."[20]

After the Gastineau rematch, Anderson said that Parker continued to threaten him, even sending "goons" to beat him with a baseball bat. The last straw for Tim Anderson was when Parker's thugs handed him a piece of paper that indicated Parker knew the home address of Anderson's sister Erin, who was paralyzed from a diving accident. Anderson, who was very close to his sister, took this as a threat against his sister's life.

Eventually, on April 28, 1995, Anderson managed to lure Parker to a hotel room in Lake Buena Vista, Florida, saying he wanted to tape an interview for a book about boxing he was working on. Along with the tape recorder Anderson brought a .38-caliber pistol. The two men argued, and Anderson shot Parker. Then Anderson called the police. These facts were all reported in the *Orlando Sentinel.*[21]

From this discussion, I identified stories about Anderson's family life and the history of incidents with Parker that he could share with reporters. The threats Parker made against Anderson and his sister were stories that the public needed to hear. I did not operate independently in determining what Anderson might safely relate to a reporter. His lawyers and I had to agree that nothing divulged would jeopardize his defense strategy.

Working with criminal defense lawyers demands a full understanding of those aspects of the case that they do not want discussed with the media. In this case, our explanation for not answering questions about the actual shooting was that Anderson did not remember many of the events that occurred that day. There are always facts in a lawyer–client relationship that must be kept confidential, and this extends to the relationship with any expert.

Reporters understand that lawyers must protect their client from discussing case strategy or ongoing investigations. It is important to make this clear before the interview begins. I generally have a pre-interview discussion with the reporter and emphasize the desire we all have to tell this story as much as his lawyer will allow. This strengthens my role as a facilitator, not a manipulator, in the eyes of the media.

In conducting media relations, there are critical boundaries in criminal matters. I let the reporter know that I am arranging the interview because I think it is important for a balanced story to run, not just a story from the prosecutor's perception. Even in a murder case, there may be facts and events that led up to the crime that elicit sympathy for the accused and his family. In the Anderson case, the defendant and his invalid sister had a very close relationship. There were numerous family photos of them, which I was able to provide to the press.

Before I left my first meeting with Anderson, I had itemized in writing the segments of his life story that he would discuss in an upcoming interview with Gerry Shields. I also asked Anderson to cut his hair, since it was nearly to his shoulders. He said he was thinking about shaving his head. "Absolutely not!" I said. I wanted his appearance to be as normal as possible. We even discussed having a professional barber brought in, but it turned out there was a competent barber available at the jail.

The purpose of all these discussions and recommendations regarding Anderson's appearance and demeanor was to humanize him, despite a prison environment that tends to dehumanize. I reminded Anderson that on the day of any interview, I wanted him to shampoo thoroughly in order to avoid flat, oily hair. I also brought foundation makeup with me the day his photo was taken for the newspaper or when a TV crew came for an interview. There really is jailhouse pallor; the very limited time in the sun and the starchy diet lacking in fresh vegetables and fruit give inmates a pasty look.

The public defender generated a letter authorizing me to visit with Anderson in a room where inmates at the county jail have private discussions with their lawyers. This privilege is very important for several reasons. As I prepare a prisoner for an interview, I need to observe and discuss his facial expressions, how he positions his body and how he will look in a photo or on camera. Access to the jail begins with a walk though a metal detector, but this still allows me to bring in cosmetics and, unlike someone visiting a family member or friend during specified hours, I am allowed physical contact with a client during visits.

Prior to any media interview, I prepare a list of answers and responses to potential questions. Before an interview, there is usually an opportunity to discuss with the reporter the questions he wants to ask or that we do not want to answer. The interview, when properly planned and monitored, will never go beyond the parameters of our objectives.

Tim Anderson was a good listener. He also had some experience speaking to sports writers while he was boxing and promoting himself. He was a genial and likeable man, and I knew I could prepare him to show this aspect of his persona in any interview.

One aspect of Anderson's outlook on life that I did *not* want revealed was his religious beliefs. Like so many people who are incarcerated, he had discovered or rediscovered religion. Even if the system does not forgive them, men and women in prison often believe that God forgives them and they are eager to share the revelations of faith that comfort and sustain them. "Do not share your faith in God with the reporter," I advised Anderson. It sounds melodramatic and too convenient for people accused of murder to discuss their new connection to God. No matter how sincere, religious beliefs typecast prisoners. I wanted the public to see Tim Anderson as an individual—someone dearly loved by family and friends, someone who committed murder after suffering uniquely traumatic circumstances. After meeting him, this is what I truly believed. So could the media and the public.

Shields interviewed Anderson for several hours before writing an in-depth feature story about his family life, his boxing career, and the events that led up to his killing Rick Parker. The story ran in the Sunday edition of the *Orlando Sentinel*, beginning on the front page and continuing with a two-page spread in the back of the first section.[22] There were two photos—a dramatically lit head-and-shoulders shot on the front page and a large photo of Anderson and his sister on the last page of the article.

Even the photo captions and headlines sent the best possible message about Anderson—"Ex-boxer faces the fight of his life." Simply stated the "fight for his life" suggested that Anderson had a defense. Headlines and captions are written by editors, not by the reporters who write the stories, so I didn't know what they would be. We were lucky with this headline, as we were with the caption to the photo of Anderson and his sister that I had provided. It read, "Anderson says thugs sent by Parker tried to intimidate him by threatening his sister, Erin (right), who is confined to a wheelchair."[23]

With this article under our belts, it was time for Anderson's television interview. When the media are aggressively interested in interviewing someone, there are opportunities to establish parameters for the interview well before it begins. It is dangerous for a lawyer or publicist to believe that he can control the tenor of news coverage. Instead, the only control available is over certain aspects what the client says to the media, the timing of access to a story and, as in this case, who interviews the client.

The advantage of dealing with someone who is incarcerated is that he or she is not easily accessible to the media, but beware of the "cooperative" guard who lets an inmate know that a reporter wants to talk to him over the telephone and is ready to accept a collect call. There are also prison personnel who will ask an inmate if he wants to agree to an interview and then put the reporter on a visitors' list. While this is not ethical behavior for a corrections facility employee, in high-profile cases, there is no shortage of people who want to be part of the parade.

In Tim Anderson's case, I ruled out the station that had broadcast the whistle-blower story about my hiring, and I also dealt out the station that had a modus operandi of sensationalism. Instead, I called the NBC affiliate who had an excellent reporter, Greg Fox, whom I knew personally to be a compassionate individual.

The jailhouse interview went well. Before the TV crew arrived, I worked on Anderson's appearance and carefully reviewed the key points that he was to bring out in the interview. I also gave the station copies of photographs of Anderson and his sister to include as stills in the segment. The story raised all the key issues: Anderson's illness following drinking from a water bottle supplied by Rick Parker, his fear for his sister's safety, his regret over the murder, and his lapses of memory during the day of the murder. The feature news story was broadcast over two evenings and heavily promoted as the exclusive interview that it was.[24]

In the wake of this publicity, there were two significant developments in the months before Anderson's trial. The state attorney's office informed the public defender that it was no longer seeking the death penalty, as it had previously intended to do. There was another development, not publicized, that is important to note. On January 18, 1996, the sister and mother of Rick Parker wrote to the state prosecutor, Lawson Lamar, and asked to "please drop the death penalty."[25]

As I mention in the reference to the article Shields later wrote about my work with lawyers, the second significant effect of the publicity became apparent during the jury selection. The first fifty potential jurors called into the courtroom were asked if they had heard or read any stories in the media about the defendant. Twelve of these jurors said that they had, nearly 33 percent—a significantly large percentage. The *Orlando Sentinel* story the following day noted how many in the jury pool had said they had read the story about Anderson.[26] This fact should be considered by all criminal defense lawyers. I am of the strong opinion, as are thousands of lawyers across the country, that not only is it ethical to respond to media inquiries in a high-profile case, but that it is unethical to ignore the effect that public opinion can have on a client during a trial and during the sentencing phase if he or she is convicted.

Tim Anderson was convicted of first-degree murder, but was not sentenced to death. We came very close to seeing a second-degree murder conviction, that would have allowed for judicial discretion in sentencing. A little-known restriction in Florida prevents the criminal defense lawyer from informing the jury that if they convict on first-degree murder, the automatic sentence is life in prison without parole. In fact, when Anderson was sentenced, there was an audible gasp from the jurors. As is usual in high-profile trials, reporters covering the story approach the jurors and ask for comments, if not immediately after they are dismissed, then the next day.

A few weeks following the trial, one juror wrote a letter protesting the fact that they were never told there would be no opportunity to voice their opinion about a reduced sentence. Shields of the *Sentinel* did a follow-up story about the juror who revealed that several of the jurors wanted to convict on second-degree murder.[27]

A few months after the trial was over, Shields profiled me and my work in an article, "More Parties in Court Find Image Counts; Specialists Said Defendants Images to the Media Is a Critical Tool in the Court of Public Opinion."[28] Regarding the Anderson case, Shields asks the question "Did the media exposure pay off?" He notes, "12 of the 50 members in the jury pool said they saw media coverage, with one woman stating that a newspaper story made her more sympathetic toward Anderson."[29]

Tim Anderson is currently serving his life sentence in prison. Instead of waiting on death row through years of uncertain appeals and living under the shadow of death by lethal injection, he exercises, visits with his family whenever possible, and pays his debt to society. Joe DuRocher, who took a chance and took the criticism on the chin, says, "In my mind, there's absolutely no question that the stories about Tim influenced the state's decision to come off death."[30]

Lawyers use expert witnesses from a number of fields to defend their clients or prove their case. In civil suits, accountants and actuaries calculate wages and profits allegedly due to a plaintiff; in many criminal cases, forensic psychiatrists present evidence regarding competency; jury-selection experts prepare questions lawyers ask in voir dire as well as advise what potential jurors raise red flags or are better choices to hear a particular matter. Public relations expertise can ensure appropriate media coverage of a defendant's actions and can save his life.

Five

The Face of a Murder Suspect

Whenever and wherever a serious crime is committed, the media begin their coverage. First reports announce the crime and may serve to warn the public that a criminal is at large. If people are being robbed at ATM machines, the media coverage encourages people to be careful when approaching an ATM. If a woman is raped in a part of town or a child is kidnapped, the media put out an alert. At the same time, the television screen often serves as a twenty-first-century wanted poster: A composite drawing of a suspect broadcast on television and printed in the paper pseudo-deputizes viewers and can help police round up suspects. Most newspapers and television news departments have specific reporters assigned to the police beat who develop relationships with law enforcement at every level. Reporters may hear both on- and off-the-record information as they monitor tips and developments in the crime and search for suspects.

Thus, when someone is arrested and charged, the media coverage that began with the crime now turns its attention to the suspects and, later, the accused. If the first person arrested for the crime is guilty or not, her prosecution begins with the arrest. In some cases, when a crime is particularly high-profile and there is no immediate arrest, the suspense builds in a community. The news media fuel speculations about the investigation and search for the person responsible for the crime. If the crime is murder and similar murders continue to occur, the search for the killer or killers will dominate the news.

Perhaps the first case to influence the popular media significantly and to result in the now all too common made-for-TV movie, was the "Son of Sam case." Between 1976 and 1977, New York City and the rest of the country followed developments in the search for the "Son of Sam" murderer, who ultimately killed six women; five were killed by a .44-caliber pistol shot at point-blank range. David Berkowitz, the twenty-four-year-old killer, wrote several letters with demented messages addressed to police and also communicated with the New York *Daily News* columnist Jimmy Breslin. In a case study developed by Dr. Thomas O'Conner, Associate Professor of Criminal Justice at North Carolina Wesleyan College, he cites the first use of the term "serial killer" as occurring in media coverage of the Berkowitz's murders.[1] In an interview with Dr. O'Connor, he further clarified that this was the first case when "serial killer" was used in popular culture.[2]

Berkowitz was arrested in July 1977, after police traced a parking ticket placed on his car near where he committed his final murder. The sensationalism of the "Son of Sam" killer spawned several books and a 1998 made-for-television movie, as well as a Spike Lee film,[3] *The Summer of Sam*, which used the time and location of the murders as the setting. Crime sprees or a series of murders and the corresponding investigation and pursuit of suspects by law enforcement have always entertained the public since the Wild West days of Billy the Kid and the crimes of Bonnie and Clyde. With the ever-expanding media coverage, finding the perpetrators becomes a peculiar form of perverse entertainment.

The Son of Sam case also launched a new literary field in memoirs publishing— the convicted felon tells all. The alleged pending sale of the Son of Sam autobiography prompted the New York legislature to pass the first law that required "the accused or convicted criminal's income from works describing his crime" be used to reimburse victims of such crime. However, Berkowitz was never paid anything, despite published accounts that he had been offered a large sum for his story.

Ten years later, when another convicted felon, mobster Henry Hill, actually did sell his autobiography to Simon & Schuster, Inc., New York State ordered the publisher to suspend payments to Hill.[4] A lawsuit ensued, and in 1991 the law was ruled unconstitutional by the U.S. Supreme Court. Although nearly forty other states have similar laws on the books, including California and Nevada, none have held up to constitutional challenges. Hudson says, "In its *Simon & Schuster* decision, the Supreme Court set such a high bar that it is highly questionable that any Son of Sam laws could survive a First Amendment challenge. These laws not only implicate the First Amendment rights of the convicted person but compromise the First Amendment rights of the reading public."[5]

As recently as December of 2005, state supreme courts continue to strike down Son of Sam laws.[6] The media coverage of David Berkowitz may have also coined mass use of the phrase "the face of a killer." According to a Web site created and maintained by Kari & Associate, KariSable.com, "True Crime Books," a news report at the time of Berkowitz's arrest stated, "The people of this city had seen many faces of the 44-Caliber Killer in a series of police composite sketches. Not one of the victims saw the Son of Sam smile. But as David Berkowitz was led into police headquarters early this evening, he broke into a macabre grin. A video for sale through this site, "The Serial Killers," has on its cover four sets of eyes, from the faces of serial killers.[7]

Media coverage of another case of serial killings in 1990 also came to focus on the "face" of a suspected serial murderer. Like the Son of Sam media coverage, the case of suspect Edward Humphrey would also create a new kind of media coverage. This coverage would result not from investigative reports or from communications from the killer-at-large, but from public relations on behalf of the first primary suspect in a series of brutal murders at the University of Florida.

In Gainesville, Florida, during the first week of fall classes in 1990, five students were murdered. The media descended on the small university town, and frequent press conferences by police provided updates on the search for the killer. On August 30, four days after the first student was murdered, police were called to the home of Elna Hlavaty in Indiatlantic, Florida, a small city on the east coast of Florida, adjacent to Melbourne. Mrs. Hlavaty's grandson, Edward Humphrey, an eighteen-year-old student at the university had driven home from Gainesville in the middle of the night and encountered his grandmother in the foyer of her home. When he bumped into her, he lost a contact lens and lashed out verbally at his grandmother. Ed was not a violent person or even a terrible teenager; he was a troubled young man who did not like to take the lithium doctors had prescribed for him since he had been diagnosed with manic depression.

There was a time in small communities, when someone came home drunk or out-of-control, people often called police to come and help diffuse the situation. Mrs. Hlavaty's daughter, Elna, Ed Humphrey's mother, made such a call to police. They were looking for help in calming down and convincing him to take his medicine. Instead, he was taken to the police station and interrogated for 30 hours. Edward Humphrey became the prime suspect in the University of Florida murders.

Mrs. Hlavaty and Mrs. Humphrey had no idea of the seriousness of the suspicions already building against him. Law enforcement had become increasingly desperate to stop the killings and calm the parents and students of the University of Florida. In his manic state, Humphrey had been acting out with erratic and angry behavior. Now they had a suspect in custody, and the killings had stopped. On August 30, the *Orlando Sentinel* reported that investigators said they were "looking very closely at many persons, who have been acting very oddly."[8]

The next day, police released Ed Humphrey's mug shot, and newspapers across the country put his scarred image on the front page. A year earlier, he had been in a serious car accident and suffered deep cuts on his face. Plastic surgery was planned, but for now, his face reflected the violence of the crash that caused his injuries. He had probably been awake for more than twenty-four hours while he was interrogated. He looked the part of a murderer, even though he had taken no part in any such crime.

Edward Humphrey was guilty of only one thing, and it wasn't a crime. He did not take the prescription medicine that inhibited the manic depressive outbursts that were so self-destructive and disturbing to those around him.

With the publication of his scary photo, he had become notorious, and many citizens breathed a sigh of relief that the killing of young people in Gainesville had also stopped. Law enforcement's treatment of Humphrey after his arrest intricately connected him to the serial murders. In reality, there was no connection at all. Media reports described several brushes with the law, including two traffic tickets. Police found a number of Gainesville residents who had seen Humphrey acting "extremely strange." There had also been an incident when he allegedly pulled a knife at someone in a fraternity house. The murdered students had been stabbed to death.

During his first week at the university, Humphrey visited several fraternity houses. His outrageous behavior was typical of someone with his bipolar disorder, commonly known as manic depression, but relatively unknown to most people. Edward Humphrey was not taking his medication because he thought it made him act funny, and he wanted to fit in. Yet not taking lithium actually made his behavior abnormal. When he visited a frat house during rush week, he was told to leave, and an argument ensued. Humphrey did pull out a knife, a small pocketknife that had him even more ridiculed.

The reason Humphrey had driven home from Gainesville in the middle of the night was that he, too, was frightened by the killings. The actual reason for his arrest was a charge of committing aggravating battery on an elderly person, his grandmother, who had fallen against the stairway banister when he bent over to find one of his contact lenses. After the thirty hours of interrogation, without a lawyer present, he went before a judge. The next day, the headline in the local newspaper, *Florida Today*, read, "Suspect's Bond: $1 Million."[9] The amount of the bail further supported suspicions that he was extremely dangerous and suspect in the serial murders.

While awaiting his hearing on the battery charge, Humphrey gave hair and blood samples for DNA testing. However, there was little evidence from the crime scenes to compare because the Gainesville killer had been meticulous before he left. Despite the lack of any close match with available evidence, investigators still believed that he was their killer. Although Mrs. Hlavaty, a strong matriarch who loved her grandson and family, refused to press charges, Edward Humphrey sat in jail and was prosecuted to the fullest extent of the law. The media set up camp outside the Hlavaty/Humphrey home, and other deranged-looking photos of Edward Humphrey continued to be broadcast and reprinted worldwide.

The local public defender that represented him did little to quell the portrayal of his client as the primary suspect in the Gainesville murders. In fact, it was odd that the actual elected public defender at the time, J.R. Russo, was handling the case. It was as if he wanted to capitalize on the publicity for himself. During the first hearing when he was in the courtroom, Humphrey was still behaving abnormally because he was in a manic state, without the lithium that he needed to offset the chemical imbalance behind his acting invincible. He was led into the courtroom in chains, but inside he was a very frightened young man. During his August 31, 1990 arraignment, in a courtroom packed with the media, he repeatedly crossed himself, a reflection of his Roman Catholic upbringing.

The judge handed down a severe sentence, nearly the maximum allowed for the aggravated battery against his grandmother—twenty-two months in a state prison. This was despite her attempts in the courtroom and her statement to the media that the events were not accurately prosecuted. In any other similar prosecution, with Humphrey's crime-free background, a pretrial diversion program and probation were the type of sentence administered.

I followed the Gainesville murders with a personal concern. My oldest daughter was a sophomore there and lived close to the campus and the crime scenes. She too was caught up in the hysteria that swept the community; one of her roommates brought home a loaded gun. At the same time, I watched the media coverage of Edward Humphrey's arrest and knew instinctively that he could not have committed the calculated murders that had been described. Someone in Humphrey's manic state was far too much out of control to commit these murders and clean up the crime scenes.

In 1990, I was working with a number of law firms and lawyers, focusing on marketing projects like brochures and newsletters as well as proactive media relations designed to raise their image in the community. One of the lawyers I represented was an impressive and successful criminal defense lawyer, Donald Lykkebak. In the spring of 1991, I attended a media law seminar sponsored by The Florida Bar Association. George Humphrey, Ed's brother, was sitting on a panel focused on the media coverage of the Gainesville murders and the portrayals of Edward Humphrey as the prime suspect.

I approached him after the panel concluded and told him that I believed his brother was innocent, and needed a new lawyer and public relations help. During the next several weeks, I met with George in Gainesville, and he asked his grandmother and aunt to meet me in Orlando. The day of this meeting, the family hired both the lawyer I recommended to them, Don Lykkebak, and me to challenge the continued suspect status of Edward Humphrey, in both the legal and media arenas. Ed was still in prison.

My representation of Humphrey marked the emergence of a new specialty in media relations. As the publicist for Edward Humphrey, I set out to correct the biased and inaccurate image that had developed since he became the primary suspect in these killings. His scarred and tormented face had become synonymous with the face of a serial murder suspect.

George Humphrey had been a dedicated and articulate spokesperson for his brother. His credibility was somewhat compromised by their family bond. My campaign on Humphreys' behalf required the strong cooperation of his new criminal defense lawyer. Without Lykkebak's expertise and commitment, my successful campaign to change Humphrey's image would never have been as effective. Perhaps this is one reason that the field in which I work is not crowded. Working with lawyers is not easy, and the number of lawyers who recognize the value of a media specialist in representing the accused is far too small.

There were several accusations and potential warrants for Ed Humphrey when he was first eligible to leave prison. During that dramatic week of the murders in Gainesville, there had been the incident when he had pulled out a small pocketknife at the fraternity house where he was ridiculed and asked to leave. Police had interviewed the fraternity members and could still file a case against Humphrey. If there was enough pressure from the task force investigating the murders to keep him behind bars, he could be arrested as soon as he left the prison system.

Other accusations had surfaced, including a woman who claimed she had been attacked by Humphrey. She called police after seeing his scarred face in the media. However, her attack had occurred before Ed's accident, when his face was boyishly handsome and unscarred. Still, he remained a suspect.

After his sentencing, Humphrey spent eight months at the Florida state prison in Chattahoochee, where there was a mental health center, formerly known as a prison asylum for the criminally insane. There, he had become stabilized on his lithium and was a model prisoner. He was a very different person from the one whose angry image dominated the news in the weeks and months after the murders. In May, he was transferred to the minimum security prison in Lake Butler near Gainesville. The North Florida Reception Center was a correctional facility where newly sentenced men were waiting for assignments to the prison where they would serve out their terms and where prisoners about to be released completed their last few months.

This is the facility where I first met Edward Humphrey in person. Lykkebak and I visited him in June 1991. Humphrey was still very much a suspect in the minds of investigators. Although police had a new suspect in Danny Rolling, who was in jail on unrelated charges, certain investigators were still fixated on Humphrey and cited one hair found at one of the crime scenes that could not be ruled out as possibly belonging to him—or thousands of other people who have hair that falls into a similar category. Hair testing is disputable evidence and hair analysis an inexact science. Despite the fact that semen found at the crime scenes completely ruled out Humphrey and despite the fact that the semen closely matched Rolling's DNA, investigators were still telling reporters that Humphrey was a suspect. A year after the murders occurred, the *Orlando Sentinel* wrote about the investigation and quoted J.O. Jackson, a leader of the investigative task force. Jim Leusner, the *Sentinel* reporter, who covered the Humphrey case extensively, wrote that "Jackson is thought to be adamant that Humphrey be considered a suspect. Investigators are also known to be examining the possibility that two killers were involved in the deaths."[10]

This kind of media attention was fueled by investigators who wanted to keep alive suspicions that Ed Humphrey was a serial killer. In less than a month after this article and other news stories like it were disseminated, published or broadcast, Humphrey was going to be released from prison. The ongoing media attention was brutal. How could he get back some semblance of his life with his booking photo still appearing on the front pages of newspapers?

After my visit with Humphrey, Lykkebak's office referred one of many media inquiries to me, an investigative television reporter from the local ABC affiliate. Rob Stafford wanted to interview Humphrey. He and I discussed what kind of an interview might be possible when Humphrey was released from prison and then wound up discussing his empathy with Ed Humphrey. Stafford explained that he had a brother who suffered from schizophrenia, similar to manic depression. He felt a kindred understanding of what Ed and his family had suffered since he began to struggle with this mental illness in high school and through the horrible year after he became a suspect in the Gainesville murders.

The telephone call from Stafford set in motion media relations plans that became a pioneering achievement in the field of public relations for the accused. Today Rob Stafford is a correspondent for the news magazine program *Dateline NBC*. He is an award-winning reporter, having received four Emmys, four Associated Press awards and a prestigious Edward R. Murrow Award for a program on racial profiling. In 1991, he was one of the best journalists in Orlando, Florida.

After discussing the possibility for a first-ever interview with Edward Humphrey, I realized that the best timing for such an interview would be before he left the prison at Lake Butler. Because of the continuing media scrutiny and law enforcement suspicions, he was going to be a marked man when he returned to his life. Still, I knew what very few other people knew. The face of Edward Humphrey, the suspect, had changed dramatically. His face, although still bearing scars from his teenage auto accident, was open, guileless and pleasant. He was a kind and thoughtful young man who had gone through an extremely difficult time. Also, his manic depression was completely stabilized with regular use of his prescribed medication during a year in a controlled environment. Edward Humphrey would never again decide not to take his lithium.

This was the person his family, friends and teachers all knew before the chemicals in his body began to produce erratic and unhappy behavior. I realized that the best way to dispel suspicions and to quiet media speculation about Edward Humphrey was to let him speak to the community he was about to reenter. The only way to accomplish this was through the media. I first had to convince his lawyer that a prison interview was the right thing to do; then, I could prepare Ed Humphrey to give the interview, and, finally, I needed to make sure that the largest number of people would see the real Ed Humphrey.

Lykkebak and I discussed the interview potential, and he agreed, with two caveats—that the list of questions the media wanted to ask was approved by him first and that we would both be present during the interview. Once the decision was made to facilitate the interview, I had to give Stafford the bad news that his was not going to be an exclusive interview. I wanted to make sure that everyone watching the television news the night Ed Humphrey's interview aired would meet the real Ed regardless of what channel they were watching.

Naturally, Stafford was not happy with my decision; however, we asked that his station provide the camera crew. The stipulation was that they would release the interview tape to each of the other stations in Orlando so that everyone could edit and air the story at the same time. Finally, Lykkebak had another stipulation; he did not want a reporter to conduct the interview. I was going to pose the questions presented by the media and approved by Lykkebak.

During the next few weeks, Lykkebak handled several critical tasks. He contacted and convinced the warden at Lake Butler to allow the interview to take place, and he also made possible my recommendation that Ed wear a civilian shirt with a collar instead of the scooped-neck prison uniform. I was busy negotiating with the local television stations regarding the timing of the taped interview release and compiling the questions that each news team put together. The ABC affiliate where Rob Stafford worked agreed to release the entire taped interview and also to distribute it to other ABC affiliates as soon as it became available.

The day that Lykkebak and I met in his office to go over the questions was the first time I realized how courageous he was in agreeing to the prison interview. During the meeting, as he reviewed the various questions the news media was going to pose, there was an unusual tension in the air. I asked him recently to reflect on his state of mind during that time. "There is always the potential for losing control when your client talks to anyone but you. It's a standard for almost all criminal defense lawyers not to let the client do interviews. They've probably already talked too much to investigators. In Ed's case, I agreed that the benefit of introducing the young man I had met in prison outweighed the standard concern as long as we followed the interview process you had arranged."[11] In the working relationship I had with Lykkebak in this and other cases, we trusted the expertise that each of us brought to the table.

On August 26, Lykkebak, George Humphrey and I meet with Ed Humphrey in the prison canteen. Having his older brother there that day helped the younger Humphrey to feel more comfortable and reassured. The ABC cameraman, Michael O'Reagan, was still in the clearance room having his equipment checked. Rob Stafford was outside the prison fence, where he would later tape his take on the interview and state, accurately, that his station was the only one allowed inside the prison.

I had brought a neutral makeup with me to soften the scars on his face that the past year had already blended. His brother George had provided a clean blue shirt. Ed was naturally nervous, so I began with the question-and-answer first. I wanted him to speak naturally and answer every question honestly. Lykkebak had already deleted certain questions that he considered leading or inappropriate. Throughout the run-through, I took notes on Ed's answers. If he rambled too much, I stopped him and asked him to restate the first thing that he had said. There were no red flags in his answers. This process was not to create or give Ed scripted answers. This was a rehearsal and a time for his lawyer to become comfortable with his client's soon-to-be broadcast comments about the horrible crime he was still suspected of committing.

I had noticed earlier that Ed had gotten a prison haircut. In this case, he had basically shaved his head. No matter how boyish his smile was, the haircut had a tendency to make him look aggressive. Thank of a Marine in boot camp. When I mentioned it to him, he naturally swept his hand across his head and said, "Yeah, it's pretty short." Ed's image was going to be so remarkably different from the arrest photos and footage from his first court appearances when he was in a nervous state of trying to make light of his situation. I suggested that during the interview he inject a comment about his hair, run his hand over his head and smile when he said he was looking forward to getting a real haircut when he was released.

The cameraman was invited into the room to set up. Ed had already changed into the collared shirt, and despite his initial self-consciousness about the makeup, he looked great. I did instruct him to sit forward and answer the questions in a normal voice, looking at me and not at the camera. This is a simple how-to tip for people who are inclined to look into the camera. If a person stops looking at the interviewer, usually a reporter, and look over or up to the camera, it appears that he is nervous and fearful of why he is on camera.

We concluded the interview and visited with Humphrey while the cameraman packed up and left.

That night, on every Central Florida television station and in dozens of other markets, the first interview with Edward Humphrey was aired.[12] The story, however, was also about the mechanism of the interview itself, about my role as a public relations specialist and the one who posed the questions while his lawyer sat close by his client. Although I knew from discussions with a news director at the local NBC affiliate that this angle was going to be included in the broadcast, the benefit of getting the interview on the air far outweighed the media announcement that the Humphrey family had hired a publicist.

The next day, the front-page article in the *Orlando Sentinel* used a photo, taken from the television screen, of Ed running his hand over his head and the caption: "In an interview Humphrey said he is doing better and looking forward to a haircut by a regular barber."[13] Sometimes it's the simplest images that give a person back some of the humanity he loses when accused of a heinous crime.

Ed Humphrey answered the seven questions his lawyer had approved; he answered in his own words that he had been "horrified" to learn that he was a suspect. By the end of the interview, he was relieved and looking forward to his release from prison in a few weeks. We knew that the news media would be waiting when he was released, so I took steps to ensure that there was not a media circus outside the prison.

If the news media descends on a person suspected of murder, there is no way to avoid looking intimidated or insensitive. No matter how unemotional the suspect appears, he looks insensitive to the victims of the crime. If the suspect looks stern or angry, that look may be interpreted as the "killer" look.

We had discussed the release timing and logistics with the prison administrator, Charles Denman. Denman explained that when his last high-profile prisoner walked out of the Lake Butler facility, an elderly gentleman who had served time for assisting in his cancer-ridden wife's suicide, the media had surrounded him as he tried to get into his car and then actually jumped on the car itself. He was open to suggestions about making Ed Humphrey's release less traumatic; he even offered to release him at 12:01 a.m. on the day he was free to leave.

Just as I had negotiated with the ABC affiliate about the prison interview and release of the tapes to other stations, I struck a deal about Humphrey's release. I set up a press conference in Orlando for the afternoon of his release to "feed the beast." I told news directors I would give them the exact time he would walk out of the prison and schedule it for the reasonable hour of 9 a.m. In return, they all agreed to stay back beyond the cul-de-sac in front of the prison, where our car would be waiting to drive him the 100 miles to Orlando for a 2 p.m. press conference.

I still get tears in my eyes when I look at the photos of him that day. This nineteen-year-old had been through a terrible fourteen months, overzealously prosecuted for a misunderstanding because he was wrongly suspected in a horrible crime. We discussed some of his experiences as we drove and over breakfast at a pancake house on the highway. Before we arrived at the building where he would be reunited with his grandmother and mother just prior to the press conference, we stopped at a strip mall where there was both a department store and a barber shop. The stop was unplanned, but we had realized that none of his clothes from the previous year were appropriate or fit properly. Lykkebak bought him a navy blue blazer, khaki trousers and a new tie to go with a white shirt that did fit. Then we stopped at the barber shop, where he did receive the foreshadowed "real haircut."

Fortunately, Humphrey's brother, George, had loaned me his camera, and I recorded the barbershop visit as well as his reunion with his family at Lykkebak's office.

The press conference played to a full house, confirming that Humphrey had still not been cleared as a suspect in the Gainesville murders. Lykkebak spoke and answered questions after I had introduced Ed and he had read a statement written over breakfast. The purpose of all of these media relations strategies and events was simple: to diffuse the notoriety of the suspicions against him and to make his reentry into private life as normal as possible.

After the press conference, I gave the film of the photos I had taken to Jim Leusner, an *Orlando Sentinel* reporter, for the paper to use if it so chose. Lykkebak had worked closely with Leusner, who covered courts for the newspaper, and he trusted him. The next day two of the photos, one of Ed Humphrey in the barber chair and one hugging his mother, appeared on the front page of the paper.[14] Although the photos credited me as the photographer, the following day, the paper printed a clarification that I was a publicist for the Humphreys who had provided the photos to the newspaper.

The next significant media event in Humphrey's life occurred when a grand jury indicted the Gainesville killer, Danny Rolling, in November of 1991. In Indiatlantic, Florida, that day, there was little media access to him or his family, because, sadly, it was also the day they held funeral services for Elna Hlavaty, his grandmother. The grand jury not only did not indict Edward Humphrey, it also issued a "no true bill," an elective legal document that stated in effect that the members of the grand jury did not believe Edward Humphrey had anything to do with the serial murders of the five University of Florida students in 1990.

Humphrey completed probation with only a few missteps, the kind of episodes that teenagers often go through, but with Lykkebak as his defender on all accounts, there were fewer and fewer stories in the media. However, a few weeks after the prison interview aired, I began to receive calls about my role in the Humphrey cases. Stories about my public relations work for Ed Humphrey appeared in newspapers across the country.[15] The then-controversial tabloid TV program "*A Current Affair*" contacted me. Lykkebak and I agreed to be interviewed about our work with Humphrey and the segment. "Makeover of a Monster" aired on *A Current Affair* in November 1991.[16]

A graduate student in public relations wrote a research paper about my role in the case in 1992, and Leonard Saffirs' book *Power Public Relations* devoted a section to the case and called me a "pioneer in the field of legal PR."[17] While working with the Humphreys I never realized that what we were doing was unique and precedent-setting. I just knew it was the right way to handle the media when the face of an innocent person was portrayed as the face of a murderer.

I've remained in regular contact with the Humphrey family because an experience like this creates a bond with the people involved. I attended his bother George's wedding in 1992 and then years later, attended Ed's wedding to a lovely woman. In August 2000, nine years after his television interview from the prison to emphasize his innocence, he graduated cum laude from the University of Central Florida with a degree in business.

Although Ed Humphrey was innocent, he could have faced arrest immediately after being released without the proactive legal representation of Don Lykkebak. Because investigators still considered him a suspect, he might well have been charged with both the fraternity incident and investigated and possibly arrested for the allegations by the woman who saw his photo. Whether he would have been convicted of either is highly unlikely, but not out of the realm of possibility. Fortunately, he never had to find out.

Are there other people like Edward Humphrey who are suspected of serious crimes and persecuted if not prosecuted? I believe that there are dozens of cases like Edward Humphrey's every year across the county. Most of these accused will be represented by overworked public defenders with no access to media relations expertise. There are also innocent people sitting on death row in states around the nation. Sister Helen Prejan, author of the acclaimed *Dead Man Walking*, recently published *The Death of Innocents: An Eyewitness Account of Wrongful Execution*.[18] She thoroughly investigated the cases of two men executed in 1997 and 1999 and cites numerous legal experts. Her persuasive analyses of these cases leave no doubt that they were innocent of the crimes for which they were executed.

Many anti–death penalty organizations try to use media relations to draw necessary attention to the highly questionable tactics of law enforcement and prosecutors and the ineffective defense that most condemned people experience in capital murder cases. However, their efforts almost always occur after the death sentence. The most critical time for media relations in a serious criminal case is before the case comes to trial. During the weeks surrounding the investigation and arrest of a person accused of a serious crime, the police will be in constant touch with the media. When the prosecutors, the state attorney or the district attorney gets the case, the media relations contact will continue unabated. These prosecuting entities have the resources, the experience, the paid expertise to move their cases against the accused in both the media and in the legal arena.

Public relations for the accused can balance the scales of justice so that justice prevails. Private citizens who are charged with crimes may never have spoken to the media in their lives. They generally do not have access to or funds for public relations advice. Public defenders need to lobby for public information personnel in their offices. Lawyers in private practice need to make public relations consulting a line item expense in their representation of the accused.

Edward Humphrey's scars and his chemical and psychological imbalances gave him the face of a deranged person, and it took only a small leap for the public to buy into the investigators' portrayal of him as a murder suspect. In September 1993, *Details* magazine published an in-depth article on Ed's prosecution titled, "If looks could kill." Don Lykkebak, who spoke with dozens of law enforcement officers and prosecutors off-the-record, recalls that "everyone had Ed nailed as a serial killer."[19] Nearly fifteen years later and a lawyer himself, the oldest of the Humphrey children and Ed's first champion, George Humphrey says, "There's no question that if Marti and Don had not stepped up to represent my brother, he might be on death row today. The wheels of justice were failing us."[20]

In this case, the accused had absolutely no part in the killings, yet he looked the part. Without the intervention of public relations and proactive legal representation, his nightmare might have continued.

Six

White-Collar Crime

A decade later, in 2001, the Texas-based energy corporation Enron collapsed and left thousands of employees and stockholders stripped of their salaries, savings and retirements. Stockholders in the company also suffered, both individuals and pension fund beneficiaries. Public sentiment was aroused by media interviews with elderly people who lost everything because of the greedy executives at Enron who concealed the company's debt level and defrauded investors.

Five years later, in January 2006, the former CEO of Enron, Ken Lay, went on trial in Houston. Before this high-profile corporate villain finally faced a jury, a number of other CEOs were tried for similar patterns of corruption, other high-profile CEOs were prosecuted, several in New York and one in Alabama. The first CEO tried during these early years of the new century, but not for defrauding stockholders, was Martha Stewart. She was investigated by the Securities and Exchange Commission for benefiting from insider trading information, specifically for selling her stock in ImClone before it plummeted in value.

In the end, Stewart was not charged with insider trading; she was tried in Federal Court for securities fraud (the one charge that the judge dismissed), lying to SEC investigators, obstructing justice, making false statements and conspiring with her broker to obstruct justice and make false statements. She steadfastly denied the charges and pled not guilty. She and her broker, Peter Bacanovic, were codefendants in her January 2004 trial.

Noted UCLA law professor and legal scholar Stephen Bainbridge, writing about the case against Martha Stewart for the online journal run by the Technology Commerce and Society chastises the government prosecution of Stewart for "having denied the very same allegations the government decided it couldn't prove."[1] He said, "I can understand why the government would want to hang a high-profile scalp in the wall, but this is a case that never should have been brought."[2]

There is widespread public opinion, including my own, that Martha Stewart's prosecution was overzealous, in part because she was a woman CEO, in part because she refused to apologize and certainly because she refused to accept a plea bargain.

As a celebrity CEO, Stewart did not handle her first media relations challenge well. In her first televised appearance after the weeks of news coverage on the SEC investigation, she showed up for her regular cooking segment on the CBS *Early Morning Show*. I watched the show specifically because I was sure that she was going to use this opportunity to reassure a national audience that she was innocent.[3]

The then CBS *Early Morning Show* host Jane Clayson summarized the ImClone stock sale and then asked Stewart for her reaction to the investigation while she was chopping cabbage. Without putting down her knife and looking up, Stewart said, "I will be exonerated of any ridiculousness." This awkward response sounded like legalistic lingo; I wondered who had advised her to make this comment. Then, without responding again, she said she wanted to "focus on [her] salad."[4]

Stewart never appeared on this show again. Then she left the public with the stiff and flustered CBS *Early Morning Show* image for over sixteen months. She did, however, give two extensive pretrial interviews with Larry King and Barbara Walters. Stewart took her mother, Martha Kostyra, with her to the first *Larry King Show* on December 20, 2003.[5] *Entertainment Weekly* correspondent Gary Sussman recapped her televised interview with Barbara Walters on November 6, 2003, "I have done nothing wrong, Barbara. I am innocent," so says Martha Stewart, talking to Barbara Walters in an interview airing on Friday's "20/20." During the ABC sit-down, Stewart's first TV talk in the seventeen months since her stock-trading scandal broke, the gracious-living guru says she's being held to a sexist double standard, both by prosecutors and by critics rattled by her drive and perfectionism."[6]

Lenard Saffir, veteran public relations executive and author of *Power Public Relations* blames her lawyer—not for her media relations strategies—but for advising her to stick to a plea of not guilty. In his opinion, avoiding time in prison was just a public relations step away for Stewart.

The Martha Stewart story is a classic public relations case study. Stewart was sentenced in 2004 to five months behind bars and five months of house arrest after she was convicted of lying to authorities about her 2001 sale of about 4,000 shares of stock. She will be on probation until March 2007, during which time she is not allowed to get drunk, own a gun, or leave the federal court district without permission or practice bad public relations.

She should have faced the crisis and admitted her mistake publicly instead of listening to her lawyer. If she did this, chances are a judge would not have sentenced her to five months in jail. More so, public opinion would have been on her side.[7]

Her lawyer Robert Morvillo was profiled and interviewed in *New York Magazine* a few weeks before the trial started.[8] Chris Smith, the author of the article, "Can This Man Save Martha," notes, "Within the legal community, Morvillo is renowned for his discretion, keeping his corporate clients out of the headlines. He's also fielded the odd high-profile case, where his signature talents are more visible." However, the article continues, "Morvillo hasn't grappled with anything like the Stewart media circus."[9]

Smith goes on to report that Morvillo has "also been involved in decisions about Stewart's pretrial PR campaign, including her 'Martha Talks' Web site and her Barbara Walters interview. 'To the extent you can do constructive things to help the image of your client or help the jury pool understand your position—or even, God forbid, be biased for you rather than against you—sure, that's great,' Morvillo says. 'So you think about those things you can do within the rules.'"[10] The Martha Stewart case is also significant for the use of Web sites and blogs to proclaim her innocence and give supporters a forum to communicate with her.[11]

Following the conviction and prior to Stewart's sentencing, the New York *Daily News* reported that one of the jurors knew fellow members of the jury were following the case in the media during the trial.[12] Michelle Wishner called the lawyer for Bacanovic and told him, among other things, that jurors discussed the hourly fee Stewart paid her lawyer and how much her pocketbook cost. She is quoted in the *Daily News* as saying, "Fellow jurors were reading media reports about the trial while serving on the panel–including reports on the $6,000 Birkin handbag from Hermes that Stewart toted to court." Wishner also expressed her opinion about Stewart's image of herself, "She couldn't separate herself from her own image, so she made it impossible for anyone else to."[13]

Perhaps the best public relations move occurred after she was no longer accused, but convicted. Stewart elected to serve her five months in prison before her appeal was decided and put the experience behind her. She used her sentencing appearance to make a highly effective and well-received statement in open court and later delivered before the media waiting outside the courthouse, apologizing not for committing a crime but for the effect her prosecution and conviction had on her employees and stockholders. The first three paragraphs revealed a very sensitive and caring Martha.

Today is a shameful day. It is shameful for me, for my family, and for my beloved company and all of its employees and partners. What was a small personal matter became over the last two and a half years an almost fatal circus event of unprecedented proportions spreading like oil over a vast landscape, even around the world. I have been choked and almost suffocated to death during that time.

I ask that, in judging me, you remember all the good that I have done, all the contributions I have made through the company I founded, as well as personally over the past decades of my life that have been devoted almost entirely to productive, creative, and useful activities. I ask, too, that you consider all the intense suffering that I and so many dear others have endured every single moment of the past two and a half years. I seek the opportunity to continue serving my country and my community in the same positive manner I always have. I seek the opportunity to repair the damage wrought by the situation, to get on with what I have always thought was a good, worthwhile and exemplary life.

My heart goes out to you and to everyone in this courtroom, and my prayers are with you. My hopes that my life will not be completely destroyed lie entirely in your competent and experienced and merciful hands. Thank you and peace be with you.[14]

Outside on the courthouse steps, she finished her statement and then looked up to speak less formally, concluding with the upbeat statement, "And, I'll be back. I will be back."[15]

Within a year, Stewart, still a billionaire, had completed her five-month prison term at "Camp Cupcake" (the nickname for the West Virginia minimum security facility), where she lost weight and gained early release. She also "reached out to the public with letters posted on her Web site discussing her daily life behind bars, the bad prison food and federal sentencing guidelines, which she thinks treat first-time offenders unfairly."[16]

She returned to work while completing her five-month house arrest sentence, and is definitely "back," with two new television programs (although one, *The Apprentice*, was panned and cancelled), a new magazine in the works and all the previous facets of her lifestyle enterprise intact. A few months after Stewart's release, New York's courtrooms were extremely busy with the trials concerning significantly more serious crimes than Stewart had faced.

In the summer of 2005, three corrupt corporate tycoons faced juries in New York City and had to pay the proverbial piper. WorldCom CEO Bernard Ebbers, Dennis Kozlowski of Tyco, and father and son defendants John and Timothy Rigas of Adelphia Communications were tried, convicted and sentenced to prison for terms of up to twenty-five years. Each of them had misrepresented the earnings of his respective company, profited from the sale of inflated stock, committed fraud, lied and ripped off stockholders.

However, during June 2005, in Birmingham, Alabama, Richard Scrushy, founder of HealthSouth, a company rocked by the very similar corporate ills of greed and scandal, walked out of the courtroom unscathed. His trial had lasted nearly five months. The Securities and Exchange Commission (SEC) prosecuted him for misrepresenting the earnings of the medical rehabilitation company he founded in 1983 and then personally pocketing over $300 million from his early sale of stock at drastically inflated prices. According to the SEC, HealthSouth's stock value was overstated by $800 million between 1999 and 2002.[17]

Before Scrushy went on trial, fifteen former top executives at HealthSouth testified in depositions that he had directed them to "cook the books." The government seemed to have an extremely strong case against Richard Scrushy.

What happened before and during this trial that did not happen when the CEOs of Tyco, WorldCom or Adelphia faced their accusers in a New York City courtroom? Public relations happened. The public relations campaign conducted by and on behalf of this accused person was one of the most blatant and unethical ever documented; it was also tremendously effective and ultimately successful.

After the collapse of Enron in 2001, American government responded to shareholders outrage at corporate corruption. According to a former prosecutor David Gourevitch, quoted in the *Washington Post* the day that the Enron trial began, "White-collar cases used to be isolated and very much on the margins." The same article went on to note the current statistics on prosecuting corporate fraud.

"The President's Corporate Fraud Task Force, formed in 2002, has filed criminal charges against more than 900 defendants—60 of them at the chief executive or president level—and won 500 convictions or guilty pleas, according to Justice Department statistics. The Securities and Exchange Commission, meanwhile, used new millions granted by Congress to boost its enforcement caseload by nearly 30 percent, from 484 in 2001 to 629 last year. The SEC won or settled 99 percent of the cases brought in 2005, according to its annual report." Richard Scrushy was one of the more than 600 defendants prosecuted by the Securities and Exchange Commission in 2005.[18]

The facts in the case against him were very similar to facts in other major corporate fraud matters that became all too common in the late 1990s. In November 2003, the SEC obtained an indictment against Scrushy on eighty-five alleged counts of fraud; he posted a $10 million bond and had to wear an ankle monitor. By the time the trial started in January 2005, the government had narrowed its case down to thirty-six counts. The original estimates of fraud were $1.4 billion; by the time of the trial, the figure had grown to $2.7 billion.

After his indictment, Scrushy hired several white-shoe corporate lawyers, including Abbe Lowell, who had once defended President Clinton and who had been named one of the best trial lawyers in America by the *National Law Journal* in 2002. However, the most important lawyer on Scrushy's legal team was also the most media-savvy: Don Watkins, a well-known African American lawyer and Birmingham businessman. In one of the earliest press releases sent out by Scrushy, he proclaimed his innocence and said, "I look forward to my day in court where the facts will show I am not guilty.... In Abbe Lowell and Tom Sjoblom as my lead trial lawyers, and with Don Watkins continuing as a key advisor, I could not have a better group of lawyers working on my behalf."[19]

Scrushy did not leave his defense to lawyers. He conducted a public relations campaign that included comprehensive and multifaceted outreach to the Birmingham, Alabama, community from which his jury would be selected. He used religion and relationships with black ministers as a springboard into the hearts and minds of people who already knew the name "Richard M. Scrushy." His solicitation of the ministers' support with large contributions gave new meaning to the term "white-collar crime."

Scrushy actually began to imprint the Birmingham community with his image as soon as his company became profitable. He started HealthSouth with a small chain of outpatient clinics in 1983; by 1986, the company had one hospital and $20 million in annual revenues. By the mid-1990s, HealthSouth was Alabama's third-largest corporation; a Fortune 500 Company that grew to become the nation's largest provider of rehabilitation services through outpatient clinics and hospitals. After HealthSouth became a publicly traded company in the mid-1980s, Scrushy, as CEO, earned a hefty salary and accumulated increasingly valuable stock options.

Over the years, he also indulged his need to be recognized and his love of performance by founding several musical bands. The first was a rock group made up of former high school friends, called Proxy. Later, he used HealthSouth money to recruit professional musicians, cut an album and produced a video for his honky-tonk group Dallas County Line, in which he was the lead singer. Finally, he spent more than $13 million to organize, promote and create a show for an all-girl band, Third Faze.

During his trial, Scrushy's lawyers claimed that he was unaware that HealthSouth executives were hiding the fact that the company was losing money. This contradicted his well-known style of micromanaging everything connected to HealthSouth. To managers and employees, the company seemed to operate as Richard Scrushy Incorporated.

HealthSouth and Scrushy were generous corporate sponsors of numerous causes and nonprofit organizations in Alabama, including colleges. Whenever a contribution was made, regardless of whether it came through HealthSouth (as did the majority of the donations) or not, he insisted that his name be prominently displayed. There was a Richard M. Scrushy Library, numerous Scrushy athletic fields, a Richard Scrushy Convention Center and Community Center. A large contribution to his former community college resulted in an entire Richard M. Scrushy Campus.

Thus, Scrushy became one of the best-known businessmen, employers and philanthropists in Birmingham, Alabama. However, after the SEC investigated and indicted him, he was forced to resign and began to concentrate on reaching out to the majority of Birmingham's population—African Americans. He was apparently following the advice of Don Watkins, who was quoted as saying, "Whites will buy into the media hype put out by the U.S. attorney and the Justice Department for two years."[20]

In a bible-belt state like Alabama, there's no better way to rub the shoulders and touch the hearts of black people than through their churches. Before his indictment, Scrushy and his family were members and big supporters of his predominantly white church in suburban Birmingham. Then, after his arrest, Scrushy suddenly began attending and supporting the Guiding Light Church, where the congregation is nearly all black. According to a *Business Week* online article that cites IRS records, Scrushy gave his new church $1 million in 2003.[21]

In 2004, the year before his trial started, the Richard M. Scrushy Charitable Foundation gave more than $700,000 to churches and organizations; another $313,000 alone went to Guiding Light. He didn't stop there. He began preaching at black churches throughout Birmingham, and gave a large contribution to another largely African American church—$300,000 went to Trinity Life Church.

In addition to his personal and monetary involvement in the African American church communities, he took to the airwaves with a religious program, *Viewpoint.*

These activities did not go unnoticed by the media. In September 2004, *USA Today* published an insightful article about Scrushy's aggressive religious fervor. The article noted that *Viewpoint* was an evangelical television program hosted by Scrushy and his wife. Commenting on the Scrushy family's sudden conversion to attending a new church where the membership is predominantly African American, *USA Today* reporter Greg Farrell wrote, "Critics of Scrushy's show see it as a cynical attempt to generate goodwill among potential jurors in the Birmingham areas, which is about 70% African American."[22]

In addition, Scrushy used the *Viewpoint* show to cross-promote a forty-day prayer campaign purportedly to unify Birmingham. One of the organizers was Bishop Dusty Hammock, head of the African American congregation at Point of Grace Ministries. There were eighteen billboards around the city announcing a prayer rally on November 1, 2004, two months before Scrushy would go on trial.

In 2003, *Fortune* magazine provided revealing biographical information about Richard Scrushy and chronicled the founding and growth of HealthSouth. Journalist John Helyar pointed out the dramatic rise of the company's stock and the timing of the government investigation into his stock sales.[23] The nagging questions in my mind as I read the media coverage of Scrushy in the months and years before his trial were, "What did the prosecution think he was going to do after he was charged? Was there a diligent effort to move the trial elsewhere?"

Following Scrushy's courtroom victory, another article by Helyar in *Fortune* magazine profiles lawyer Don Watkins, noting that he had come out of semi-retirement (he had not practiced law for over five years) to defend Scrushy.[24] Helyar describes the tactics used by this head of Scrushy's legal team by saying, "He employed a brilliant, if controversial, racial strategy in a city where blacks and whites still . . . view certain things very differently."

Don Watkins not only advised Richard Scrushy on his religious and community outreach, he was also comfortable with his client's media relations abilities from the start. Soon after his indictment, Scrushy began blasting the government on radio shows he hosted with a minor former child star Jason Hervey, from the nineties sitcom *The Wonder Years*, whom he had recruited to work at HealthSouth. Later, Scrushy chose a well-known national program for his first television interview after he was arrested. In October 2003, his interview with Mike Wallace aired on CBS's *60 Minutes*.

Whenever a high-profile defendant appears on a national news program like *60 Minutes*, his hometown media will promote the appearance from the moment the film crew arrives in town. There was coverage that the interview would take place at the Scrushy home, additional reports announced when the show was first scheduled to air, and even more coverage after it was rescheduled for another night. Following the show, there was media analysis about what Scrushy said and how the interview went.

The people who watched from the Birmingham area were the defense team's most important viewers, since they were members of the potential jury pool. Anyone who tuned in that night heard Scrushy say, "I'm not going to jail. I'm an innocent man. I'm not going to jail." If they missed it, it was printed in the next day's local newspaper.[25]

CBS conducted an unscientific poll of 1,200 viewers following the program. The results of the poll showed that 95 percent of those who watched the interview did not believe Scrushy's claim of innocence. While there is no proof that the 5 percent of the viewers who said they believed him were from Birmingham, Alabama, the opinions of the local viewers were the only ones that mattered.

The next day, the *Birmingham News* headline stated "Watkins Happy with Interview." Watkins knew before Scrushy agreed to the interview that his client would play well in the local demographic. One of the most important aspects of the relationship between a lawyer and his high-profile client is an accurate understanding of the accused person's media relations skills. Don Watkins recognized that Richard Scrushy was an effective self-promoter and played to his strengths.[26]

Between January and July 2005, Scrushy was tried in a very different setting from the New York City courtrooms, where Ebbers, Kozlowski and Rigas were convicted by respective juries. Scrushy's jury was selected from a much smaller population in a community that had been exposed to Scrushy's charitable works for twenty years. He was a very big fish in a small pond. The defendants tried in New York City were well known in the business and investment worlds but were merely exotic fish in the city of more than eight million people.

During the Scrushy trial, the prosecution presented testimony from more than a dozen HealthSouth executives, including five of the former chief financial officers who had helped to run the company under Scrushy's direction. These were his day-to-day managers and closest peers. Although they admitted guilt, almost all were sentenced to prison. They testified that Scrushy not only knew about the inflated earnings, he told them to make the numbers correspond to what he had projected even after Medicare reform dramatically reduced those earnings. Jurors were given detailed accounting documentation that showed HealthSouth reported earnings that did not exist.

Scrushy never took the stand. However, he did create and maintain a personal Web site to proclaim his innocence and attack the government's case. Naturally, he had his own way of looking at every development in his case and the operation of HealthSouth. After he was fired by his company in April 2002, every effort was made to remove him from the HealthSouth profile. The company Web site was cleansed of Scrushy references. However, on www.richardscrushy.com, he claims he resigned and continues to write about how well the company is recovering—as if this proves his innocence.

In some ways, the success of Richard Scrushy's defense included the very same public relations tactics that I have practiced in the legal arena for over twenty years. However, six months after Scrushy was acquitted at his trial, reports that he engaged in blatantly unethical activities in the name of 'public relations' were confirmed.

On January 19, 2006, the Associated Press reported allegations by an influential church leader of one of Birmingham's largest black congregations. According to Pastor Herman Henderson of the Believers Temple Church, Scrushy hired him through a local public relations agency both to organize black pastors to attend the trial and to provide public relations services. In fact, Pastor Henderson said Scrushy still owed him $150,000.[27]

These public relations services included work done by Mr. Henderson's assistant. Prior to and during the trial, she wrote favorable articles about Scrushy (articles that

Scrushy reviewed and edited) that appeared on the front page of *The Birmingham Times*, the local newspaper with a predominantly African American readership.

Although Scrushy denies that he had any agreement to pay Pastor Henderson through The Lewis Group, a local public relations firm, to perform community relations work, *Business Week Online* reports that Scrushy did pay the Lewis Group $20,000 for "marketing and public relations as discussed."[28]

The hiring of this firm may have been one instance where Scrushy did not follow the advice of Don Watkins, his lead lawyer. The same *Business Week Online* article reports that a note from Watkins was affixed to the first contract that Scrushy says Watkins turned down. It read: "There is too much of a chance that the government will use this event to ask for a mistrial." Finally, Scrushy's spokesperson, Charlie Russell, admits he also directly gave Pastor Henderson's assistant a check for $2,500 that he claims was to be used to attend a funeral out of state and later to provide public relations services after the trial was over.[29]

The fact that Scrushy paid for "favorable press coverage" as the Associated Press headline reported on January 19, 2006, should come as no surprise to those who worked for him. Whenever one of his rock groups, Proxy, was scheduled to perform, HealthSouth employees knew to help pack the venue.[30] As the *Fortune* magazine article described it, "This was known at the company as 'purchased applause.'"[31]

Scrushy and his designated spokesperson deny that any of their self-styled community relations actions are unusual or unethical. However, public relations guru Richard Edelman recently wrote that the "sleazy behavior" of a public relations firm and image consultant hired by Scrushy "is a deplorable example [of] what can happen when there is no enforceable code of ethics in the public relations field."[32]

Edelman is referring to the work of Charlie Russell, Scrushy's spokesperson and the head of a Colorado-based PR firm. On his public relations firm's Web site, Mr. Russell claims to be an award-winning professional, an accredited member of the Public Relations Society of America, and a member of its Counselor's Academy—an organization with a code of ethics.

The omission in Mr. Edelman's blog essay "Enough Already," January 20, 2006, is his failure to recognize that in the legal arena the stakes are different. I am also appalled by the blatant payoff to a newspaper writer and a so-called community relations outreach that gave large sums of money to local black churches in return for their attendance at Scrushy's trial. However, I am reminded of the old adage that "you cannot legislate morality."

On July 3, 2005, Scrushy's jury found him not guilty. Ultimately, Richard Scrushy paid out $30 million to his legal team, plus an untold amount in public relations fees as well as "contributions" of millions to black churches. Even for someone who walked away from his company with multimillions, this is a significant expenditure. After his indictment, the government had frozen $70 million of his assets; then, in an early win for Scrushy, his lead lawyer convinced a federal judge to release $17 million.[33] The rest was unfrozen in May 2003.

In November 2005, Scrushy actually sued HealthSouth for back pay and benefits. There is no end to his belief in his own worth. HealthSouth, slowly but surely showing signs of financial recovery, countersued its former CEO. Scrushy's run of success changed course on January 4, 2006, when a federal judge ordered him to repay $48 million in bonuses he took from HealthSouth since he was paid those bonuses while the company was hemorrhaging money, not posting profits.

Although the Alabama Supreme Court has put the repayment on hold, there are a number of lawsuits and settlement negotiations over investor losses. Shareholders, including large pension funds in various states, are also suing Scrushy.

Even though Scrushy obtained a not guilty verdict in the criminal trial, the SEC has filed a civil lawsuit against him. Many Americans first observed the success of a civil lawsuit against a person found innocent of criminal charges in the O.J. Simpson matter. Even when a defendant is acquitted in a criminal court, his victims may still file suit in a civil court to recover monetary damages.

There are more issues than money ahead for Scrushy. In October 2005, prosecutors filed felony charges against him alleging that he raised $500,000 for former Alabama Governor Don Siegelman to gain positions on a state health panel that oversees hospitals. That trial is scheduled for 2007 and is to be held in Montgomery, Alabama, a different venue from Scrushy's home court.

Although there were several articles in the months before the 2005 trial began that raised questions about the effect of Scrushy's activities and recognition on the potential jury pool, the prosecution never requested a change in venue in the HealthSouth fraud case. In fact, when asked about this omission after the trial, U.S. Attorney Alice Davis said, "We had a strong case. You can't run off to New York for everything."[34]

The fact that Scrushy beat the government in the court of public opinion is indisputable. As already referenced, according to the *Washington Post*, the same year that Scrushy survived the SEC's dogged prosecution by winning an acquittal, "The SEC won or settled 99 percent of the cases [it] brought . . . according to its annual report."[35]

Whether the government could have done anything to balance the scales of justice in this case is questionable. Scrushy had a plan to influence the jury pool and a lawyer who apparently agreed that he needed to do the increasingly unethical things he did.

In the post-verdict article in *Fortune* magazine, Don Watkins, Scrushy's lead lawyer and chief advisor justified his successful efforts to try the case before a mostly African American jury with a reference to the prosecution's "media hype."

Watkins said that "Black people are more open to receiving their information in the courtroom."[36] Although the initial investigation into this case as well as the indictments of HealthSouth and Richard Scrushy were announced in press releases issued by the U.S. Securities and Exchange Commission, the resulting press coverage of the government's case falls far short of "media hype."

After Scrushy's acquittal, there were other CEOs still facing trial. The most notorious and infamous was Kenneth Lay, CEO of the failed energy corporation Enron.

Of all the investigations into the major defrauding companies, one that continued to resonate with public sentiment was Enron. In the months after this Houston-based corporation collapsed in December 2001, four thousand people lost their jobs. The fraud wiped out their savings and pensions. The media carried dozens of gut-wrenching stories about these people. "The pain and suffering aren't forgotten, even three years later," observed CBS Correspondent Scott Pelley on *60 Minutes* in a segment that aired March 13, 2005.[37]

In this segment, Mr. Pelley interviewed Ken Lay, the former Enron Chairman who maintained his innocence up until and throughout his long-awaited trial that began in January 2006. Mr. Pelley gave Mr. Lay ample room to claim he was fooled at Enron, and then noted, "As he prepares for trial, Lay is trying to improve his image. And that is probably why he chose to talk to *60 Minutes*."

Mr. Pelley stated the obvious about Mr. Lay's reason for participating in the interview; after all, Lay, like Scrushy, had refused to testify before the U.S. Senate in 2002. This interview, while obviously self-serving, is the very kind of exchange that gives the viewing public what it wants—an up-close television look at a high-profile man accused of a high-profile crime.

When Enron collapsed and Lay was indicted, there were numerous deals struck and testimony gathered from those who worked for him at Enron. There was even the suicide of a former Enron bigwig. The case that the SEC built and brought against Richard Scrushy had very similar elements. More than a dozen of Scrushy's subordinates struck deals with the government and testified against the former HealthSouth CEO. There was a suicide in the Scrushy case also.

One reason the government was in a much better position to pick the jury that convicted the former Enron CEO was that Ken Lay was not half the self-promoter that Richard Scrushy is. Lay's trial lasted nearly four months. After he testified for six days in April 2006, the *New York Times* asked, "Can the Man Who Charmed Houston Do the Same to the Enron Jury?[38] The answer was a resounding "no," and on May 25, 2006, Ken Lay was convicted on all ten counts of fraud.

In all likelihood, Lay faced a life in prison after his sentencing hearing, scheduled for the fall of 2006. He also faced the forfeiture of all remaining riches he had gained from his Enron days. On July 1, 2006, the SEC demanded he and his co-defendant Jeff Skilling repay $183 million. Then, five days later, at his Aspen, Colorado, home, one of three he still owned, Ken Lay died of coronary artery disease. As a result, any appeal was rendered unnecessary, and he and his estate avoid any criminal or civil penalties since without an earthly appeal, his conviction is vacated. These circumstances certainly benefit his remaining family, but, considering his medical history, his death was apparently not a planned way to escape prison or financial ruin.

The high-profile case of the SEC versus Richard Scrushy clearly illustrates a two-pronged successful criminal defense—in and out of the courtroom. The defense took full advantage of the trial location in Scrushy's hometown of Birmingham and the pro-defense rulings of several federal judges, especially the refusal to freeze his assets. Press coverage of the trial regularly mentioned that the jury did not believe the testimony of government witnesses. The former HealthSouth executives who testified against Scrushy had received relatively light prison sentences, fueling juror speculation that these sentences were in exchange for testimony.

That the defense courted the media is indisputable. In a post-verdict article, *USA Today* quotes Don Watkins as saying, "We recognized that the court of public opinion was just as vital to Scrushy's life and freedom as the court of law is. He has to go on working and living and providing for his family. We made sure we kept the public educated, as well as the jury."[39]

In 2007, Richard Scrushy will go on trial again. It remains to be seen if the government and stockholder lawyers have taken notes on the successful community and media relations strategies employed by the defense.

The Scrushy case illustrates how public relations for the accused in a community clearly defined by geography, history and demographics can have such an impact that lawyers, public relations executives and journalists across the country sit up and take notice.

Seven

Empowering the Disenfranchised

There are four primary ways that an individual person in America can have a lawyer represent him. First, a person accused of a crime may hire a criminal defense lawyer or any lawyer in private practice and pay the lawyer's fee and the costs of the defense.

If someone is injured and accuses another person or company of causing the injury, a civil trial lawyer, commonly known as a personal injury lawyer, may agree to represent the injured or the family of the injured and accept a contingency fee. Except in rare cases, this lawyer receives his fee and reimbursement of money spent to investigate and litigate the case only after the lawyer recovers an award through a settlement or jury verdict. For this reason, civil trial lawyers do not take on a case unless they believe they will recover a monetary award.

The third and least likely way people can get legal help is through pro bono legal representation. There are law firms throughout the country who require that certain members of the firm work pro bono, for "the good" of the public, on a certain number of cases every year. The accused person who receives pro bono legal help may be appealing a wrongful conviction and he may face the death penalty or life in prison unless the appeal is successful.

Finally, the fourth way an individual may become represented by a lawyer is to have one appointed for him. Since 1963, people accused of a crime are guaranteed a lawyer, regardless of the ability to pay for one. In that year, the U.S. Supreme Court handed down a decision in the case of *Clarence Earl Gideon v. Wainright*, ruling that every accused person has a "fundamental and essential" right to a lawyer regardless of the ability to pay for legal representation.[1] On the Fortieth Anniversary of the *Gideon* decision, in March 2003, there were numerous events commemorating the ruling. At the same time, there was also a great outcry that the constitutional principles of the decision were largely unfulfilled.

The National Association of Criminal Defense Lawyers compiled a number of significant editorials and essays about the continuing failure of many states to provide adequate representation to accused people. A *New York Times* editorial, "Gideon's Trumpet Stilled," states, "In many of the 22 states that pay for such legal services at the state level, the level of financing is so low that lawyers cannot afford to investigate and prepare proper defenses. In the 28 states that rely on local financing, the quality of representation is even worse."[2]

In the *Atlanta Journal-Constitution*, one columnist, Bill Rankin, noted deplorable failures to provide timely representation and serious deficiencies to legal representation of the accused in Georgia, Oregon, California, Florida and Mississippi, where thousands of poor defendants sit in jail for months, many of whom are forced to plead guilty or negotiate with the prosecution without their having ever seen a lawyer.[3]

Those accused of serious or capital crimes may be appointed legal counsel, but the quality of the legal representation is largely inadequate. In fact, even in death penalty cases, when a poor person is accused and stands trial, he may be represented by a court-assigned lawyer without any criminal defense experience or any basic knowledge of the case law that affects their clients' cases. The *New York Times* editorial calls for "accepted standards . . . and that there are sufficient resources for investigators and expert witnesses."[4]

The way the legal system works in many states is that indigent people accused of a crime are assigned a public defender. For example, in Florida, counties elect a public defender to run a publicly funded office. Depending on the amount of money budgeted by the government responsible for funding, the public defender must hire lawyers and staff to serve the thousands of people who cannot afford to hire a lawyer when they are accused of a crime. In states where there are no public defender offices, the courts usually assign lawyers from a pool. These lawyers are paid an hourly fee, dramatically lower than the usual fee charged by criminal trial lawyers who are usually more experienced in defending the accused. Some of the lawyers who take court-assigned criminal cases do not have adequate training and work unsupervised on cases where their clients' freedom or even their lives may be at stake.

In Chapter 5, I recount the case of Tim Anderson, and the decision of the public defender of Central Florida to request funding from the county to pay for an expert to assist in this capital murder case. What made this request unusual was that he wanted a media relations expert. The county agreed to pay the fee; yet, this precedent-setting use of a public relations specialist has not paved the way for other public defenders to have similar assistance in high-profile cases.

In the field of personal injury law, the use of public relations experts is much more common, although still not a standard cost incurred when litigating a claim for damages in a high-profile matter. Many civil trial lawyers invest in marketing to promote their services and encourage the injured to hire them. I have worked for several of the best civil trial lawyers and firms in America. While my ongoing marketing services for the firm often include newsletters, Web sites and advertising, I am also in constant communication with key lawyers about high-profile personal injury cases and clients.

In 1998, my law firm clients included a prominent New York City personal injury law firm, Schneider, Kleinick, Weitz, Damashek & Shoot (SKWD&S). I had been handling marketing and media relations for this outstanding group of lawyers for several years. In June 1998, Antoine Reid was shot outside Yankee Stadium on a Sunday evening following another win for the Yankees. The next day, the newspapers accurately identified him as a "squeegee man," since he had been trying to wash windshields of cars backed up after the game on the 138th Street exit ramp on the Major Deegan Expressway. When one driver he approached got out of his car and shot him, he had not just shot a squeegee man, he had shot a beloved son, brother, cousin and boyfriend. And this was not just any shooting in the Bronx. The shooter was an off-duty police officer in a city where police misconduct had reached a new low in 1997 when an officer used a broom handle to sodomize Abner Louima in a police station bathroom.

While news reports papered the city, Antoine Reid lay in intensive care at Lincoln Hospital in the Bronx, where his family and girlfriend stood watch over him. Tony, as those who loved and befriended thirty-seven-year-old Antoine Reid called him, had been shot point-blank in the chest by Officer Michael Meyer with his official service revolver. The gun wound necessitated removing Reid's spleen and also damaged his liver.

The Reid family spent most of the next week at this public hospital in the Bronx, a public hospital operated by the New York Health & Hospital Corporation. A few days after the shooting, the family retained the services of lawyers at SKWD&S.

New York City's three major dailies reported the shooting Monday morning, June 15, in their respective styles. The *Daily News* was typically down-to-earth and a little inaccurate: "Cop Shoots Squeegee Man, Critically Hurt in BX Face-Off" was the headline;[5] the story said that the shooter, Officer Michael Meyer, "was with his wife and child on their way home from yesterday's Yankee game"; the *New York Times* correctly and formally reported "Off-Duty Officer Shoots Man on Freeway,"[6] and the next day followed up with a story that Officer Meyer was with his girlfriend and her child.

As for the *New York Post*, a newspaper in a class of its own, it reported the shooting briefly, in typical tabloid fashion, notably with reactionary editorializing by the police-loving columnist Steve Dunleavy. On Tuesday, June 16, two days after the shooting, Dunleavy wrote "Hero officer vs. a lowlife: you choose." He also had the nerve to include Antoine's mother, Ethel, in his column, referring to her as a woman praying for her son, described by Dunleavy as "the rat" and "a nasty piece of work." The *Post* also offended Mrs. Reid by describing Tony as a "homeless" man.[7]

The SKWD&S lawyer handling the case, Cliff Stern, called me on Tuesday night, June 16, to begin the process of setting up the press conference to announce the firm's representation of Antoine Reid and the intent to file a lawsuit against the City of New York for, among other things, allowing an officer like Michael Meyer, who had been removed from regular police service because of his violent history, to retain his service revolver. My media relations plan included several objectives: to introduce Reid and his family to the public through the media; to promote the expertise of the law firm they hired to represent him; and to prepare Tony Reid himself for his new high-profile public image.

First, I had to meet the new client. I was in my Florida office the day after he was shot, so I pulled up his news coverage on the Web. The first article I reviewed was from the *Washington Post*, a story that focused on reactions to the fact that this shooting was another tragic instance of the police abusing their power and the police department not policing its own.[8]

Squeegee guys were already scapegoated by then-Mayor Rudy Giuliani. Before he became the hero leader during 9/11, this mayor was widely considered a bully who targeted those who committed nuisance crimes. He tried to get rid of squeegee guys like Tony Reid as part of his quality-of-life platform plank in the city campaign beginning in the early 1990s.

No one really knew what set off Officer Meyer when he decided to shoot Tony for the unpardonable sin of putting liquid soap on his car window; however, it was clear that the officer had a problem with his temper and a record of allegedly abusing people while he was wearing his police badge. According to the law firm's investigation in the case, Officer Meyer had been removed from duties as a police officer that involved interaction with the public. However, he still carried his service revolver.

When I arrived in New York on Wednesday, two components of my media plan were already in place. I had contacted reporters at the *New York Times* and the *Daily News* about an embargoed interview with Reid at the hospital. I did this after speaking to Rennie Reid, the older brother, on the telephone and discussing his brother's state of mind and personality. It was not news to anyone who knew him that Tony was a drug abuser and that some drugs, certainly cocaine, negatively altered his personality. I also knew that after four days in the hospital, Tony was going to be more of the beloved son, although perhaps somewhat sedated. Rennie

Reid informed me that his brother's humanity and gentle personality were clearly evident.

He also let me know that his brother was normally friendly and open, even somewhat childlike. He was also aware of what had happened to him and incredulous that he had been shot. Ethically, I needed to discuss the media attention with the client himself before I introduced him to reporters.

Managing successful media relations always depends on effectively managing the timing, preparation and delivery associated with an interview, and thinking on your feet. My plan was to bring the reporters from the *Times* and *Daily News* into the hospital for a brief interview with Tony, with the understanding that they would hold their stories until after the press conference scheduled for the next day, Thursday, June 18. It was not possible to include television media in this process because they would not be allowed into the intensive care unit. Actually, if I had known how strict this hospital was regarding any media access, I might have been less proactive about inviting the two reporters to the hospital.

I set up the two interviews one hour apart. Each was promised a visit with Reid and his family at the hospital in return for holding the story until the day our press conference announced the lawsuit. I also negotiated a promise to print the full name of the law firm representing Tony. While this might seem outside the parameters of what this case was about, it most certainly is not.

SKWD&S was a trial law firm handling personal injury and wrongful death cases on a contingency basis. The competition among these firms is fierce. Some firms advertise, or pay, the media to get their message out. Others market with newsletters and brochures, as did SKWD&S, and the really savvy ones also use media relations to get out the message about their high-profile clients and obtain news coverage about the types of cases they handle. There is an adage in the public relations business that one inch of editorial coverage in the newspaper is worth ten inches of paid advertising. When a high-profile case like Tony Reid's comes along, the smart law firm will stay in constant communication with the media.

There are two reasons to be aggressive is media relations. First, after the tremendous publicity about Antoine Reid, people in New York were going to remember his shooting for a long time. These people were part of a future jury pool who might be asked, "Do you remember reading anything about the squeegee guy being shot outside Yankee Stadium?" The longer the coverage continued, the stronger the impression we could make. Furthermore, we wanted to completely wipe out the snide comments of Steve Dunleavy saying that the cop was the good guy.

Second, there are so many personal injury law firms in New York City; many of them do not do a thorough job of representing injured people. I've written about numerous cases in firm newsletters that report on significant results obtained for a client who had come to the firm only after another, less capable, personal injury lawyer told her that her case was worth far less. If a civil trial lawyer is very good at what he does and consistently obtains the highest result possible for a client who has been injured, this firm has an ethical obligation to make sure as many people as possible know that they will get great representation for this firm. SKWD&S was such a law firm.

For this reason, I was very direct with the newspaper reporter about identifying the law firm. In return for early access to the client, I wanted them to make sure that the full name of the firm was not edited out for space or whatever reason. This law firm had a very long name: Schneider, Kleinick, Weitz, Damashek & Shoot (SKWD&S). The lawyer who was assigned to the Reid case was not a named partner; therefore, if the newspaper stories quoted only the lawyer, few people would make the connection that the firm representing Tony Reid was, in fact, SKWD&S.

The *New York Times* reporter who covered the police beat, Michael Cooper, was young and very sharp. I spoke to him on the telephone and explained that I was arranging this interview with the *Times* and also one with the *Daily News*. There was no question that the *New York Post* was not contacted. The inflammatory, unfair and highly critical column by Steve Dunleavy had angered the family.

I arrived at Lincoln Hospital around 5:00 p.m., Thursday, having come directly from La Guardia airport. I had already informed the managing partner and the assigned lawyer of the interviews I had arranged and the press conference details. I confirmed the interview time with the *Times* and *Daily News* by calling from my mobile telephone from the car service sent by the law firm to get me to the Bronx hospital as soon as possible.

I met Rennie Reid in the lobby, and we proceeded through the metal detector, past the guards, and up to the intensive care unit. After asking about his brother's recovery progress, I succinctly explained the purpose of the two interviews: to make his brother real to the public, to allow him to tell his side of the shooting, and to refute the attacks in the *New York Post*.

As we entered the intensive care unit, the Reid family was gathered in a tiny, low-lit waiting area. I introduced myself to his mother, Ethel, and his sister, Sharon Clemente Reid, explained my relationship with the law firm, the purpose of this visit, and then verbalized the explanation I would give directly to Tony about why I had arranged to introduce him to the media and allow the public to hear his voice about what happened.

A few minutes later, Rennie and I walked to Tony's glassed-in room, where he lay hooked up to the standard wires and tubes. Fortunately, the hospital staff had just removed the feeding tube from his mouth. If this had not occurred, he could not have communicated with the *Times* reporter, who was, by this time, in the lobby, waiting. Sometimes, the timing of these interviews is facilitated by pure luck.

Before I left Florida, I packed my small, high-8-mm camera and a compact 35-mm camera, both of which I was carrying in my briefcase. In the back of my mind, I had considered getting the *Times* interview on videotape and releasing it to the television stations. Tony had his eyes closed when Rennie and I positioned ourselves on either side of his bed. He awoke at the sound of Rennie's voice and listened while his brother explained who I was: someone from the law firm who would help him tell what happened when he was shot. Now it was my turn to talk.

"Hi, Tony. I'm so glad you're starting to recover." I placed my hand gently on his arm. "I want to make sure that everyone knows what a horrible thing this cop did to you. Do you remember the Rodney King case?" He nodded and whispered, "Yeah." "Well, the only reason they got those cops is that somebody videotaped them beating him and released it to the TV stations. We want to let the media tell people about you, how badly you're hurt and how wrong it was for that guy to shoot you. Do you understand?" He nodded. I told him I was going down to get the reporter from the *New York Times* and asked if he would mind speaking to him for just a few minutes. He said that was okay. I had my clearance, so I told him we'd be right back. His brother and I immediately went down to the lobby.

Mike Cooper was waiting; he had arrived at the hospital bearing a small green plant. It was camouflage for visiting a sick friend. Again, we went through security. Rennie Reid knew the guards by then; he'd been at the hospital every day for three days visiting his brother. They knew him and about his high-profile brother.

On the way up, Cooper said that he had a photographer on the way. When I asked him if we needed to meet him, he said the photographer would find us.

We stopped very briefly in the anteroom to greet Ethel Reid, but then wisely went directly to the intensive care cubicle. Rennie Reid left us, and I introduced Mike, who began writing immediately. I pulled out my camera. Perhaps because I knew the camera was forbidden, I kept glancing outside the room to see who was watching. When a nurse looked up from the station in the middle of intensive care, I put away the video camera, deciding it was more important to let the *Times* get its interview, before drawing too much attention to us.

About five minutes after Mike was into his interview, a black man in a Dashiki stepped into the room and took out his camera. This was the *New York Times* photographer Chester Higgins, Jr., dressed for the environment and for the ease of fitting in at this Bronx public hospital. He shot off six or seven frames as Mike continued his interview PBS has called Higgins "one of the world's premiere African American photographers."[9] Tony responded clearly and quotably. About Officer Meyer, he said, "He got out of the car and started walking towards me. I told him he ain't got to get out of the car. I would take it off his window [meaning the soap]. He was still arguing and screaming." Tony continued, "We was [sic] touching. He put his gun on my chest and shot it. The gun was on me. He was standing right there. Finally, he said, "I was holding these two Spanish girls' hands, and I was going, 'Oh God, don't let me die here. Don't let me die like this.'" Cooper's observations, which appeared in his story two days later, described Reid speaking in a faint voice, "He had an oxygen tube strapped to his nose and green and purple rosaries hanging around his neck."

As he wrote down Tony's comments, I saw a nurse speaking to two hospital security guards. I alerted Cooper that the interview had to wrap up and stepped outside the cubicle. I walked toward the guards, who were fast approaching. "Hi, I'm from the law firm who represents Reid. Can I help you?" They wanted to know who was in the room with him and if they were taking photos. I said that Tony had asked to speak to this reporter, and we were just leaving. "Was there a problem?" They said there were no reporters allowed, and I truthfully replied that I was unaware of this rule and apologized. Meanwhile, Mike and photographer Higgins had left the room and were moving past us toward the exit. I joined them, and the guards walked behind us. I then had an epiphany and whispered into Higgins' ear "Do you have another roll of film?" He nodded. "Let's change it out. They might want to take your film." We stopped in the narrow waiting room, where the family was keeping vigil, and after ostensibly introducing himself to Sharon, surreptitiously exchanged out the two rolls. He slipped the film in his pocket as the guards closed in and said that Higgins would have to go upstairs to the administrator's office. Cooper and I were free to go.

Then, as we walked with Higgins down the hallway, I saw him slip the roll of film into Cooper's hand.

On the way out, I used a pay phone to call the *Daily News* and explain that there was no way on earth they could get into the hospital for an interview because the guards were on high alert. They were not happy, but I assured them I would try to level the media access as the Reid story progressed.

I rode the subway downtown with Mike Cooper, who was obviously delighted that the *Daily News* was out of the picture for an interview with Reid, making this a real exclusive for the *Times*. I assured him that there would be no other interview opportunities before the press conference the next day and reminded him that the *Times* was going to print the entire name of the firm at some point in the story. We all have our priorities.

When I told the film caper story the next day to Philip Damashek, the managing partner at SKWD&S, he was as delighted as I had ever seen him. He also cautioned me that we had to be very careful in allowing the media access to Tony Reid. I assured him that, having met the entire Reid family, I felt confident I could prepare them and Tony for any interview in the next few weeks. I recommended that we maximize Tony's story, restating my impression that he had given an excellent interview, albeit being sedated at the time.

Damashek, who lost a long battle with cancer in January 2006, was a pioneer in the field of law firm marketing. In the early 1980s, when few law firms took advantage of the Supreme Court decision that lifted restrictions on advertising for lawyers, doctors and other professionals, he began a campaign called "Fact Law" that essentially said, "You tell us the facts (about your accident) we'll tell you the law." Just understanding the power of advertising was not all Damashek knew. He also respected the power of the press. He trusted me with the Reid case and that filtered through all my recommendations to the lawyer running the case and the final decisions made about media access.

The day before the press conference, I contacted all the local media, including the Spanish newspaper *El Diario*, with an embargoed alert. What this means is that, although the media knows what the press conference is about, they agree not to run a story until after the actual press conference. *El Diario* had a special interest in the Reid case, not only because he was a minority victim, but because the teenage girls who comforted him after he was shot were Spanish. In Chapter 11, I discuss how important it is to include the Hispanic media.[10]

The day of the press conference, I arrived at the fifth-floor Woolworth Building offices of SKWD&S at 7:30 a.m. and supervised sending out the press conference announcement. In 1997, most press releases still went by fax; by 2003, all communication was either electronic or spoken. When I work in a law firm, I try to use all the support services necessary to make the project we're working on a success. Essentially, the law firm and I become a team with the same goal of representing our client in the court of public opinion as well as the court of law.

The Reid family had arrived at the Woolworth Building offices of SKWD&S an hour before the press conference was scheduled. I took them into the lawyers' room, ordered refreshments, let them know what to expect, and reviewed the key points that we wanted made at the press conference. Most of the non-lawyer clients I work with have never dealt with the media. In this kind of high-profile case, if I have done my job, their first experience may well be before dozens of reporters.

I planned for a full contingent of media, what I call a grand slam event: radio, TV—network and independent—all the print dailies, at least one weekly, even a monthly publication. Members of Tony Reid's family who were present included his mother, Ethel, his sister, Sharon, her daughter, Tessa, Rennie, his brother, and Lisa Wilson, Tony's girlfriend. She had been with him outside Yankee Stadium, but was instructed not to say anything because she was a potential witness. We decided that Sharon, a professional woman who worked at a downtown utility company, would be the family's spokesperson. This did not mean that no one else would answer reporter's questions, just that she would make a statement on behalf of the family. Press conferences include introductions, opening remarks and a question-and-answer session.

I also discuss facial expressions with participants. There is a natural tendency in all the uninitiated to smile at the camera. Think of the starving children in third world countries, their ribs poking out of their sides, their bellies distended. When they see the photographer, they grin. I often mention this story to the press conference participants, and it usually gets a smile, the last one we want until after the media have left.

The time of the press conference approached, and I made sure that the media were in position in the large conference room. I go around introducing myself, handing out my card and collecting theirs. As I stand in front of the microphones to do a sound check, and perhaps hold up a white sheet of paper for a late-arriving TV camera operator, I always state that I do not wish to be quoted and will be available for help in arranging any follow-up media inquiries. At the Reid event, after distributing a background sheet and identifying in advance who would be speaking at the press conference, I let the lawyers know it was time, rejoined the family and lined up the family and lawyers outside the wooden side door of the conference room.

I have heard press conferences described as a performance; however, when confined to a conference room, I'm less theatrical, opting more for organization and proper demeanor. We all knew that we were here because Tony Reid had been shot and was lying in a hospital without his spleen.

Because Tony could not be with us for this press conference, I asked the Reid family to bring photos of him with them. This is an important tactic when introducing an injured person or an accused client to the media. If the client is incarcerated, it's a way to show him as a regular person, living life with family and friends. It humanizes him or her. The same is true for someone who has been injured. How did he look before he was shot? In Tony's case, how did he look when he wasn't being a squeegee guy? One photo his mother brought was of him dressed to go to church.

In this particular case, I knew that the *New York Times* had also had a photo of him in the hospital that was likely going to be in the next day's story, after the embargo had passed. The *Daily News* was already defensive about its lost access, denied when the hospital guards were put on alert. There was also another group, unrelated to the media, who would be surprised to see the hospital photo in the *Times* the next day: the administrators who thought they had confiscated the film from, Chester Higgins, the *Times'* photographer.

Earlier that morning, before the Reid family arrived for the press conference, I had called Sister Mary Caulfield, a patient advocate at the hospital, who, in a fairly remarkable coincidence, knew Tony and his girlfriend, Lisa Wilson. In addition to working at the hospital, Sister Mary worked with a Bronx drug clinic where

Tony and Lisa had gone for help in the past. In fact, I knew that she had helped Lisa put together an attractive outfit for today's press conference.

I had received a message from Sister Mary that morning regarding the film from the hospital interview. I knew that the film was basically blank. The photographer did click off a few frames while pointing the camera at the floor. She told me that the hospital bigwigs had decided to return the film after it was developed. She had sent it out that morning. I must say that I felt a tad guilty lying to a nun, even by omission, when I avoided talking about what I knew was *not* on that roll of film. Late that afternoon, she called me to express her puzzlement that the developed photographs were blurs of nothing. I declined to speculate with her about what had happened, although I knew she would see the photographs in the next day's *Times*.

The press conference started after I introduced the managing partner of SKWD&S, Philip Damashek. We had briefly discussed his comments that morning, but this was a lawyer who needed little direction on how to speak to the media. He included in his remarks the fact that this firm handled many police brutality and misconduct cases and was dedicated to holding the City of New York responsible for the actions of its police officers. He then introduced the lawyers who were handling the case for the Reid family as well as his family.

I digress briefly to explain that the way personal injury and wrongful death firms usually operate is that the lawyer who gets the call, either directly from an injured person or a representative of that person, family member or another lawyer, is entitled to a percentage of the fees when the case is successfully resolved. As the advertisements for personal injury legal services have largely educated the population, if there is no recovery, there is no fee and, for the lawyers, this means nothing for the time they put into the case. This is why trial lawyers, the good ones, are careful not to accept a case unless they determine that the case has merit and that the potential for a monetary recovery is feasible.

While I'm handling media relations for a law firm on an ongoing basis, I have a responsibility to balance the needs of the injured client and the client's family to speak with the importance of giving the lawyers a forum for describing what the case means and what kind of lawyers they are for taking it.

During the press conference with Antoine Reid's family, his family described a gentle and much-loved young man who had, like so many in the Bronx, fallen under the grip of drug use, but who had always managed to maintain his friendliness and family ties. Reid was well represented by his family, and the lawyers spelled out how they would aggressively pursue justice in the civil courts. In fact, they announced they were seeking over $100 million from the New York City Police Department.

This kind of number is great for headlines, and it's actually not as outrageous as it might sound to some people. A few years later, Harvey Weitz, a founding partner of SKWD&S, would convince a Brooklyn jury to award $105 million to two brothers who had become paraplegic after they were injured when they dived off a pier into shallow water, in an area where warning signs had been removed and never replaced. I was assigned to manage media relations in this case, *Brown v. City of New York*, after a Brooklyn jury found New York City 100% liable for the accident. Lawsuits against the City are bifurcated, which means that the liability portion of the lawsuit is tried first, and if, the City is held liable in any way, then the damages are tried before the same jury. When the jury came back with the 100% liability, Weitz knew that a precedent-setting verdict was possible.

The facts in the case were compelling. The Brown family was picnicking and swimming on Memorial Day in 1992. Virgil Brown, then 27, saw other people diving off the pier into the water below. When he dived in, however, he struck a shallow area and broke his neck in the fall. His brother, John Brown, seeing him floating face-down immediately dived in to save him and, as a tragic coincidence, also broke his neck. With the exceptional trial skills of Weitz, the New York Court of Appeals, Appellate Division, 2nd Department, ultimately upheld $38 million of the $105 million to the brothers in September 2000. At that time, the $38 million was the largest amount ever upheld by this court.

Although Tony Reid's injuries were very different from the Brown brothers' permanent quadriplegia, the circumstances and timing of the shooting by an off-duty-cop were headline news. The law firm's best shot at publicity in the case was at the front end of the lawsuit.

When the Reid press conference concluded, and after the clients left to speak with the lawyers, I wrapped things up with the media. The *Times* reporter, Mike Cooper, wanted to make sure no one else would have the chance to see Tony Reid. He was concerned because Tony's brother, Rennie Reid, had spoken to the *Daily News* yesterday, and it ran a story in that morning's paper that quoted him and implied it had been in communication with Tony Reid himself. I assured him that his story was an exclusive, and he said it was scheduled to run as the lead story in the Metro section, Friday, June 19, 1998.

I also took a few minutes to speak to the *Daily News* reporter and asked him to convey my intentions to his editor that I would give them special access to Reid the day that he was released from the hospital.

There were a few radio interviews to complete for the lawyer assigned to the case, and after I had given him written directions on how to phone in for the interview, my job was done for the day.

Friday morning, I stopped at my local news stand for the papers, the three city dailies and *Newsday*, a newspaper that then focused both on Long Island news and some news from Manhattan. The coverage was terrific, and the full name of the firm appeared in the *Times*.[11] The managing partner was also quoted in all the papers. The family's photographs appeared on the front page of *Newsday*.[12] It was time to plan ahead for Tony's release from the hospital, our last big opportunity for high-profile case management this year.

One of the most important readers of the newspapers sold on Friday, June 19, 1998, was Tony Reid, and I made sure he saw all the stories and photos about his press conference. Something very important can happen when a regular person is thrust into the media spotlight; he may start believing what is written about him. In Tony Reid's case, he was able to see the real person behind the troubled young man who had a tendency to live his life wandering in and out of drug use and joblessness. As he went through his near-death experience, he saw how much his family loved him and how dear life was.[13]

As Reid continued to recover at Lincoln Hospital and his family and lawyers made the news with our lawsuit announcement, the media investigated Mike Meyer, whose civilian complaint record was publicized in the *Times* and the *Daily News*.[14] Naturally, this complaint record was published alongside the various infractions of the law that Tony Reid committed over the years. His record included nine minor charges between 1989 and 1998, from going to the bathroom in public, that is, indecent exposure, and drug possession of marijuana and cocaine that resulted in serving three to five days imprisoned on Riker's Island with one extended sentence of thirty days. These were victimless crimes except for two charges on possession of stolen property. On the other hand, Officer Meyer had seven charges filed against him by civilians between 1994 and 1997, six involving complaints of physical abuse. The first and the last two were substantiated by the Civilian Complaint Review Board, and he was relieved of his law enforcement duties. At the time he shot Antoine Reid, Officer Meyer was assigned to work in building maintenance, painting and repairing police stations; however, the police powers that be did not ask him to turn in his gun.

Two weeks less one day after Officer Meyer used that gun to shoot an unarmed squeegee man, Tony Reid was released from the hospital. A few days earlier, I began to set up both an exclusive interview with the *Daily News* and a press conference, this time at his family home in the Bronx. While it was appropriate to have the first press conference at the law firm's downtown offices, the media and the people who read or see their stories respond well to hearing from them in their personal environment.

I met Rennie Reid at the hospital. We went up to his brother's floor, where he was still recovering after his release from intensive care. His room contained the plant that Mike Cooper had brought, and, like the story, was still alive. Tony was in good spirits, but already a little nervous about the Sunday press conference he had learned about yesterday from Rennie. While we waited for the nurse to bring a wheelchair, I asked to see the scars on his stomach and back. They were wide red scars. When someone is injured violently, with a gun shot or knife, surgeons at the hospital have to act immediately to stop the bleeding and find out the extent of the internal damage. In Tony's case, they had to get in to repair his liver and remove his spleen.

As we gathered up his few things, Tony shared with me several letters that had been sent to him at the hospital, including two from the young women who had witnessed the shooting and held his hands as he thought he lay dying. He also told me about a truck driver who called him from Chicago to wish him well. The origin of the call shows just how far and wide a media story can travel.

This truck driver had met Tony when he came off the highway ramp into the Bronx several years ago. Out-of-state long-haul truckers know to ask for directions from a local, and a squeegee man would know his neighborhood. He had read about the shooting from wire service stories, remembered the friendly man who helped him get around the big city and tracked Tony down in the hospital, calling to wish him a good recovery.

On the way home, I explained to Tony that he would have a sit-down, one-on-one interview in a little while that I had set up with the *Daily News*, a make-good arrangement for the missed opportunity at the hospital.

I am not a proponent of exclusive interviews in breaking news stories. Allowing one newspaper or TV station access and denying the others create a hostile media environment for both the high-profile client and the law firm that may represent him or her. It's also counterproductive. I want the maximum exposure for the client's story. If a national show like *20/20* or *Prime Time* wants to do an in-depth story on the case, that's different.

On Saturday, June 27, the *Daily News* reporter and photographer were due to arrive at the house around 11:00 a.m. This gave me time to evaluate the location for the next day's press conference. The front porch and driveway looked ideal. There was also a lovely backyard where we could have a follow-up after the news conference if that was appropriate. Since Ethel Reid, his mother, had been very concerned that Tony was called "homeless," I also took a moment to look at his downstairs bedroom and living area. It is always important to scope out the physical setting for a media encounter, if a site visit is not possible, then to speak to someone who knows the environment and try to plan for whatever is needed to make it suitable.

Before the *Daily News* team arrived, I sat down with Tony and his family. I had reviewed a few key points that he would make specifically about the injustice of the situation, the indefensible action of Officer Meyer and how he was suffering from his injuries. The one-on-one interview with *Daily News* reporter Patrick O'Shaughnessy and a photographer from the paper went well; I sat near Tony on the living room couch. His mother and brother sat in the same room. During questions about his injuries, he lifted his shirt to reveal the scars. A description of those wounds was in the Sunday story that ran on page 5 the next day.[15]

The Sunday edition of a newspaper garners the maximum audience. People who never read the paper during the week will buy the Sunday paper, some specifically for that week's TV guide. The story was warm and included the account of the friendly truck driver. When Tony elaborated, I learned that he had washed this truck driver's windshield for seven years! Who says a squeegee man cannot have a customer base?

As promised by the *Daily News* editor to whom I spoke when arranging this Saturday interview, the article also contained the full name of the law firm, Schneider, Kleinick, Weitz, Damashek & Shoot.[16]

On Sunday, June 28, the sky was sunny and blue, perfect for an out-of-doors press event. The lawyer from SKWD&S, Cliff Stern, was driving down from his Westchester County home. Meanwhile, rather than let Tony focus on his nervousness, we looked at family photo albums and talked about other things.

After Cliff arrived and spoke to Tony alone for a few minutes, we all sat around the table. The media were gathering out in the front, and I asked friends of the family, who were not known to the media, to go outside and set up a folding table and chairs. I stayed close to Tony; he began to describe his nervousness. "My heart is really going fast. I'm afraid I'll choke up and not be able to talk."

I told him what I tell all my high-profile clients, "Your heart is going to beat fast, and that's a good thing because you've got stage fright, like all good performers. Even though you will be yourself, you have to perform in front of all the cameras. When you walk out, just focus on me and your sister, who will sit at the table with you. As soon as you start to speak, you will feel in control and you will stop being nervous. I promise." I also told him to think of the smiling, starving children story and to be serious when he faced all this unusual attention. Think of the bad cop.

As we walked out to meet the press, Reid leaned carefully on his cane, and this was one of several photos in the next day's newspapers. The *Daily News* ran a photo of Tony leaning on his cane as he walked out of the house[17]; *Newsday's* coverage of the press conference showed a close-up, with Tony leaning forward on the top of the cane while sitting down.

The *New York Post* also covered the press conference, and its article was a balanced story, very different from the columnist Dunleavy's attack mode.[18]

This coverage was a great ending to the two-week media relations effort conducted on Tony Reid's behalf. By making him available and maximizing the news coverage through two exclusive news stories, we had created a lasting impression of an innocent man, shot while trying to earn a few dollars performing an urban street service, washing car windows. Before he was shot, Tony looked forward to some happy people leaving Yankee Stadium, where the home team had won that night. Instead, he encountered an angry, violent off-duty cop who deliberately shot him. Eight years later, people in New York still remember his story and him as a victim.

A year later, in June 1999, a Brooklyn judge, Justice John P. Collins, would dismiss the attempted murder charges and on July 8 would acquit Officer Meyer of any charges. A jury never heard the case; the defense wisely opted for a nonjury trial. The *New York Times* reporter who wrote the story on the acquittal was Michael Cooper. His article included specific criticism of the judge's decision by high-profile Bronx District Attorney Robert T. Johnson: "Judge Collins's New York, in which an unarmed individual who merely possesses a squeegee and puts soap on a person's windshield can be shot, is not the New York that is my New York." Cooper continued to quote Johnson: "Antoine Reid's crime is one that has continually been referred to a quality-of-life crime. If somebody can be shot down for a quality-of-life crime, what does that mean for the rest of us?"[19]

Although Antoine Reid and his family were angry and disappointed, his lawyer Cliff Stern knew that there was another court outside the criminal court, and I don't just mean the court of public opinion. The lawsuit filed in civil court was continuing on its course and eventually this civil lawsuit could punish the City of New York Police Department and Officer Meyer with monetary damages. There was also another obstacle for Officer Meyer, a Police Department administrative hearing that would take place in November 1999.

At the administrative hearing, the police department tried Michael Meyer with attempted murder, assault and misuse of his firearm. Unlike the criminal court trial, in this hearing, Officer Meyer's past was admitted into evidence. A Long Island man described a beating by Officer Meyer that left him with a broken jaw, missing teeth and a dent in his skull that almost killed him. Like Tony Reid, he had filed a multimillion-dollar civil lawsuit against the City and Officer Meyer.

Another witness to Meyer's violent history recalled a 1996 neighborhood dispute during which Meyer refused to make a report, handcuffed the complainant, and began punching and hitting him while he was restrained. In January 2000, the trial commission ruled that Meyer overreacted when he shot Antoine Reid and recommended that he be dismissed. On February 25, 2000, the Police Commissioner fired Officer Mike Meyer.[20]

Tony Reid began drug and alcohol treatment in the months after his release from the hospital. His civil lawsuit continued; the average time for such a lawsuit to be resolved is six years. Because he had a loving family, and because his law firm retained a media specialist, Tony Reid was accurately portrayed as the victim in the squeegee man case. His humanity and his suffering were conveyed through every possible medium to the public who came to know and appreciate his ordeal. If there comes a day when a jury pool gathers to consider his civil case, there will be many whose memories are awakened when his story unfolds in the courtroom. Tony Reid won his case in the court of public opinion. Officer Meyer was convicted in this court and dismissed in the court of his peers.

In 2006, I tried to find out what had happened in the civil lawsuit. The SKWD&S firm had merged with the national firm founded by Johnnie L. Cochran Jr. in 1999. A few years later, after 9/11, the New York office of SKWD&S downsized to fewer than ten lawyers. Soon after this, many of the cases on the firm's docket were transferred to another law firm. Although I have heard second-hand that Antoine Reid was unable to kick his drug habits completely and that his civil case was not as aggressively litigated by the new firm, I do not know if this is true.

What I do know is that the media relations campaign clearly established that Antoine Reid was an innocent victim of an angry cop who should not have been allowed to keep his service revolver. The early accusation that Tony was a "low life" never surfaced again.

Eight

Sexual Abuse: Accusations and Motives

Any time a sex crime occurs, the media will cover the story aggressively. Just as advertisers employ the "sex sells" adage to push new cars, clothing and perfume, the media uses sexually charged stories to sell papers and improve ratings. When allegations of sexual abuse are made against a celebrity, the media have a story with double the impact. Add America's obsession with sports celebrities, and the story becomes a media World Series or Super Bowl. When basketball star Kobe Bryant was arrested for allegedly sexually assaulting a hotel clerk in 2003, he needed a lawyer with outstanding strategic skills in and out of the courtroom.

The police and prosecutor from the small Colorado city where Bryant faced charges by a nineteen-year-old resort hotel employee reacted as best they could to the intense media coverage. They held a press conference and accused Bryant of raping the young woman after she willing went to his hotel room. Within days, Kobe Bryant and his wife went before a full spectrum of media and side-by-side made several simple and effective statements: "I'm a man just like everybody else;" "I love my wife so much;" "we don't want to try the case in the press."[1]

His first two statements as an accused man ring true. The third excuses him from future statements about the charges. However, that does not mean he will not be represented in the court of public opinion.

Bryant did not have to deny that he had a sexual encounter with his accuser or announce that the rape charge was not true. In the twenty-first century, extramarital affairs are all too commonplace. For celebrity superstars, sexual encounters with adoring female fans are expected, if not universally condoned. Denying the rape charge was implied in Bryant's public mea culpa that he had confessed and repented to his wife his infidelity with a hotel employee.

The prosecutors were at some disadvantage without the accuser or an effective representative to step into the media spotlight and point the finger at Bryant. Although more and more rape victims eventually go public with their accusations, it is usually after the case is closed. The mainstream media protect their identity. After the prosecution had its media blitz around the arrest and indictment, it requested and got a gag order from the judge. If it thought that a gag order might actually curtail access to public opinion by Bryant's defense, it was wrong.

The only effective way to limit public opinion in high-profile cases is if interest in the case has geographical boundaries. For example, a local politician in a small city kills his wife during a violent domestic dispute. It will be big news in the community where they live, but a change of venue to a different part of the state a year later will make it unlikely the potential jury pool will have heard about the murder. When the accused is an international sports star, there is no venue in the known world that is insulated from the media message.

To a good lawyer in a high-profile case, a gag order can be like the red flag waved in front of the bull. Kobe Bryant had such a lawyer. A highly successful criminal defense lawyer, Pamela Mackey, partner in a Denver law firm, was experienced in the media games typical of law enforcement and district attorney offices. On July 6, 2003, her law firm issued a press release that included, "Mr. Bryant is innocent and expects to be completely exonerated."[2]

Even police in small communities like Eagle, Colorado, are versed in releasing information about the people they prosecute. If they do not have someone working full-time with the media and advising lawyers on media strategy, they have someone so designated. One or more officers or prosecutors have probably attended a convention or professional meeting where they hear from a media expert about tactics to advance their prosecution in the court of public opinion.

One of the more egregious uses of leaking evidence to the media occurred in a case I worked on involving a dedicated and skilled pediatric orthopedic surgeon in 1992. A community-minded, soft-spoken doctor, he performed sports physicals at no charge to high school athletes and also taught seminars on treating orthopedic injuries in young people. He often photographed his patients' injures, following the protocol of a textbook on presentations for medical research and instructions that included using specific colored backdrops for certain injuries.

When the parents of one patient told a friend who was also a police officer that she was uncomfortable with her child being photographed, the police investigated and began a process of insinuation and dissemination that destroyed the doctor's reputation.

The doctor had several large portfolios of slides used for research and instruction. Never had the slides been turned into photographs. The police took several slides from his office after a search, had them enlarged and printed as 8 × 10 glossies and went to the local media. The appearance of these photographs was misleading and dramatically different from the slides. Aggressive media coverage ensued, and the editorial board of the paper published a call-to-action from the politically conscious state attorney.[3]

Although the doctor was never convicted of a crime, the media coverage was professionally devastating and drained his family of resources and faith in the legal system.

In the Kobe Bryant case, Pamela Mackey seemed well aware of how law enforcement leaks and prosecutorial media relations are used in any high-profile case worthy of a sound byte or byline; the media opportunities were critical to both sides.

Because court hearings are public and the media will get whatever message is embedded in an open court statement, Pamela Mackey used the open courtroom in a preliminary hearing to request that the alleged victim be tested for other sexual activity, clearly implying that she may have had multiple partners in the hours or days before she went up to Bryant's hotel suite.[4]

Before the Judge responded angrily to Mackey's making these court statements, the media have their new angle and a reason to investigate the alleged victim. When the defendant in a high-profile case is a celebrity by virtue of their achievements, not by the heinousness of his alleged crime, the media will agressively investigate both sides. National media, newspapers, magazines and radio and television shows must continue to come up with stories to simulate the water-cooler conversations across America in the months before a case comes to trial and *CourtTV* takes the lead. In the Kobe Bryant case, he wasn't talking; his lawyers can talk only in the courtroom, so the media are looking for anyone who can comment. One mention of the victim's possible checkered past, and the media have doubled the news fodder for the rest of the case.

Mackey had an ethical obligation to raise the possibility that the accuser was lying as early in the case as possible. Bryant's accuser had a jumpstart on the case and the media focus on the accusation was going to be undeniably influential in the area from which Bryant's jury would come. She knew that the accuser would have to testify in the same courtroom where Bryant was sitting. Her investigation of the accuser's past was necessary. Therefore, it was right to let the public know what the investigation could involve. This case went all the way to trial but was won in the court of public opinion, when prosecutors dropped the case during jury selection after the accuser refused to testify.[5]

Reactions to Kobe Bryant's case by several traditional public relations professionals demonstrate the different views of handling media relations for a corporation or even for a law firm that does not specialize in non–white-collar criminal defense.

One PR professional reacted to Mackey's open court request for background on the accuser's sexual activity by suggesting that it would draw additional attention to the cases, as if there was any chance that the Kobe Bryant's case was not going to be a huge media circus from start to finish. "It was terrible," says Magnet Communications Kate Casey Foley, who works with law firms, "Without a doubt, the information that was provided in court was disturbing."[6]

I do not know what kind of law firms Foley represents, but I find her statement naïve. When the accused person facing a rape charge and prison time is a superstar, his lawyer must be able to do what it takes to fight the charge publicly.

Paul Holmes, the author of another article in *PR Week*, includes professional opinions that there is a "downside" to Mackey's announcement that she wanted the sexual history of the accuser in the hours and days just prior to the time she willingly went up to Bryant's hotel room.[7] Her request was not only appropriate; she would have been seriously remiss if she neglected to investigate the background of Bryant's accuser. Making the announcement in the courtroom was providing her client the best representation on every level.

What I find disturbing is that 99 percent of the men accused of rape do not have lawyers who question the accuser's past. These men are tried in the newspapers and in the electronic media in their local communities because the police and the prosecutors use every opportunity to release incriminating information about their past before they ever get into a courtroom. Even if they are innocent, public opinion is stacked against them by prosecutors' use of experienced media relations.

In *PR Week*, opinions on media relations in the Kobe Bryant case were featured in several articles. In one article, Anita Chabria notes that "For many communications experts, that downside far outweighs any positives brought out in the preliminary hearing. Forcing the story onto the alleged victim's past was like squirting lighter fluid on a lit barbeque. It spread the fire to new territory, but also has the potential to blow up. Perhaps that is inevitable—details had to come out at some point."[8]

Yet, this is exactly what Bryant's lawyer needed to do.

Details about the alleged rape had already come out. These details were provided by the prosecution to advance their case through media coverage. The positive for Bryant in the preliminary hearing was that his lawyer leveled the playing field in the rape charge he had to fight in the public and legal arena. There is no downside to that. When someone is facing a felony conviction and prison time, the battle for a fair trial begins at the time of the arrest.

However, Ronn Torossoan, who is quoted in Chabria's article, is correct when he says, "To be the guy who was found innocent but everybody thinks is guilty is not good enough for him. If he's [Kobe Bryant] found innocent in the end and the public perception is that he was manipulated and the woman has slept around, it is very beneficial to him."[9] That is precisely why reaching the public through the media and addressing the obvious possibilities that Kobe Bryant's accuser was not raped and is manipulative are key to his defense in a court of law, where a jury exposed to the media will hear the case.

Holmes, who critizes Mackey, responds: "Perhaps it would be beneficial, but it would not be honorable. Even if the evidence fails to support the rape charge, it points to a Bryant very different from the role he cultivated as basketball's good boy."[10] I disagree with Holmes' statement that there's honor involved once a man is charged with rape and prosecutors work to convict him on every level. He and his lawyers must fight the charges in every forum. As regards his reputation, despite Bryant's marriage status or endorsement profile, he is a professional sports star, and the general public takes that into account when there are allegations of sexual misconduct.

There was no downside to any of the strategies employed by Bryant's lawyer. In fact, I suspect that the tall, black athlete and his very wise advisors selected the petite white woman as his lawyer for all the best reasons, from the way they looked walking in and out of the courtroom, to her thorough knowledge of the Colorado criminal justice system, to her exceptional media savvy.

While Mackey's lawyer skills preempt any other reason for hiring her, race is a factor in America's judicial system. Race is closely linked with image, and image influences public opinion and sways juries.

In the mid-1990s, criminal defense specialist Don Lykkebak represented a businessman accused of exposing himself, a felony in Florida, to young boys at a water park in conservative Central Florida. The facts in the case were that the accused was wearing a pair of gym shorts while sitting on the edge of a pool. His shorts had no built-in support. Several youngsters in the pool swam up to the edge and saw his exposed genitals.

Following his arrest, the accused interviewed several lawyers and hired Lykkebak. Although Lykkebak's legal skills are well known in the area, he was hired because of image. He said that he selected him because he looked like Mr. Clean and the former Marine officer that he is. Lykkebak projected the image that the accused wanted to project. The businessman knew that he needed more than just a good lawyer; he needed to project a clean-cut image. Lykkebak recalls, "In five minutes flat the jury returned with a verdict of not guilty; the fastest verdict I've ever had." During his more than thirty-five years representing the accused, he has also frequently heard from black clients who say their race was already one count against them; they did not want a black lawyer.

The references to image discussed in Holmes' article do not address the image of Bryant's lawyer, but comment on the reputation of the basketball star himself. A reputation-management specialist states: "It doesn't matter if Bryant is guilty. The trial hasn't even started yet, and huge decisions are being made that have nothing to do with a court of law," said Mike Paul, president of MGP & Associates PR. "He has sponsors that are starting to drop him. He's had fans that are starting to drop him."

While there is certainly some truth in what Paul says, concern over reputation never matters more than fear of a conviction. When you are a basketball superstar facing a prison sentence, you want a lawyer who will push the envelope in media relations.

For every sponsor who drops him, there's another out there who will want him after he is exonerated. For the rare fan who takes umbrage when a sports star is charged with rape, there are thousands who figure it goes with the game.

Reputation is much more important to someone who lives in a small community and, at the fragile age of sixteen, is facing exposure in the local newspaper that he molested young boys. This is particularly true when he is the son of a prominent local pastor. I worked on such a case in 1998.

That year, Central Florida criminal defense lawyer Mark M. O'Mara was notified that the high school student he represented was going to be "outed" by the *Orlando Sentinel*, whose reporter, Rene Stutzman, had obtained juvenile records of the sexual acts that occurred when the student was twelve years old.

O'Mara's client was the son of a pastor at a large affluent church in a small city near Orlando, Florida. When he was a preteen, he had engaged in what many might describe as immature sexual experimentation with younger boys, behavior that included pulling down their pants and touching each other. One of those incidents occurred on church property during school hours.

When the parents first brought the incident to the pastor's attention, he took immediate action to chastise and counsel his son about appropriate and inappropriate behavior. There were no more incidents. Then two years later, parents went to police to complain, and criminal charges were filed.

The timing of the charges brought against the boy is significant: two years after the sexual playing had occurred and three weeks before a civil suit was filed against the family. The civil suit alleged not the original incidents but made recent allegations, stories alleged by the families now suing the pastor and his son, and, of course, the church, which had a $1 million insurance policy.

Because the sexual acts occurred with younger boys, the allegations eventually brought to the police by their parents resulted in charges of felony sexual abuse. O'Mara negotiated a no-contest plea with the prosecutor, whereby both sides agreed to follow the recommendation of a court-appointed psychologist.

Nearly a year after the then sixteen-year-old began counseling, supervised by the Department of Juvenile Justice, and four years after the sexual activity had occurred, the parents of the younger boys began to approach the media.

The possibility that an article publicizing sexual acts that had occurred when our client was twelve years old was a devastating invasion of privacy and an emotionally stressful event for the high school senior, a popular athlete on the basketball and track teams who was also musically talented and involved with choirs at both school and his church.

The family wanted to protect their son from being publicly profiled as a sexual abuser of young boys. They were very concerned about how their teenage-old son would react to the media, his friends and fellow students and teachers. They were also concerned about legal issues related to both the criminal case and the pending civil lawsuit.

Mark O'Mara, their son's criminal defense lawyer was experienced in media relations. He and I had worked together on an earlier high-profile murder case with positive results. After we discussed the case and media scrutiny, he advised them to use my services.

Within a few hours of my first meeting with the family and their son, I recognized that the information obtained by the newspaper was biased and incomplete. The reporter's information included police records and reports by the Department of Juvenile Justice, but not the positive psychological evaluations. She had listened to the exaggerations and untrue allegations of ongoing sexual contact proffered by the families suing the church, but had not heard from the pastor, his wife and son, who were naturally as opposed to an interview as they were to the publication of the story itself.

After interviewing the pastor, his wife and son, and reviewing the police records and the comprehensive psychological evaluations of the seventeen-year-old, including a recent court-ordered reevaluation, I contacted the *Orlando Sentinel* reporter to discuss her research and the article she was preparing for publication.

I evaluated the reporter's and her editor's intentions to proceed with the story as well as considered the fact that a television reporter had also called O'Mara about the case. Then, I began to create a strategy that was best for the family.

I always feel a serious responsibility for advising the accused or the accuser, their family members and involved friends. Getting them to accept that the story is very likely going to become public is the first step in preparing them for an interview. At the same time, convincing the family that an interview with the *Sentinel* reporter was judicious and necessary did not mean that we were going to give up trying to persuade the reporter and her editors that the story was old news, that this juvenile deserved to be protected from public scrutiny. I was convinced that he was absolutely no danger to anyone, as his most recent evaluations clearly stated, and that the motives of the accusing families were questionable.

I asked both O'Mara and the family to agree to release the psychologists' reports to the reporter. These were not available to her, and by making them available I accomplished two goals: first, she now had access to very positive and accurate evaluations about the young man and a report which included that it was unlikely that he might engage in such behavior again. The potential for future sexual misconduct was the reason the reporter said that the *Orlando Sentinel* had decided to use the name and records of a juvenile. Second, she recognized that we were being honest and open with her. This created a more personal and trusting connection with the reporter and her editors and my client's family.

O'Mara and I worked as a team to prepare for the newspaper reporter's interview. His role was to assure the family that all of their son's legal rights were protected and to explain discrepancies between what the victims' families had told her and what was factual and what was unsubstantiated in the criminal and civil legal proceedings.

A few days before the scheduled sit-down interview with the *Sentinel* reporter, I assisted the pastor in answering written questions submitted to them a month earlier by the reporter. I also spent several hours in the weeks before the interview and on the day of the interview preparing the now seventeen-year-old and his parents for what to expect. I stressed that it was important to ask the reporter and repeat the request throughout the interview: "Why does this story have to be in the paper?"

Prior to the interview, O'Mara and I contacted editors at the *Sentinel* and asked them not to vary from their ethical standard of not to publish the name of an accused juvenile. We stressed that the incident occurred fours years earlier and that psychological counseling and the counsel of his parents had made the young man aware why his behavior was unacceptable. I also emphasized that the reason they were informed about this case was that the personal injury lawsuit against the church had moved closer to a trial. The media recognize when someone is trying to use them to carry out a publicity campaign to advance their monetary agenda. I simply reminded the editors of this fact and provided supporting documentation that the client was not a danger to his community.

As the day of the interview approached, the *Sentinel* seemed determined to publish the story. However, I've learned that just because an interview takes place, it doesn't mean that the story will actually run.

In this case, as in every case where the media aggressively pursue an interview from a reluctant person, I stressed the importance of truthfulness, direct and succinct responses and a strongly worded series of statements, rehearsed for clarity and emphasis.

Four weeks after the family retained me to assist them in managing the media inquiry into their son's case, their lawyer, O'Mara, and I sat down at the pastor's home for a three-hour interview with the parents, their son, and two older siblings, there to support their brother. There were repeated opportunities to correct and refute information already given to the reporter by the families pursuing the civil lawsuit.

Both the pastor and his son directly asked the reporter to consider not pushing for publication of the story. Throughout the interview, even the most intrusive questions were answered honestly and without shame.

I left the interview convinced that this intrusion into the young man's juvenile history was terribly unfair, and worked closely with O'Mara in the following week to keep up pressure on the newspaper to refrain from publicizing this case.

At the same time, I advised the pastor to alert the administrators and teachers at their son's high school to put in place a plan to counsel other students and protect him from unfair ridicule should a story actually run in the newspaper. A newspaper story would be much more destructive than a story on the local radio or TV news, because any student who saw the story could clip it out and bring it to school. The story could be passed around for weeks.

Ten days later, there was no story in the paper, but a news truck from a TV station we had hoped was not yet informed about the case, pulled up outside the pastor's church and began taping as well as asking for an interview. Clearly someone representing the family suing the church had contacted them, perhaps because they had become frustrated with the newspaper's delay or reluctance to run the story as yet.

The family called me immediately. Although we were indeed ambushed by the sudden appearance of the TV truck, we were also completely prepared to handle the ambush.

Because O'Mara was sequestered in depositions in an upcoming first-degree murder trial, he was unavailable to participate in a response to the TV station. I discussed the importance of balancing the TV segment with a position statement from the family if all efforts to delay or postpone the airing of the story that night failed. After a pointed discussion with the news director, and a telephone consultation with O'Mara and the pastor and his wife, I set up an on-camera interview in time to be included in the segment.

At the same time, I contacted the local NBC affiliate WESH TV-Channel 2 news department that had earlier expressed an interest in the story. Realizing it was going to air on the local CBS-Channel 6 at 6 p.m., I proceeded to educate the second TV station and make plans to schedule an interview for later that evening with the pastor and lawyer present. That interview to Channel 2, which, along with the pastor's interview, was included in the 11:00 p.m. newscast.

Each TV news segment included the same father of one of the younger boys suing the church, who appeared, by his reported request, in shadows. Channel 6 repeated the young man's name and aired his mug shot; Channel 2, in a sensitive, balanced and ethical report, did not use his name, but naturally, as we intended, showed the pastor as a concerned father, speaking clearly and directly to the reporter, explaining that his son's behavior had been immature and that he had received extensive counseling.

Both news segments aired that night and were repeated during the morning TV news shows. The next day, our client, a seventeen-year-old young man who had grown and matured with the love and support of his family and the professional counseling of trained psychologists, went to school and studied separately while appropriate discussions with his peers took place. That afternoon, he decided to attend track practice, where he was immediately surrounded with a show of support and friendship from his teammates.

There was another responsibility that I carried out the day the news truck showed up at the church. I knew that this station was unlikely to delay its sensationalist, self-promoting "exclusive," and immediately called the Rene Stutzman at the *Orlando Sentinel* to give her the heads-up that she was going to be scooped. She had to know that we were reluctant participants in the TV news segments, and I was determined to give her the same honest and ethical consideration that I had been asking from her for the last month.

The newspaper never ran the story. However, as Mark O'Mara recalls, "Before the hearing to confirm the court's acceptance of the psychologist's recommendation, our client made a terrible mistake. He skipped a class to talk with a friend about his depression over some school problem. This relatively minor infraction was brought to the court's attention, and, as a result, the judge insisted that he be placed into a juvenile institution for mandated psychological oversight until he turned eighteen."[11]

Fortunately, the young man and his family no longer faced print publicity. They met the difficult intrusion into their lives; actively and thoughtfully considered professional advice and experience; and kept their strong faith and family support intact as they handled the media investigation of their son's youthful errors with the same careful consideration as they used to find him the best legal representation they could.

Whether the accused is a sports star, a sensitive teenage boy or a businessman, allegations of sexual abuse or rape are insidious and sensational. If there is any defense at all, the defense must take place in the court of law and the court of public opinion. For lawyers to represent their clients fully, they must pay appropriate attention to both.

Nine

The Mea Culpa Press Conference

Any lawyer worth her salt will advise anyone who is arrested to keep quiet and not say anything to police or investigators until a defense lawyer is present. "Anything you say, can and will be held against you" is a critical part of the Miranda warning that police are supposed to read to the accused. Perhaps the least recommended response a criminal defense lawyer wants his client to make when he is suddenly arrested for a crime is, "It's my fault" or "I'm sorry."

However, in certain cases, a public apology can be an excellent public relations component of defense strategy. When someone is charged with a crime, the accusations may be unfair, inaccurate, misconstrued or just plain untrue. In cases where an accusation was made administratively and a person is facing civil proceedings, saying "I'm sorry" personally to the injured person may help the accused show appropriate compassion and, at the same time, help him to protect his interests and defend his actions.

For example, a family member once had a doctor prescribe a drug to treat anxiety. The pharmacist misread the handwritten prescription, in part because the handwriting was so messy, and the patient took an unhealthy dose. He became so drowsy that he fell and slightly injured himself. After speaking with the doctor and learning that the prescription was filled incorrectly, he wanted to hire a lawyer and sue the pharmacy. First, however, he called the pharmacist, from whom he received such a genuine, heartfelt apology, that he decided not to pursue legal action.

Apologizing can include acknowledging a degree of fault and accepting some responsibility for what happened, but does not necessarily mean admitting guilt. Although, in cases when the accused is culpable, guilty on some level, a genuine apology may be rendered in hopes of influencing the prosecution's decision on how to charge the accused and thus affect the type of sentencing and the length of time in or avoidance of prison. In a far less serious matter, when an accused person is culpable but not guilty of a crime, an appropriate apology may help him to preserve his reputation and explain the circumstances of what really happened.

When someone commits a crime on any level and is contrite, apologizing may be essential to the healing process for both the accused and the victim. However, the timing and manner of making an apology must not contradict the criminal defense lawyer's successful representation of the accused.

In the following three cases, the alleged crimes are very different. In one, a young schoolteacher is involved in a hit-and-run accident that leaves two children dead and polarizes a community. The second case concerns a kind dentist who inappropriately tries to calm a hysterical child, and the media coverage threatens his reputation and dental practice. Finally, criminal behavior by the parents of a topless dancer who kills her abusive boyfriend draws the attention of the national media and leads to a murder trial. In each of these cases, the accused mounts a mea culpa (my fault) defense with the approval of his criminal defense lawyer.

While visiting a friend in Tampa, Florida, in November 2005, I opened the Sunday newspaper and read the front-page story about a case that had been one of the city's top stories two years running.[1] In the early morning hours of that Sunday, a judge had sentenced a twenty-nine-year-old white dance teacher to house arrest and probation for her part in the hit-and-run accident that killed two black children in March 2004. The story in the *St. Petersburg Times* mentioned that the circumstances of her arrest were unusual. Before she turned herself in to the police, she and her high-profile lawyer had held a press conference during which she apologized to the mother of the children. The reference to a press conference—what I call a mea culpa press conference—a few days after Jennifer Porter left the scene of the accident is what caught my eye.

Porter's lawyer is Barry Cohen, one of the nation's most successful trial lawyers. He is a lawyer who has a thorough understanding of media relations and how media coverage affects public, prosecutorial and judicial opinions and decisions. Cohen explains that he makes his media relations decisions carefully and consciously balances "the legal ramifications, public perceptions and politics" before speaking to the press. "Public perceptions of the facts in a high-profile case influence the political considerations underlying prosecutorial and judicial decisions."[2]

Cohen has been known for his willingness to conduct media relations on behalf of his clients for more than eighteen years. In 1989, he attended a Florida Bar Association seminar that focused on lawyers and the media. An article in the

St. Petersburg Times, "Lawyers Learning to Plead in Court of Public Opinion," reported

Tampa defense lawyer Barry Cohen didn't build his successful practice on knowledge of the law and good trial skills alone. A certain media savvy also helps when Cohen defends people uncomfortable with publicity or whose public personas draw extra attention to a case. In fact, some lawyers say that to ignore the media's coverage of a case is a failure to represent the client in the best way possible.[3]

After a May 27, 1989, boating accident that killed four teenagers near Indian Rocks Beach, Cohen was on the media offensive. His client was William A. LaTorre, a St. Petersburg chiropractor, and the driver of a Cigarette boat that struck the teens' boat. Before a single charge was filed, Cohen assured reporters his client was not at fault. (Several civil suits had been filed in the case, but no charges had been filed against Cohen's client.)

Two months after the accident, Dr. Latorre was arrested in the early morning; outside reporters, alerted to the arrest, captured the image of him led out of the house in handcuffs. Cohen says that the arrest, like many, was political, and his client was innocent. "Sometimes prosecutors will use the system to gain political eminence," Cohen said, "over the bones of anyone they can bury."[4] Later that day, Dr. Latorre and his wife appeared at a press conference in Cohen's office, where Mrs. Latorre spoke, "I know that there is a lot of pain involved to the families of these teens," she said. "There's also a lot of pain involved for my family. . . . My husband will be exonerated."[5]

Even before U.S. Supreme Court Justice Kennedy's 1991 opinion in *Gentile v. Nevada* (see Chapter 1) that lawyers "represent clients in the court of public opinion," Cohen was one of the lawyers described in the *St. Petersburg Times* article as believing that "defenders have to try to balance an inherent media advantage enjoyed by prosecutors."[6]

Like many top-notch criminal defense lawyers, including Johnnie Cochran, Cohen eventually began to focus on civil trial law, suing on behalf of injured people. The same investigative, negotiating and trial skills that made him an outstanding defense lawyer also made him an excellent personal injury lawyer. In fact, according to his Web site www.tampalawfirm.com, he has obtained multimillion dollar results from $6, $8, $10 and $25 million to a wrongful death verdict of $500 million in 1995.

These kinds of results and the fees his law firm received for these cases put Cohen in a position to handle whatever kind of case he chooses, regardless of the client's ability to pay his fees and investigative expenses. Although he focuses primarily on civil matters, he says he took on the defense of Jennifer Porter because he saw that she was also a victim and believed she did not deserve to be sent to prison.

The impact of this case on the West Coast Florida cities of Tampa and St. Petersburg was tremendous. The story of Cohen's representation of Porter and the lives and characters of the people affected by the tragic hit-and-run deaths of thirteen-year-old Bryant Wilkins and three-year-old Durontae Caldwell is chronicled in a five-part series that ran in the *St. Petersburg Times* in the year after the judge sentenced Porter. Unlike many newspapers, the *St. Pete Times* does not charge for access to its archives, and this fascinating series can be accessed at www.stpetetimes.com. Just enter the name "Jennifer Porter," and there are nearly 30,000 words in the five-part series (almost half the length of this book!) that provides a detailed account of this fascinating high-profile case.

According to the *St. Petersburg Times* series, Cohen saw the pain and suffering of his client and allowed her to go before the press and apologize to Lisa Wilkins for the deaths of her two sons and the injuries suffered by two others. At the same time, he was engaged in negotiations with the state attorney's office regarding the process for Porter's surrender and conducting his own investigation to determine what happened on March 31, 2004.

Cohen accepted the cases after meeting with Porter and her parents. When he initially heard about the hit-and-run on the news, he reacted like everyone in the Tampa area, condemning the person who was so callous as to run over children and then leave the scene without trying to help the children; he planned to offer a $10,000 reward to help find the guilty driver. However, as with almost every case, circumstances of the accident were complicated and unexplained, and Porter's reaction when it happened was not malicious.

The daughter of a postal worker and his Cuban-born wife, twenty-eight-year-old Jennifer Porter was living at home and had just started a teaching job at a new elementary school in a decrepit part of Tampa. An extremely quiet and obedient daughter, she was known for loving children and her dedication to helping her fellow teachers. The circumstances of the hit-and-run accident were never fully explained. Witnesses saw two vehicles leaving the scene; one was a white van and the other a small car, model unknown. Porter's first realization that something had happened was a body hitting her windshield. She panicked and then used her mobile telephone to call her mother. Hearing the hysteria in her daughter's voice, she told her to drive to the nearby dance studio they owned and stop the car.

Her father's first reaction, when his wife called him about the incident, was to say their daughter should return to the scene. A short time later, however, he called his wife back, who was on her way to meet Porter, and said that if their daughter had hit someone, perhaps they should get her a lawyer first. Meanwhile, ambulances were taking the children who had been struck to area hospitals, their mother riding in one of them. The next day, Porter called the lawyer he had seen on television many times, Tampa's best-known advocate for accused people, Barry Cohen.

When Cohen first met with the Porters on April 2, he realized that they could not afford to pay his fee and the costs that are essential to mounting a successful defense. He also saw a grief-stricken and contrite Jennifer Porter who was still extremely distressed and suffering from what numerous psychologists would describe as posttraumatic shock. Cohen decided to represent her; later he would also defend the parents from criminal charges that they failed to report the crime and took steps to conceal the evidence by pulling her car into the garage and cleaning off the blood.

That same day, Cohen notified the state attorney for Hillsborough County, Mark Ober, that he was representing one of the drivers of the two cars. He then called the local sheriff's office to direct its investigators to the location of the car, but not before he sent his own team of investigators to gather evidence. Over the weekend, he also informed the sheriff the name of the driver of one of the cars reported at the accident: Jennifer Porter.

In addition, in these very early stages of the case, Cohen made an initial outreach to Wilkins. The *St. Pete Times* reports, "That weekend, Cohen drove Mrs. Porter to Lisa Wilkins' apartment. It was an impulsive decision. Cohen said he thought the parents should tell Wilkins how sorry they were. He described it as a gesture of respect. He also believed it could not hurt their case. Jennifer was in no condition to join them. Cohen believed she might be suicidal and arranged for her to see a psychiatrist."[7]

Although someone at the Wilkins' home turned away Cohen and the Porters, citing Ms. Wilkins' state of mind, the first overture had been made. That Sunday night, Jennifer Porter drafted her own mea culpa statement. She had decided to speak through the media to Wilkins. Monday morning, at 10:00 a.m., she did just that.

"I want to express my deepest sympathies to Lisa Wilkins, her family, friends, and the whole community. I'm sorry. I'm so sorry. I wish there was more that I could say to ease her pain. I know there's nothing I can do to bring your two precious sons back, Bryant and Duronta. And I will continue to pray for the speedy recovery of your two other children. May God bless all of you."[8]

Jennifer Porter apologized to the children's mother as directly as she could. Her apology did not specifically admit to any role in the accident that killed and injured her children. It didn't have to. Why else would she be speaking from a criminal defense lawyer's office about a hit-and-run accident? There were a number of important reasons for Porter to apologize. One reason was, as the *St. Pete Times* characterized the attempt by Jennifer's parents to apologize to Lisa Wilkins, Cohen felt "it could not hurt their case."[9]

There are two newspapers that dominate the Tampa area, the *St. Petersburg Times* and the *Tampa Tribune*. Both reported every development in the hit-and-run case and Jennifer Porter's defense. In addition, columnists for each paper weighed in with strong opinions. Judy Hill, who has written a column for the *Tampa Tribune* for fifteen years, was critical of Porter. After the first press conference, Hill's column "'I'm Sorry' Is Sorrowfully Inadequate" called for Jennifer Porter to "take responsibility." She quoted from the mea culpa statement, but wanted the *culpa*, that is, the culpability, to have been overt, not implied.[10]

In her column after the sentence of house arrest and probation was handed down, Hill criticized the leniency but indicated that her broader concern was that justice be "equally imposed, regardless of race, color, gender, age." She acknowledges that the judge must have felt compassion for Porter.[11]

In fact, eliciting compassion for Jennifer Porter was what Barry Cohen knew was going to be her best defense. When he tapped into the intense public interest in the hit-and-run case, and allowed his client to apologize to Wilkins and speak to her community through the media, he demonstrated his outstanding skills in the court of public opinion.

However, when Cohen went into the sentence hearing, he was armed with legal ammunition that he did not report to the press. He relied on his trial skills to elicit testimony from the state's experts that his investigation and his deposition of one of the children who survived the hit-and-run accident that there was indeed a second vehicle, a white van, involved. The facts that Cohen presented in court were powerful. Without this evidence, he believes that the judge might well have given Jennifer Porter prison time.

The evening that the children left the park, according to Cohen's investigative report, "they were running across the busy highway and ran right in front of the white van. When they jumped back, they jumped back into Porter's car." Cohen says he kept quiet about this evidence because he wanted the investigating officer to agree on the stand that this is what happened.

This case perfectly exemplifies the strategic balance of legal procedures and media relations. From the press conference in March 2004 when Jennifer Porter apologized to a public who was judging the unknown hit-and-run driver as callous and uncaring to the sentencing hearing in November 2005, Barry Cohen made all the right moves for his client. "Changing the image that the public had of her was never inconsistent with our legal defense. They were intertwined."[12]

The benefits and components of an apology are analyzed in a book by California psychotherapist Beverly Engle, *The Power of Apology*. There are actual health benefits to apologizing, according to Engle.[13] In Porter's case, she began to talk of committing suicide the night of the accident. Psychiatrists who examined her the week of the accident and the following year concluded that she suffered from severe posttraumatic stress. This first apology might have helped to begin the process of reducing her debilitating posttraumatic stress.

Engle also says that people who cannot apologize have serious character flaws. Among her family, friends and coworkers, Porter was known for her good character. For her entire twenty-eight years of life before the accident, Jennifer Porter had always tried to do the right thing. When she spoke at the press conference, her apology included two of the components of a successful apology as described by Engle: regret, responsibility and a wiliness to remedy the situation. At this point, there was no remedy for the deaths of Wilkins' two sons.

Porter's apology expressed sincere regret; the fact that she was apologizing clearly acknowledged that she had some responsibility or role in the hit-and-run accident. The timing of the apology was also important. Engle says that "the sooner an apology is made to the person who has been wronged, the more genuine and meaningful" the apology.[14] Wilkins, who watched Porter on television from her home, likely believed that the missing component of the apology—the remedy— included punishment for Porter. However, while nothing could bring back her two sons, there was the distinct possibility of compensation.

Within days of the hit-and-run accident, Lisa Wilkins was represented by legal counsel. Well before the state's prosecution of Porter was over, Wilkins' life and the lives of her remaining five children changed dramatically. Although the amount of compensation she received remains confidential, she and her five children (one was born after the accident), moved into a new five-bedroom house in a predominantly white gated community miles away from the rental apartment where she had lived.

After the Monday morning press conference, Cohen entered into a series of negotiations with the State Attorney's Office. Jennifer Porter's role in the hit-and-run accident called for one of two criminal charges: leaving the scene of a crash involving death or vehicular homicide. The sentencing guidelines varied from fifteen years to sixty years in prison, but Cohen "had no intention of pleading Porter out with prison time."[15] When the decision was finally made to charge her with leaving the scene, Cohen arranged for his client to turn herself in on April 28, 2004.

A few days after Porter surrendered to police, another prominent columnist, Bill Maxwell, of the *St. Petersburg Times*, wrote his opinion. Maxwell, like the victims, is African American, and had a unique perspective of the case. In his column "Do We Really Know What We Would Do?" he comments on Porter's apology and reveals that he lost a sibling in a hit-and-run accident in 1963, "I have no way of knowing what was going through her mind, but I am certain that raw fear and surprise prevented her from doing the right thing. . . . I suspect that too few of us examine our own lives and motivations before we harshly judge other people. Because I lost a nine-year-old sister to a scared, genuinely remorseful hit-and-run driver, I am reserving judgment of Jennifer Porter, who has expressed what appears to be sincere remorse."[16]

Cohen was unusually fortunate to be able to arrange a mea culpa statement by his client before she was accused and arrested. He knew, as do all criminal defense lawyers, that once someone is arrested, the mug shot of the client will be broadcast and printed. Almost anyone's mug shot looks either defiant, guilty, or both. In the first part of its series on the case, the *St. Pete Times'* published reactions to her expression ranged from cold to numb and despairing. "At the jail, Jennifer Porter gave her fingerprints and stood in front of a camera for the image that would follow her forever. Her long brown hair was shown hanging over her shoulders. Her eyes stared slightly downward, big and dark and dead. It became the test. Some, seeing the photo, would say Porter appeared cold and self-absorbed. Others insisted they saw numbness, despair, a sense of something irrevocable."[17]

In March 2005, while the negotiations between Cohen and the state attorney's office about the Jennifer Porter case were ongoing, the second opportunity for an apology was arranged at the office of Lisa Wilkins' lawyer. This was a private meeting, and the timing was very different from the televised apology.

During the year since the accident, Wilkins, who had been evicted from five apartments in seven years, had received a substantial amount of money, enough for her new five-bedroom home with a pool in a gated community, a new car and the ability to maintain this style of living without working. She was also pregnant with her eighth child. This apology was important to Cohen's continuing effort to eliminate the possibility of jail time for Jennifer Porter. The feeling and desires of Wilkins would be considered by both the state attorney and the judge who ultimately imposed her sentence.

Apparently, the two young women communicated well during the meeting. Jennifer Porter apologized, and Lisa Wilkins told her she forgave her. Both of them cried. After the meeting, Porter followed up with a thank-you letter to Wilkins, but the letter was never delivered. Wilkins' civil lawyer did not give it to her because his client had changed her mind again and wanted more answers, about the crash and why Porter left the scene—answers that Porter couldn't give her.

Cohen had taken his client to be interviewed and examined by the country's foremost expert on posttraumatic stress. His evaluation surmised what had happened when the body of one of the children hit the windshield. "The part of the brain that thinks, plans, understands and reacts . . . can become dysfunctional during extreme trauma. . . . She shut down and went on automatic, and then she drove like a zombie for eighteen minutes. . . . [What] woke her out of her stupor was the cracking of her windshield."[18] At this point Jennifer Porter, the obedient daughter, had already turned to her parents and followed their advice despite suicidal thoughts and a desire to turn herself into the police that night.

This was not what Lisa Wilkins was willing to accept as the whole truth. It was, however, at the crux of Barry Cohen's defense. In May 2005, he had a meeting with prosecutors and tried to persuade them not to seek jail time for Porter. Soon after this, the state attorney invited Lisa Wilkins into the office to tell them what she thought. Her opinion was indecisive: According the *St. Pete Times*, she said "she wouldn't ask that Porter receive probation. But she also wouldn't stand in the way of any plea deals that made probation possible. 'Y'all do your job,' she told prosecutors."[19]

The prosecution decided it was its job to seek three years in prison for Jennifer Porter. Cohen had always known it was his job to make sure she did not serve any prison time.

Jennifer Porter did not go unpunished. She is a convicted felon who will never be able to teach school, the job she loved above all else.

Ten years before Barry Cohen invited the media to his office so that Jennifer Porter could apologize for what happened to Wilkins' children, I organized a mea culpa press conference in Sanford, Florida, a small Central Florida city midway between Daytona Beach and Tampa. Originally, I was called by a criminal defense lawyer, Mark O'Mara, who wanted help negotiating a deal for his client to tell her story on *Inside Edition*, the nationally televised tabloid program that completed with *A Current Affair* for viewers.

In 1992, Michele Roger, a twenty-six-year-old topless dancer with the stage name "Sunny" had yet another fight with her twenty-eight-year-old boyfriend. They had lived together for eighteen months, although her father had tried to change the locks for her three times to keep him from coming back after abusive fights. According to Roger, her boyfriend, David Richmond, was a cocaine abuser. Violent exchanges in their relationship were often witnessed by Roger's family and her coworkers at an adult club in Cassleberry, Florida. The night of September 6, Roger stabbed Richmond with a fruit knife as he was allegedly trying to push her face onto a hot stove burner. While he was bleeding from the mortal wound, she fled the home and called her parents, who were familiar with their daughter's previous injuries from altercations with Richmond,

That night, instead of calling police, Roger's father and brother returned to her condominium where they cut a wide circle in the carpet, rolled up Richmond's body and transported it to an isolated area. Then, to destroy the evidence and to protect their beloved family member, they burned the carpet and the body, further reduced his remains and disposed of what was left. The gruesome details of their actions surfaced a year later when Michele Roger confided to a coworker that she had killed Richmond This woman, who was studying to be a paralegal, called police who asked her to wear a recording device and discuss the matter with Roger again.

Based upon the recorded evidence, police arrested Roger in September 1993. The headline on the front page of the local section of the *Orlando Sentinel* screamed "Stripper Charged in Lover's Death Police Say her Family Burned the Body and Mixed Bones with Cement They Broke into Concrete Chunks and Threw onto 1-95."[20] Needless to say, this was the kind of story the tabloids love. (In actuality, the final resting place of Richmond's burned remains was the Atlantic Ocean as Roger's father would later explain.)

Michele Roger was released on bail and her family hired an excellent criminal defense lawyer, Mark O'Mara. In the months following her arrest and leading up to the trial, Roger and her lawyer were repeatedly contacted by various television producers who will were willing to pay for her story. This "pay to tell" policy directly conflicts with accepted journalistic standards, but the tabloid shows of the 1990s were paying for exclusivity, sometimes thinly masked as a contribution to the high-profiles client's legal defense fund.

In July 1994, O'Mara called me to request help with both selling and telling the Roger's story. I met with his notorious client and her parents in his office early one evening to discuss my recommendations. Roger was not currently working as a dancer, although she had returned to the condominium where the crime scene had been erased with help from paint and eventually a new carpet. Now, however, after her arrest and release on bond, she had returned to live at her parent's home. The family's position was that the media and the tabloids were going to cover her trial, why not try to make sure that their side of the story was told accurately and give an exclusive to one show in return for monetary payment. Apparently, the family was feeling a little cash-strapped but wanted to mount a full-defense, including media relations.

This case was going to be watched very carefully for reasons other than the manner in which Richmond body was handled. The same year Roger was arrested, 1993, Kimberley Soubielle was the first battered woman in the nation to be released from prison after she was granted clemency. In 1987, Soubielle, coincidently also a nude dancer, shot her husband six times while he was asleep, reloaded and shot him again. She argued it was self-defense because her husband had repeatedly abused her and she was afraid for herself and their two-year-old daughter. Soubielle had been convicted in 1988.

The 1990s were a decade when the laws affecting battered women were changing. Florida was the first state in the nation to change clemency procedures to allow a woman who raised a battered woman's syndrome defense to seek commutation of her sentence before a special panel. By 1993, sixteen women had petitioned for clemency; Soubielle was the first released. O'Mara was preparing a far-sighted self-defense case for Roger. He knew that the more publicity about Michele Roger's abusive relationship with David Richmond, the better case he could mount, if an appeal for clemency became necessary.

The family agreed to hire me and paid one-half my fee up front; the other half was due before the trial. I left the meeting with a file of news clippings and copies of the letters from television producers. There wasn't much time; her trial was due to start in five weeks. My first outreach was to a producer for *Inside Edition* who had contacted the Roger family. Over the next ten days, I negotiated with this producer and ultimately obtained an offer of $7,500 for Michele Roger's story. In return, she promised to participate in interviews with their correspondent. I notified her by telephone that the show was sending a contract and offered to meet with her at her home to determine whether this was the best place for setting the first interview.

When I arrived at the Roger home, I met with Michele and her mother; they agreed with my recommendation that the first interview take place in their living room. The setting was a good one, I thought, because it was lovely, had great light and was tastefully decorated. We agreed to meet at O'Mara's office that evening to go over the contract from *Inside Edition* that was due to be faxed there that afternoon. The fee from the show was going to offset my fee and some would be left over for legal expenses.

During that meeting, with Michele Roger and her parents both present, O'Mara went over the contract with them while I listened. Then he asked me how the first interview was going to proceed. At this point, we were less than 10 days before the trial start date on August 15, 1994. I explained that having her interview in the Roger home was the best locale and that the first interview would take place this coming weekend. At this point, Michele sat up in her chair and said something to the effect that "I won't do this before the trial. I'm too stressed thinking about the trial." I looked at O'Mara and probably dropped my jaw. I had assumed that she understood that the program wanted to get her side of the story before the trial. Besides, I cautioned her, after the jury was selected, any account of the murder she had been accused of committing had less impact on public opinion. I was reluctant to point out that after the trial, there was also the possibility she would be in custody.

Despite my recommendations and O'Mara's gentle explanation that she had asked for the chance to sell and tell her story and this was the only window of opportunity, she declined to go any further with the program. I gave him the telephone number for the producer handling the agreement. We retreated to his office for the call and his explanation as to why Roger reneged on her verbal agreement included the phrase "seller's remorse." The producer had already scheduled a crew to arrive in Orlando and was angry at the turn of events. I explained to O'Mara that no matter what happened at this point, the program was going to do everything possible to skewer Michele Roger. He agreed, but there was no explaining this to Roger. It would have been highly inappropriate to try to persuade his client to do an interview she didn't want to do.

During the rest of our meeting that night, I proposed a fall-back media relations strategy for the accused and her parents, a mea culpa press conference. Both Mr. and Mrs. Roger and Michele Roger's brother faced criminal charges for their part in concealing a crime and for disposing of the evidence—Mark Richmond's dead body. The state attorney had not yet decided whether or not to file formal charges. I knew from previous conversations with Mr. Roger that he felt sorry for Richmond's parents and family, who had no way to bury their son since he had disposed of it in an attempt to protect his daughter from prosecution. The Rogers never denied their role, but they felt justified in trying to protect their daughter from police, who might not have believed her story of abuse that night.

They agreed to take part in the press conference that I scheduled for Monday, August 8, one week before the trial was due to start. That day, in a meeting room at a Sanford, Florida, motel on the St. John's River a few miles from the Seminole County courthouse, there was a full contingent of media. Interestingly, in addition to the *Orlando Sentinel* reporter Beth Taylor, her editor also attended the press conference. I asked him why he was there, and he explained that this was an unusual event and he wanted to monitor it.

I knew the local NBC affiliate's reporter, Dave McDaniel, well and approached him off-the-record regarding a videotape of David Richmond. Ever since Michele had been arrested, the only photos the media had printed or aired were photos supplied by his family. In them, Richmond looked like a quiet schoolboy in horn-rimmed glasses. When he and Michele Roger were a couple, Richmond was also a heavy metal rocker and, according to Roger, a cocaine user. He wore dozens of silver bracelets on his arm that he used to make striking her more painful. I offered a copy of the videotape of Richmond performing at a concert to McDaniel with the agreement that the circumstances of his obtaining the tape remain confidential.

That night, local television stations carried the story and comments from both Michele Roger and her father. McDaniel's story on WESH-Channel 2 was the most in-depth, and the videotape of Richmond painted a very different picture from that of a smiling, well-groomed young man. The newspaper story the next day quoted both Michele and her elderly white-haired father dressed in suspenders, clearly evident in the photo of him sitting next to his daughter standing at the podium. Both of these statements supported the battered woman defense.

"I had to protect myself. If I hadn't, I wouldn't be here now. He tried to kill me," said Michele Roger. "I had seen my daughter all bloody with a broken nose and a burned eye from David. I wanted to keep her safe. I didn't trust the police," said Mr. Roger.[21] As regards his disposal of the body, Roger said: "I just made a wrong decision. I shouldn't have done it, but I did it and I can't retract it."[22]

Thus, Roger and her lawyer began her defense before the media one week before her trial. The news account also included a description of the state prosecutor's response: angry. The state attorney handling the case, Steve Plotnick, also said that the news conference "might prejudice potential jurors and possibly violate a judicial order not to talk to the media."[23]

I had already discussed the judge's viewpoint of the media with O'Mara. Although the judge had said in a pretrial conference "not to try the case in the media," there was no formal gag order.[24] Furthermore, O'Mara had not hired me. The family had hired me directly. Although my fee is usually paid through the lawyer's account so that I am covered under the confidential fiduciary relationship as an expert consulting on the case, O'Mara wanted the family to hire me directly. I now realized why he had made this decision.

Two days after the press conference, I was subpoenaed by the state attorney's office to appear in court with any information I had about the case of Michele Roger. I was not concerned that I had done anything wrong. As the newspaper had reported, "Little of the information released [at the press conference] was new, either to the media or to prosecutor Steve Plotnick."[25]

What was new was the appearance of Michele and her father, speaking to the public through the media a week before the trial, and Roger's apology that he was sorry that Richmond's family did not have the chance for a final good-bye with a proper burial service.

In order to fully protect myself, I decided to hire a civil trial lawyer who specialized in contracts to represent me at the hearing I had been subpoenaed to attend. Having a respected lawyer by one's side is always a plus when you go before a judge or even into a deposition with the opposing counsel. At the hearing, my lawyer simply explained that anything I knew about the case was in the evidence shared between the two opposing counsel in the Michele Roger case or had appeared in media accounts of her case. That was it. I never even had to testify.

During the two-week trial, O'Mara presented a number of experts who testified about medical treatment rendered Michele Roger for injuries from a burned eye to multiple nose fractures. According to testimony from Roger's mother, Richmond had a habit of shoving his fingers up her daughter's nose to abuse her. The prosecution countered with testimony that the relationship was mutually abusive, that Roger told coworkers she was going to kill him, and that Richmond wouldn't try to kill her because he valued the income she earned stripping at the adult clubs.

The jury deliberated fourteen hours. During that time, they came back once to announce that they could not reach a verdict. The judge sent them back to reconsider; whoever was holding out for a not guilty verdict caved into pressure from the other jurors, and Roger was convicted of second-degree murder. Although the trial result was disappointing, O'Mara's defense, the intense media coverage and the mea culpa press conference laid the groundwork for a campaign to have Roger's sentence reduced through an application for clemency.

In November 1995, the judge sentenced Roger to seventeen years in prison. In September 1997, O'Mara submitted the first application seeking clemency for Michele Roger. In September 1998, he argued before the Clemency Board on behalf of his client. He was just in time. The Florida Clemency Commission that was established under Democratic Governor Lawton Chiles was not likely to survive under the newly elected, conservative Republican governor Jeb Bush, who was due to take office in January 1999.

By December 1998, the governor—who died suddenly on December 12, 1998—and two of the three Florida cabinet members who needed to approve the clemency application, had approved her request. On December 28, a third member of the cabinet, Secretary of State Sandra Mortham, completed the approval. According to the *Orlando Sentinel,* "Mortham said she decided to support clemency papers after receiving a letter from Roger's attorney, Mark O'Mara, outlining his client's assertions that she was a victim of abuse. Included with the letter were polygraph results."[26]

Her sentence was commuted to time-served. Michele Roger left prison for a halfway house in 1999, and was released on probation the following year, having served a total of five years, the same length of time served by Kimberly Soubielle.

O'Mara says that Michele currently lives with her elderly parents and works at a low-profile job in the Central Florida area. The sensationalism of the manner in which the Roger family disposed of Richmond's body fueled the already heightened interest in this case because of the prurient nature of her career as a nude dancer. If Michele Roger had been a secretary in an insurance office or a teacher's aide in an elementary school, she would have had a much more sympathetic public. She had to overcome the stigma of her profession as a topless dancer in a conservative community as well as address the cover-up that her father and brother executed the night of the altercation that resulted in Richmond's death.

The pretrial press conference not only afforded Roger the chance to apologize for her role, it demonstrated that she was a beloved daughter and sister. By injecting humanity into the case, the publicity softened her image, thus making it more believable that she had indeed stabbed David Richmond in self-defense.

However, a less-than-sensational profession is not a shield when certain behaviors are misinterpreted, sensitivities overlooked and a self-proclaimed victim goes public with the details. A few years after the Roger's trial, I worked on another case where a mea culpa press conference was effective. In 1996, I consulted with a dentist whose reputation was being attacked and his practice threatened for an incident that never resulted in criminal charges.

Dr. Alan Guy was a successful dentist in Altamonte Springs, Florida, who became embroiled in a very unpleasant and potentially career-damaging matter. He was accused by Wendy Allen, the parent of an eight-year-old dental patient, of slapping her son during a procedure. Within a few weeks, he received a letter from a lawyer retained by the boy's family demanding $150,000. To put some "teeth" into this demand, Allen went to the police to allege that not only had Dr. Guy slapped her son, he had come out to the waiting room and slapped her too.

A few months after the incident and subsequent complaint, the Seminole-Brevard (Counties) state attorney's office decided not to file battery charges. Dr. Guy agreed to a year-long pretrial diversion agreement that included anger-management classes. Apparently not satisfied or $150,000 richer, Wendy Allen turned to the media. The *Orlando Sentinel* published an article on May 8, 1996, with the inflammatory headline "Boy's Mom: Dentist Still Unpunished: Slapping Her Son Should Have Led to a Charge of Battery against Dr. Alan Guy, a Longwood Woman Says."[27]

By this time, Dr. Guy had hired a young associate at a prominent Orlando corporate law firm, Fred Barnes, a lawyer who now practices construction litigation in Maitland, Florida. When the reporter called Dr. Guy to get his side of the story, he referred her to Barnes. His response appeared in the May 8 story: "Dr. Guy has been practicing for 25 years and never had a problem like this. Dr. Guy has many, many loyal patients, some of whom have called him today to tell him they will continue seeing him."

Certainly it was important for someone to respond on behalf of Dr. Guy in this article; however, Barnes' comments at this point were purely defensive and also secondhand. During the next few days, Barnes recalls, "A local talk-radio commentator began an on-air tirade about Dr. Guy, ridiculing him and completely sensationalizing the matter." He and his client recognized that there was the "potential for this incident to get really blown out of proportion and affect his business."[28]

Barnes told Dr. Guy that they needed to explore whether they needed assistance from a media expert. When Barnes called me the day after the article appeared on May 9, he had already spoken to a partner in Orlando's best-known public relations firm, Joe Curley, of Curley & Pynn, who represented Walt Disney World and other large Florida corporations. He told Barnes that this type of matter wasn't what they handled and referred them to me, someone who specialized in media relations involving legal issues.

The radio ridicule and *Orlando Sentinel* article had also prompted many of Dr. Guy's loyal and happy patients and friends to call and offer him their support. I realized we needed to act quickly to counter the negative publicity. I met with Barnes and Dr. Guy that evening. As soon as I met the genial dentist, I recognized that he could be an effective and persuasive spokesperson for himself. As long as we stayed within the parameters that his lawyer dictated to protect him from any legal backlash, Dr. Guy was capable of stemming the negative publicity and responding to the media directly.

Dr. Guy already had an excellent marketing program. In 1987, he was featured in the *Orlando Sentinel*, "Dentists Wooing Patients with Marketing Magic."[29] Dr. Guy had opened his dental practice in 1975 and developed a "marketing personality" with a distinctive red-and-white logo. He had an excellent internal marketing campaign that included staying in touch with patients all year, sending birthday and holiday cards and distributing referral thank-you gifts like travel mugs. He also made helpful books about a healthy diet and dental care readily available.

With this sudden, infamous notoriety because of Allen's accusations about her and her son, Dr. Guy's successful dental practice was under assault. During the meeting, I interviewed Dr. Guy and his lawyer about every possible accusation that Allen or anyone else might make about him. All too often, accused people who are ready to deal with the information that has been made public will not want to bring up other aspects of an incident, hoping that if they say nothing, nothing will happen. This can be a very damaging mistake.

For example, although it did not appear in the first newspaper article, Allen had also accused Dr. Guy of slapping her on the face. The facts of the incident were straightforward.

While Dr. Guy was in the process of pulling a decayed tooth from the mouth of Allen's son, the boy became hysterical, screamed and began thrashing about in the chair. Dr. Guy was holding a sharp instrument in his hand and was concerned that the child might cause injury to himself by thrusting his mouth toward the instrument. His first reaction was to get the boy's attention, and he tapped him firmly on the cheek. The boy did refocus, and Dr. Guy completed the procedure. There was a dental assistant in the room the entire time.

He then went to the waiting room to explain to the mother what had happened. He said that he then demonstrated to her just how he tapped the boy's cheek by tapping her on the cheek. She recoiled and told him that she was a battered woman and any kind of touching her face was very disturbing. Dr. Guy says he apologized to her, and they hugged. A few weeks later he got the demand letter.

I proposed a public relations plan that included the following:

1. Prepare for a press conference in two days' time.

2. Contact and invite supporters to come to his office during the press conference.

3. Make and announce a contribution to a battered spouse's organization.

4. Rehearse a statement that he, his lawyer and I would write.

5. Correct the inaccuracies of media coverage.

6. Publicly apologize to Allen.

7. Hold a press conference in his office waiting room.

I told Barnes and Dr. Guy that it was imperative to address all the issues, even if the tapping of Allen's cheek had not been covered by the media as yet. As a lawyer, Barnes initially did not want to release the information about Dr. Guy's demonstrative tap on the cheek and Allen's startled reaction. Lawyers always want to protect their clients from new allegations.

However, we discussed the downside of not admitting to everything that had happened. After holding the press conference and saying and doing all the right things, if we did not preemptively address the waiting room event, Allen or her lawyer would. Then it would appear as if Dr. Guy was being untruthful by omission, continuing to hide something about the incident; this would undo the positive effect of our public relations efforts. Also, the media would have a new angle to continue to cover the story.

The next day, we put the media strategy in motion. I drafted a statement for Dr. Guy's consideration. Having met with him for a few hours, I wrote the statement "in his voice." I have developed this skill during the more than twenty years I have worked with lawyers and their clients on high-profile cases. During each meeting with the accused people I agree to represent, I establish a relationship of trust, assuring them that I am on their side, no matter what they have been accused of doing. I will not work with someone unless I can accept them for who they are; if I believe that they are truthful and I can feel compassion for them, then I can make sure that the next time they meet a reporter or go before a camera, they will emanate these same characteristics that I discern in the first interview.

I take notes as they describe what has happened to put them in the position of being accused. In every instance, the first responses they make will be the most natural and the most genuine. From these notes, I can provide them with key statements, "in their voice," that help them reflect the best of their human nature and effectively express—in quotable language—responses to the media that best represent them in the court of public opinion.

Lawyers have a tendency to pepper their statements to the media with legalese. Clients like Dr. Guy who have never faced a media inquisition are fearful of addressing accusations before a television camera. Although I always make sure that the client's lawyer reviews every statement and may have to make changes, my job is to craft comments that will be appropriate responses to almost any question posed by the media about the accusations.

I did just this for Dr. Guy and faxed the statement draft to his office the day before the press conference. He reviewed it; his lawyer looked it over; we made a few minor changes. Finally, I told him to take it home and rehearse in front of a mirror. By the next day, I had pre-qualified the media interest and confirmed the time of the press conference with each of them. In addition, Dr. Guy's staff had put out an invitation to supportive patients and friends.

It was important to keep Dr. Guy busy that morning so that he did not have too much time to let his nervousness eat him alive. He was able to see several patients in the morning. I arrived two hours before the 2 p.m. press conference. I asked his staff in advance to have lunch brought in for everyone. I did a read-through with Dr. Guy before lunch. We discussed what to expect over a sandwich, and just before 1:00 p.m., did a walk-through of his office with Dr. Guy and Fred Barnes, showing them where to stand when we walked out into the waiting room.

Finally, we rehearsed his statement in the privacy of his office. I had him practice rephrasing his statement to answer a variety of questions that the media might pose. By 1:30 p.m. the waiting room was already filling up.

We had all the key players there from the local media, including the *Orlando Sentinel* reporter, the two television stations that had first broadcast their stories from the frontage road that ran in front of his office. The Dr. Guy red-and-white mouth logo was on the air for those stories because they had no one to interview.

Today, however, Dr. Guy was ready to meet the press. I told him what to expect from the media fear factors, as I do with all clients; this helped him to focus. I told him to expect but not to dwell on the butterflies and heart-in-the-mouth symptoms that usually hit right before walking out in front of the cameras. Find a friendly face or two, I advised, and look directly at them when you speak.

A short time before the press conference, I circulated among Dr. Guy's friends and supporters, advising them to be silent and, if they were willing, to be available to answer any media inquires after Dr. Guy had left the room. I greeted the media, helped with a microphone check and went back to get Dr. Guy and Barnes. We entered the waiting room; his lawyer and I sat off to the side, and Dr. Guy stepped up to the microphones.

He overcame his nervousness as soon as he began to deliver his statement; having carefully rehearsed, he was comfortable with the words that succinctly explained the truth, emphasized his apology to Allen and mentioned the $1,000 contribution to Spouse Abuse, Inc. The crux of his statement was, "I believe that I did the incorrect thing for the right reason."

The next day's story was the last one to appear, either in the *Sentinel* or on the television news. The headline read: "Dentist Says Slapping Accusations Exaggerated."[30] Even the aggressive radio talk-show host found someone else to berate. Through the advice of an open-minded and media savvy lawyer who knew enough to hire and trust an expert, a compassionate dentist delivered an effective mea culpa to his accuser. The last I heard of Dr. Guy was that he sold his successful dental practice and retired.

Although the mea culpa press conference by Dr. Guy accomplished everything we intended, it occurred six months after the incident. In the Porter case, the first apology was given within just a few days, but on television. The subsequent face-to-face apology after the sentencing had mixed results. In the Roger case, the apology by the accused parents was one of several components of a pretrial and postverdict campaign to use the battered woman's syndrome defense effectively.

If I've left anything out, mea culpa.

Ten

Andrea Yates, Insanity and Gag Orders

There are news stories so heart-wrenching that turning off the television and switching to an old movie is my first instinct. Yet horror can also be compelling, and like millions of others I watched and read about Andrea Pia Yates, who drowned her five children in June 2001. Initially, her act of "filicide" reminded me of another crime by a mother who drowned her children in 1995. In the earlier case, Susan Smith, a twenty-three-year-old South Carolina mother, drove her car off a pier with her two children strapped in car seats, killing them. She got out of the car just in time to save herself and then tried to blame a mysterious black man for carjacking them. Smith confessed ten days later, was tried for and convicted of murder.

The critical difference between the two cases was that Andrea Yates was insane, and Susan Smith was not. Smith's ex-husband, the father of their two young sons, testified at her trial and asked the court to "put her to death."[1] Yates' husband dedicated himself to defending his mentally ill wife in every public forum that he was permitted to use.

After Smith was found guilty, she was sentenced to life in prison. What probably saved her from execution was that the jury believed she was sorry. A South Carolina state law enforcement agent, Pete Logan, testified in Smith's murder trial. His testimony, coming from a state investigator, was powerful. He said Smith showed remorse, "probably the greatest I've seen in 35 years."[2]

In the Yates case, however, police and prosecutors in Houston, Texas, actively pursued the death penalty despite Yates' history of severe mental illness.

Yates, who was diagnosed as psychotic and suffering from severe postpartum depression, had been deprived of the medication that stabilized her for days before she drowned her five children in the bathtub one summer morning. Within a few hours, the media swarmed outside the Yates' home in suburban Houston, Texas.

By the early afternoon, the story broke on every television network. News crews arrived in time to capture Russell Yates in agony, prevented from entering his home, now circled by the bright yellow crime scene tape, where his thirty-seven-year-old wife of twelve years had murdered their four boys and baby daughter, laid the four of them side by side on a bed, and then called both her husband and the police. Viewers saw this scene repeated over and over, including the pictures of police leading Andrea Yates out of her house in handcuffs.

The crime scene footage was soon interspersed between photographs of the smiling faces of the children and one of a seemingly happy family. These were not images likely to leave the public consciousness anytime soon.

As details of Andrea Yates' diagnosed psychosis, suicide attempts, treatment center stays and antipsychotic drug dependency became public, her insanity seemed undeniable. Focusing on the "How could they let this happen?" instead of the "What did she do?" was easier than reading about which child she drowned first and how she chased the oldest child before forcing him into the water. By the time the children were buried a week later, anyone who listened to a news report or who read a newspaper knew that the circumstances of the Yates' lifestyle were unusually demanding for a mother of five young children.

Andrea Yates home-schooled the children; they were with her all day while her husband worked a full-time job at NASA. They were religious fundamentalists, believed in Satan, evil and the death penalty. Before they moved into their house, they had tried giving up material things and lived in a converted bus with four toddlers. The most disturbing news was reported in the stories detailing Andrea Yates' mental illness and her admission in jail that "[she] had to kill the children, as Satan demanded, so that [she] would receive the death penalty."[3] Articles also described her medication for psychosis, her diagnosis of postpartum depression, the unadvised fifth pregnancy and the recent death of her father.

Finally, there were other facts that supported Andrea Yates' insanity when she drowned her children: two days before, her husband had tried to get her treatment, and the psychiatrist refused to continue the prescription medications or to readmit her to the treatment center. Instead, as Russell Yates later reported, the doctor gave her a pep talk and told her to think more positively.[4]

The Yates tragedy and murder trial took place in Texas, one of the most difficult states in America in which to put on an insanity defense. Criminal defense lawyers who practice in Texas know what they're up against. I followed her case and hoped that the lawyer who defended Andrea Yates would know that educating the public through aggressive media relations is essential in her kind of defense.

Remarkably, the person who emerged as Andrea Yates' best defender in the court of public opinion was Russell Yates, the father of their children, and her loving and supportive husband. In the limited media relations he was permitted to engage in before the trial, Yates was highly effective, but his hands were soon tied—his lips sealed by a gag order, which the court eventually ruled unconstitutional after Yates defied it.

Yates, a computer specialist at NASA in Houston, spoke about the gag order on one of the two Web sites, www.yateskids.org and www.yatescase.org, he created to report on his wife's case. On www.yateskids.org, launched on August 20, 2001, two months after he lost his five children forever and his wife to the judgment of the Texas court system, he wrote,

> Immediately after Andrea was arrested, Judge Hill quickly found Andrea in-
> digent and appointed an inexperienced attorney who immediately requested
> a gag order. Judge Hill wrote a gag order that prohibited all witnesses from
> speaking to the media about the case. I was served Judge Hill's gag order
> during the visitation for our children, the night before their funeral.
>
> When an article appeared in the *Dallas Morning News* that implied I may
> have spoken to its author, Judge Hill appointed an independent prosecutor
> to determine whether or not I'd violated her gag order. A few days later,
> an officer appeared at my door and handed me a subpoena to appear at
> Andrea's competency hearing. When he handed me the subpoena, he said,
> "Now you're a witness, and under the gag order." Eventually, the state
> subpoenaed every member of our family who had spoken to the media.
> Immediately after reading the verdict in the competency hearing, Judge Hill
> passed out copies of her gag order to all of our family members and warned
> us not to speak to the media. None of our family members were called as
> witnesses during the competency hearing, as expected.
>
> After I appeared on *60 Minutes*, Judge Hill again appointed an indepen-
> dent prosecutor to investigate whether Chuck Rosenthal (Houston District
> Attorney) or I had violated her gag order. Shortly after the trial was com-
> pleted and the gag order had expired, the independent prosecutor found the
> gag order to be unconstitutional. Note also that she appointed much more
> prominent attorneys to determine whether or not I'd violated her gag order
> than she did to defend Andrea's life.
>
> Our constitution is our highest law and grants each of us certain pro-
> tection from our government. Namely, if we feel the government is pro-
> ceeding wrongly against us, then we have a civil right to publicly object.
> Every member of our family believed that the state was proceeding wrongly
> against Andrea, and Judge Hill prohibited us from speaking.[5]

This is an excellent first-hand account of how the judicial system's use of a gag order denied the accused equal access to the hearts and minds of the community from which the jury would be chosen. It also demonstrates just how effective Yates was in representing his wife in the court of public opinion during the few times he spoke out before the trial. If he had felt secure in his right to speak out concerning his wife's prosecution in the weeks and months leading up to her January 2002 murder trial, there were any number of media opportunities to make a significant impact on public opinion.

I discussed the Yates gag order with Brian W. Wice, a well-known Houston criminal defense lawyer and regular legal commentator on local and national programs. "In twenty-seven years of practice I've yet to see anyone—lawyer, witness or party—ever spend a day in jail or pay a cent in fines because they violated a gag order in criminal cases, but, a civilian, unlike a lawyer, is less likely to challenge a judge's order."[6]

Russell Yates was such a civilian, but he and his mother-in-law had hired an established Houston criminal defense firm. Their family had never before needed a criminal defense lawyer. Now, the all-encompassing tragedy that suddenly put Russell Yates in the dreadful position of burying his five children also demanded that someone undertake effective legal and media representation.

The lead defense counsel was George Parnham, who took over the representation of Yates from her original court-appointed lawyer, Bob Scott. It was Scott who actually requested the gag order during Yates' first court appearance. Wice calls him an "old-timer," one of a group of lawyers who do not understand how media relations work in a high-profile case.[7]

At the same time as Parham met with his new client, he realized that the gag order had not yet been entered by the court. He quickly became fluent on the issue of postpartum depression and the type of psychosis Yates suffered. He recalls appearing on several talk shows over the weekend, including *CNN*, *Good Morning America* and the *Today Show*. "I literally spent all day Sunday at various televisions studios in Houston to take advantage of every media opportunity to refute the damning statements released by law enforcement about Andrea's case."[8]

Meanwhile, it seemed that Andrea Yates was getting better medical care in jail than she had received in the weeks leading up to her insane crime. After she was stabilized on antipsychotic drugs, police were able to interview her about the manner in which she murdered her children. Of course, the interview was released to the media by the prosecution. It was public record.

The *Houston Chronicle*[9] detailed the methodical way in which Mrs. Yates drowned each child. According to the reporters who wrote the article, they got the details from a police officer who "spoke to the *Houston Chronicle* on condition of anonymity."[10] The media repeatedly broadcast and reprinted this leaked information. Parnham says the reports were factually incorrect and prejudicial.[11]

As horrific as these deaths were, Yates felt driven to defend his children's mother. He often cited the failure of the legal system and the medical specialists who treated her. "They never tried to understand why this happened. They treated Andrea like a hardened serial killer for no reason," Yates said in June 2002.[12]

By December 3, 2001 Russell Yates asked Houston defense lawyer Edward Mallet to help him challenge Judge Hill's gag order. Yates wanted to publicize his belief that his wife and the mother of their five children should not be prosecuted for drowning them. As frequently happens, family members of an accused become steadily more educated about the justice system and the language of the prosecution. In many cases, the accused herself may become a "jailhouse lawyer," studying the law and trying to help defend her case. However, Andrea Yates was in no condition, mentally, emotionally, spiritually or in any other way to do anything to help herself.

Mallett's motion to lift the gag order stated that "Yates strongly believes that Andrea should not be prosecuted because she did not have felonious intent."[13] On December 4, 2001, he requested that Judge Belinda Hill release Russell Yates from the gag order she had imposed five months earlier. Although she denied Mallett's motion, Yates had already defied her order with a September interview with Ed Bradley of *60 Minutes*. "Rusty felt emboldened to go on *60 Minutes* when its producers assured him that Chuck Rosenthal had already given an interview on the Yates case," Ed Mallet said.[14]

On December 9, 2001, Yates' courageous appearance on CBS's *60 Minutes* aired. During the interview, Yates stressed his wife's undeniable mental illness and the fact that her doctors took her off the medication that inhibited her psychosis. A few days later, Judge Hill appointed a former prosecutor, George "Mac" Secrest, to determine if Yates and Rosenthal had violated her gag order. Ten days after Yates defended his wife on national TV, her lawyers, George Parnham and Wendell Odem also requested "equal access to the public's ear."[15]

During the months when the media covered the prosecution's deliberations over seeking the death penalty, Parnham neither defended Yates in the court of public opinion nor did he fight the gag order so her family could speak out. The day the prosecution announced it was going to ask a jury for the death penalty, Parnham, with Andrea Yates' family by his side, said at a press conference in his office, "We share your frustration at not being able to address the issues that you're asking us about."[16]

Wice is an experienced criminal defense lawyer and extremely familiar with the media, both as a commentator and as a lawyer defending clients. In addition to serving as a legal analyst for the Houston affiliate KPRC TV, he also frequently appears for *CourtTV* and on other national news programs. In response to my question about the importance of a criminal defense lawyer's knowledge of media relations and willingness to make sure an accused is adequately represented in the court of public opinion, Wice said, "Generations of jurors have grown up on episodes of *Law & Order*, *The Practice* and *Baretta*. At some level, they expect a defense attorney to be able to get out on the courthouse steps to talk about his client at five, six and ten. [These are the hours when TV news airs in the Central Time Zone.] And if he can't, won't or don't, he doesn't serve his client. I don't know if it's unethical; it's certainly moronic."[17]

However, when I asked Wice if he ever prepared his accused clients to speak to the media, he said, "Rarely, if ever, because the typical criminal defendant, when he sees the red light, he panics." When asked to respond on exceptions to "rarely," he allowed that some accused people are very good with the media. For example, "NBA star Calvin Murphy—accused of sexually assaulting his step-kids—was one of the best at dealing with the media. His lawyer let him speak repeatedly because he was used to answering tough questions." Wice also mentioned the media skill of another high-profile defendant: Ken Lay.[18]

Wice's position on allowing clients to speak to the media is held by a majority of lawyers. I, however, am convinced, as are lawyers who have worked with me, that, whenever possible, the accused must be prepared to speak to the media about his innocence of the crimes he is charged with committing. I am not suggesting that Andrea Yates could ever have spoken to the media and been her own best spokeswoman, but she is the exception—the insane client who should be in a medical treatment center, not in the courtroom.

Unlike Ed Humphrey, who was unfairly suspected of a series of murders, Yates committed murder. Humphrey's mental illness was far less severe and, when stabilized on lithium, he was able to participate in media interviews. Yates, even if her psychosis was under control, is also in a Catch 22 situation. When she is stabilized on the appropriate medications, her psychosis diminishes, and she may become sane enough to recognize what she did and to grieve. However, any image of her speaking to the media is unethical; it would be like drugging someone so she could give an interview.

During Yates' initial confession in the Harris County jail, she was not stabilized on antipsychotic medication. She explained to the investigators that she killed her children "because she realized she was a bad mother and they were hopelessly damaged." Yates was interviewed any number of times in jail, including the same day of the drownings. More importantly, she was interviewed by investigators trained to elicit a statement or confession that would stand up in court. They used words like "intent" when asking questions like, "As you drew the bath water, what was your intent?"[19]

The best description of Yates' state of mind was given in court by Dr. Lucy Puryear when she stated that "Andrea was 'grossly psychotic' and lacked rational thought the day her five children died.... As she drowned each one of the children, she thought she was doing the right thing."[20] Dr. Puryear, one of the first psychiatrists to examine Yates in the weeks following the June 20 deaths felt that Andrea was so psychotic that she was unaware she needed a lawyer to advise her during her confession.

During Andrea Yates' treatment in the county jail, she regularly received the medication and counseling that diminished the psychosis behind her insane crime. Unfortunately, her brother, Andrew Kennedy, made extremely misleading comments to the media about her response to psychiatric treatment. He remarked that she had gone from a nonverbal stupor to "completely normal," and "I've never seen her this happy even."[21] No one, even members of the community who thought Andrea Yates was insane and should not be charged with murder, wants to hear that she is "happy." This demonstrates that even with a gag order, Yates' defense lawyers needed to meet with every member of her family and instruct them on what (if anything) they ever said about their loved one to the media.

In high-profile cases, there must be an intense educational session with the accused's supporters about the policy and procedures for speaking to the media and exactly what may or may not be stated. Certainly, it was essential to respond to the media in any way possible—around, despite, or in defiance of the gag order. It was the lawyers' responsibility to provide the expert media advice and training that Andrea Yates needed in the court of public opinion.

Before the trial was over and the jury had convicted Andrea Yates of murdering three of her children (the prosecution reserved charging her with two of the children's deaths as back-up cases if the first trial didn't go the way they wanted) the defense challeneged the testimony of a key witness. The star expert forensic psychiatrist, Dr. Park Dietz, who testified that Andrea Yates was not insane, used an example that was proven false. He stated that *Law & Order*, a program that Andrea Yates regularly watched, had aired an episode about a woman drowning her child and successfully claiming the insanity defense. It wasn't enough for Dietz to interview and examine Andrea Yates' mental condition during several meetings with her at the Harris County jail. He had to bolster his opinion with—that's right—a media portrayal of a similar crime![22]

Because no such episode ever aired on *Law & Order* or any other program at the time, Andrea Yates' lawyers filed a successful appeal of her conviction. The court apparently recognized the powerful influence of a television program on the jury. On November 9, 2005, the Texas 1st Court of Appeals—that state's highest criminal court—reversed the murder convictions of Andrea Yates, stating that the testimony of Dr. Dietz that included the reference to the nonexistent *Law &*

Order program "could have affected the judgment of the jury."[23] A new trial was scheduled for March 2006 with the same judge who presided over her first trial.

Meanwhile, despite the fact that the gag order was ruled unconstitutional in January 2003, there were rarely proactive media updates about Yates in the next two years. However, Parnham recalls speaking to a number of nonmedia groups. After he accepted an invitation to speak to one of the Houston Rotary Clubs about Andrea Yates, multiple opportunities arose to address other organizations. Parnham estimates he made over 50 presentations in 2003 and 2004, and, periodically, the media came and covered these speaking engagements.[24]

Parnham frequently responded to the media after the appeals court overturned Andrea Yates' conviction. However, he often spoke about his emotions over a new trial for Andrea Yates.

Brian Wice recalled, "Once the case was to be retried, he [Parnham] went on a dozen different talk shows and repeatedly said he was terrified, mortified at the prospect of putting Andrea through a second trial and opening up all the old wounds. There was nothing positive about getting her released from prison and into a mental health facility. The public face that George [Parnham] put forth was that the defense was absolutely terrified about the prospect of a second trial. You can be compassionate toward your client and still project an air of confidence."[25]

Although there were updates in the local media about the Yates appeal and the favorable rulings that granted her a new trial, there did not appear to be an ongoing media outreach. One ideal time to have addressed Yates' psychotic postpartum depression was missed.

In 2003, the actress Brooke Shields went public with her battle with postpartum depression. This was an opportunity for Andrea Yates' defense to address her mental illness. There is nothing like a beautiful actress to arouse public interest. The fact that Yates suffered the more dangerous form of depression—postpartum psychosis—after having four children is newsworthy. According to Laurence Kruckman, a professor of medical anthropology at Indiana University of Pennsylvania, "If you are in that category, there is a high likelihood of hallucinations."[26] Professor Kruckman, who heads Postpartum Support International, stated immediately after the Yates children were killed, "Mothers hear voices that say kill yourself or kill the baby, or both."[27]

Russell Yates successfully sought a divorce in 2003 and remarried on March 20, 2006, the Saturday before his ex-wife's second trial was scheduled to begin. By that time, his e-mail on the Web site he created to memorialize the children and use as a forum for his opinion no longer reached him. Messages were returned, marked "undeliverable." The other Web site, www.yatescase.org, no longer covers the Yates case or protests the injustice of her conviction; the domain name was obviously purchased by someone else and now promotes airline tickets and ring tones.[28] Andrea Yates' name and illness became used to link visitors to this misleading site to high school reunions and doctors. Ironically, one advertising link asks, "Want a quality doctor?" Except for the "quality doctor," these are things that Andrea Yates will likely never need.

In March 2006, when Yates returned to the same Houston courthouse where she was found to be sane, convicted of murder, and sentenced to life in prison, the judge granted the defense motion to postpone her trial to July 2006. When the trial finally began, a very different jury heard from the experts, the prosecution and the defense. The media coverage of the Yates case intensified in the weeks before the jury pool reported to the courthouse. The local newspaper, the *Houston Chronicle*, published an editorial "Test of a Just Society: We Have 2nd Chance to Do Right by Yates," written by Jennifer Bard, an associate professor at the Texas Tech University School of Medicine. The timing of her opinion was perfect; it ran the weekend before jury selection began.[29]

According to Brian Wice, "Public opinion and public sentiment had shifted radically since the first trial. There had been acquittals by reason of insanity in two other of the most conservative Texas counties in trials of mothers who killed their children. These were aggressively covered by the Houston media, doubtlessly because of the Yates case."[30]

During the nearly four-week retrial, Yates was represented by the same lawyers, George Parnham and Wendell Odem. Her staunchest defender in the court of public opinion was still the father of her children. Although remarried, Rusty Yates continued to stand by his ex-wife, visiting her in jail and sitting in the courtroom every day.

The twelve-member jury and three alternates were exposed to another aggressive and emotional prosecution. Among the gut-wrenching evidence they saw was the clothing the children were wearing when they were drowned. Their outfits were mounted on display boards, from the tiny baby girl's clothing to the little boys' pajamas. However, this time, instead of taking less than four hours to convict Andrea Yates of murder, the jury deliberated over three days and found her not guilty by reason of insanity.

At the press conference after the verdict, the lead prosecutor, Harris County Assistant District Attorney Joe Owmby, said that the heavy media coverage, including a series of editorial opinions in the local paper, "must have had an effect, in a general way, on the jury." He said he was not accusing the jurors of not following instructions, "But they're human beings, and they have been living with this for the past five years."[31]

Parnham agrees with this observation. In fact, he takes it a step further. "The public is now aware, because of the print and television media, that mental illness and especially post-partum depression must be dealt with. The jury not only understood this but understood the parameters of the delusion Andrea Yates experienced. Her reality is not the reality that most of us enjoy."[32]

Owmby was likely referring to editorials published in the *Houston Chronicle*. When the editorial board of the local newspaper takes a position supportive of the accused, this is the purest form of media coverage. Not only did the *Houston Chronicle* run the Bard opinion piece, its editorial board called for the prosecution to settle the Yates case a few months before the new trial. On March 22, 2006, an editorial stated that the district attorney's insistence that Andrea Yates serves her time in a prison rather than a mental health hospital "is not enlightened justice."[33] The message to the Houston community is that continuing to try and convict Andrea Yates of murder is wrong.

Editorials are written after the editors and columnists who make up the board decide to take a position. There is no byline on the editorial. In the five years between the time that the Houston District Attorney Chuck Rosenthal first sought the death penalty for Yates in 2001 and the not guilty verdict in July 2006, the *Houston Chronicle* endorsed a challenger to Rosenthal and cited the Andrea Yates case as "an example of overzealous prosecution."[34]

The not guilty by reason of insanity verdict on July 20, 2006, was national news. The next morning, from a studio in Houston, Rusty Yates appeared in an exclusive interview on NBC's *Today Show*. He said he was happy about the verdict and called it a victory for Andrea and once again shared the painful explanation of his feelings. "I hate what she did; I support her. She's a kind and loving person. I can't blame her for being sick."[35]

Before the interview concluded, Yates also shared his opinion that he resented "the fact that the state prosecuted her at all. It made it that much more difficult; all the media associated with that."[36]

Despite the difficulties of facing the intense media coverage under such tragic circumstances, Rusty Yates recognized the importance of speaking out for his psychotic wife, fought the gag order and met the challenge of representing her in the court of public opinion.

Eleven

Lawyers and the Media

In 1991, I developed a seminar, "Lawyers & the Media: Skills for the '90s," and sent my brochure to one hundred presidents and former presidents of state chapters of the Association of Trial Lawyers of America. One of the first to respond to this mailing was Willard Techmeier, whose law firm was negotiating what was then the largest settlement in Wisconsin history for a young boy who had lost his arm in an unlocked transformer unit owned by Wisconsin Power & Light.

During the six-hour training I conducted in his law office conference room one Saturday in 1992, I assured them that they were farsighted in preparing to publicize the $25 million settlement they expected to obtain and that they also needed to hire a local public relations firm to assist them when the settlement was approved.

I was wrong.

Despite the qualifications and experience of the PR professionals at the firm they retained, these generalists did not understand the ethical considerations of publicizing a personal injury or wrongful death case. When the $25.2 million amount was approved, the PR firm held a press conference and made the mistake of "overselling" the image of the law firm instead of letting the settlement speak for itself. Media coverage not only focused on the settlement amount, the victim's compensation, and admissions by the power and light company that the transformer boxes were unsafe, but it also talked of a brochure about the law firm that was distributed at the press conference by the PR firm.

Techmeier and I worked that same day to counter the criticism that the law firm was using the case to bolster its profile. We wrote letters to editors of newspapers in Milwaukee and Madison. Afterwards, the local NBC affiliate, WTMJ-TV, broadcast a positive editorial about the firm's announcement that it was pledging part of its fee from the case. Ed Hinshaw, of WTMJ-TV, delivered the editorial.

> The usual personal injury cases leave us with images of fighting, ugliness and sleaziness. This is to acknowledge one case which appears to have been handled with competence, grace and care.
>
> The Wisconsin Electric Power Company and its insurers agreed to pay more than twenty-five million dollars to settle the case of Matthew Brown. He was critically injured when he reached into an unlocked electric transformer box.
>
> We should also note that the lawyer representing Matthew Brown and his family—Willard Techmeier—has pledged a part of his firm's fees to establish a foundation to help disabled children such as Matthew Brown. That, too, is a classy act.
>
> Without a doubt, there is a lot of pain in this story. There is also a reason to smile.[1]

Techmeier learned from this experience. "Turning a high-profile case into the spectacular human emotion one that it really is requires the skill of experts like Marti Mackenzie, who literally taught me how to embrace, not shun, the media. I carry this lesson with me every day," he says.[2]

Flash-forward to 2006 and an even more serious gaffe regarding a settlement negotiated by the New York office of The Cochran Firm. When Johnnie Cochran was alive, I handled media relations for the office he merged with in Manhattan, then known as Schneider, Kleinick, Weitz, Damashek & Shoot. Shortly before he became ill with the brain tumor that caused his death in 2005, that firm dramatically downsized. Today, The Cochran Firm, New York, still handles several high-profile cases each year.

On March 22, 2006, the *New York Times* reported that a press release announcing that a $25.6 million settlement on behalf of a Cochran Firm client in a high-profile injury case was inaccurate.[3] The case involved injuries a passenger suffered during the crash of the Staten Island Ferry in 2003, and The Cochran Firm client was a victim who had lost his legs. The *Times* noted that "the City's Law Department soon issued a terse statement of its own, saying: 'There is no settlement. Any discussions that we had with plaintiff's counsel had not been concluded, and the settlement amount set forth in plaintiff's press release bears no relationship whatsoever to the number that had been discussed.'"[4]

Settlements are extremely delicate matters. Many are confidential and can be vacated if the plaintiff's lawyers or the plaintiff violates the confidentiality. However, when a government agency is the defendant, then the settlement eventually will be public record and not protected by confidentiality. When the Staten Island Ferry case was actually settled a week later, the law firm again made a big splash. However, a premature press release can be a serious matter. During my career, I've announced dozens of settlements; however, no press release is ever sent without the written approval of the lawyer on the case.

In the same article, the publicist was interviewed. The publicist's response was, "All I can give you is what The Cochran Firm has instructed me to give."[5] When these kinds of situations make the news, lawyers who avoid the media like the plague pat themselves on the back and think no good will ever come of working with a PR firm or publicizing a case.

Handling public relations work for lawyers is a highly specialized field. It is not for the faint of heart. In the legal arena, a media relations professional must adhere to the same standards that govern lawyers. This is true when representing lawyers for either the accused or the accusers.

The media training seminar I first developed in 1991 has been updated and individualized for special groups. I always address all the basics, and I will review many of them in this chapter. However, a handbook approach to learning media relations skills is ill advised. In the court of public opinion, as in the court of law, lawyers are held to a higher standard than in the commercial marketplace, where most pubic relations firms operate.

Managing public relations projects in the legal arena is far removed from handling media relations to help market banking services, dog food, or even sleeping pills. Conducting media relations for the accused and accusers in the twenty-first century is not a skill that a lawyer or client can "practice" with a chance of making an inexperienced error. The media relations strategy in any high-profile cases must be perfected before any contact with the press occurs. The stakes are just too high.

There are numerous how-to media guides available in book form; some are self-published, some commercially produced, and many available at Amazon.com.[6] Prices range from a used media how-to book for $6.99 to an average new-book price of $30.00; however, the same tips and tactics are available free, from our government and on any number of Web sites run by universities and law schools.

Easily available on the Web is a PowerPoint presentation and five pages of media tips at www.usinfo.state.com. One of the tips involves responding to "feeling" or emotion questions; the illustration shows a large pink unhappy face with a big teardrop under the right eye, with the caption "How did you feel when you saw those dead children?"[7] The tips provided might be good for a soldier in Iraq; however, the tip doesn't work well in a criminal case like, say, the Andrea Yates case.

A few of my favorite Web sites are www.mediatrust.org[8] (many lawyers might call this an oxymoron) and one run by North Carolina State University, www.ncsu.

edu/news/homepage/guide.htm. On the latter Web site, there's a good section, "When a Reporter Calls, What Do I Do?"[9]

A site run by a Missouri library organization has a rather naïve opening, "Most reporters are ethical, trained professionals who want to help you tell your organization's story—especially when it comes to First Amendment and freedom of information issues," tempered with cautionary statements introduced with a nice quotation. "Some however, adhere too closely to H.L. Menken's quote, 'A journalist's job is to comfort the afflicted, and afflict the comfortable.' A few unscrupulous reporters are often looking for an exposé where there's nothing to expose. The purpose of this brochure is twofold. First to give you ... tips, hints, and assistance when working with representatives from the media, and second, to help you better grasp the importance of having a coordinated media relations plan."[10]

One government-run site, www.mhr.gov.bc.ca/docs/mediarel.guide, proffers some misinformation, "1. Remember there is no such thing as 'off the record'! 2. Resist the temptation to "be candid" with the media."

There is indeed such a tactic for going "off the record"; I have used the tactic to release sensitive and influential material in several cases, including during the Michele Roger case (Chapter 9). There are guidelines that, when closely followed, minimize the risks of a reporter's violating the agreement. Of course, the how and when of going off the record must be subordinate to the lawyer's threshold for exposure.

As a final example, the University of Southern California Law School lists some important media tips on its Web site for professors, www.lawweb.usc.edu/news/media/guide/mediaguide. Under the heading "Dos and Don'ts," there are several examples.

Do

During an interview, speak conversationally and avoid jargon and legalese. Answer questions in layman's terms and illustrate with relevant analogies whenever possible. Explain any legal terms you use.

Don't

Allow your assistant to "pre-screen" a reporter's questions. This will slow down the interviewing process and annoy the reporter. You can always ask reporters directly about the direction of their story before giving them an interview.

All of the above Web sites provide a degree of educational information on how to engage in media relations; however, remember the adage, "A little knowledge can be a dangerous thing."

In the preface to his 2003 book *In the Court of Public Opinion*, lawyer, publicist, and author James Haggerty says, "This is the first book of its kind." He may be right, although I know that I wrote an article on media relations for lawyers in 1989. Also, I was featured in the 1992 book *Power Public Relations* as an expert in defending criminally accused people, specifically my campaign on behalf of Edward Humphrey (see Chapter 4).[11] In the same book, veteran PR professional and author Leonard Saffir includes a full chapter, "From Lawsuits to Murder Trials: PR and the Scales of Justice," with an analysis to a civil lawsuit he handled in 1988–1989 on behalf of a Texas hotel that sued the Metropolitan Life Insurance Company.[12] After Saffir's client obtained a settlement from Metropolitan, he says, "A Metropolitan Life lawyer in its New York City headquarters told a *Wall Street Journal* reporter that [it] was getting clobbered in the media by some small hotel in Texas [and] pointed to a stack of clippings on his desk."[13]

The difference between what Saffir did in that case and what Haggerty covers in his book is that they are writing predominantly about business-driven lawsuits, commercial litigation, not criminal cases. Nor do they provide much advice on handling media relations in personal injury lawsuits. Haggerty devotes a few pages to analyzing why the defense lawyer in a high-profile case erred by mounting an affirmative defense in court pleadings. These pleadings were reviewed by the media, who then attacked the defense arguments.[14] He creates a catchy campaign system called CIR—Control, Information, Response—and provides many useful tips for lawyers and the clients who respond to media opportunities regarding their cases.

However, Haggerty writes about extending the kind of public relations that corporations already practice into the litigation process. It's just not that easy.

Media training for lawyers begins with addressing existing prejudices against the media. Whether that prejudice is rooted in inexperience, self-determined ethical boundaries, or a bad experience, I try to dissipate that through education, an explanation of the media's objectives and modus operandi. If a lawyer does not trust the media to report accurately on a case, it is because he does not have the skills and does not trust himself to ensure that his client is well represented in the resulting coverage. Most prejudice is tied to a fear of the unknown. When a lawyer expands his knowledge of the media and corrects some misunderstandings and presumptions, he can begin to represent clients in the media arena ethically and effectively.

It's also persuasive to show lawyers that, in some ways, lawyers and reporters have much in common. Both lawyers and members of the media today see themselves as effecting change. A lawyer's representation of someone may effect changes in people's lives individually and by setting precedents.

The media also effect change as well as report news and events of interest to audiences. Lawyers and journalists have something else in common. As *Orlando*

Sentinel columnist Charlie Reese wrote in 1995, "Societies need groups to hate, and better lawyers than journalists, through to tell the truth, the two vocations are nip and tuck in the race for most public scorn in a public role."

The media believe that they are fair and impartial. Despite the scandals during the last ten years at the *Nation* and *The New York Times* involving journalists who made up facts and sometimes whole stories, newspapers make efforts to regulate themselves and maintain journalistic ethics. The mainstream news media largely respect the separation of editorial writing, which is their opinions, and news reporting, which they maintain is totally fair and balanced. Of course, there are notable exceptions, commonly at small independent papers whose editors ignore certain standards (see Chapter 6, regarding the Richard Scrushy pay-for-columns scheme).

Lawyers become more comfortable with the media and more proficient at speaking to the media once they have a fuller perspective of the profession. Studying journalism may provide some insight, but the real learning takes place when the lawyer is in front of reporters. Lawyers cannot sign up for "Media Know-how 101" in law school; perhaps they need that elective option. My experience as Executive Director of the American Civil Liberties Union of Mississippi made me aware that the public does not easily understand the lawyer's role in protecting individuals from government agents who would deprive them of their liberties.

The media are there waiting for lawyers to come to them or calling the lawyer for comments in high-profile cases. There are both general strategies and specific tactics that lawyers need to understand thoroughly and practice repeatedly before they conduct public relations for the accused or the accusers.

If someone is injured and needs a law firm to accuse, to investigate, and file suit against the person or corporation who caused that injury, there are far too many personal injury lawyers who will accept an early settlement rather than invest in a costly investigation and lengthy litigation. If a lawyer is an exception to that generalization, I advise him to make his name known both to other lawyers and to the public who may need him. Although there are personal injury lawyers who do not regularly promote their services, those who achieve the best results can best publicize those results through media relations, not advertising.

In the area of criminal defense, there are lawyers who claim that they will never engage in media relations. Miami lawyer Roy Black, who successfully defended William Kennedy Smith in 1991 (one of the first trials televised live), never spoke to the media about the case. Smith's family did, however, hire an extremely experienced public relations professional, Barbara Gamarekian. According to her 2004 obituary, "Gamarekian had a twenty-five-year career at *The New York Times* after she left the press office in [during] the presidency of John F. Kennedy."[15] In 1991, *Media Watch* wrote this about her role in the William Kennedy Smith defense: "The Kennedy family hired her to serve as press relations representative for

William Kennedy Smith, who went on trial for rape in Florida in early December. In the *Boston Globe*, correspondent Christopher Boyd summarized Gamarekian's PR line: 'She has told interviewers that he attends Mass, is a handyman around the house, and enjoys playing with his six-week-old puppy, McShane.'"[16]

This case is a perfect example of a criminal defense lawyer adhering to his personal choice of not speaking to the media, yet, undoubtedly, fully aware that public relations is ongoing for the accused person he represents. How a lawyer or accused person appears in the media may not have an immediate or discernable influence on the outcome of a high-profile case, but lawyers may not ignore the fact that the media are there and the prosecution is ready. When only one side of the legal system speaks out, it affects public perceptions and opinions and filters into jury pools.

The effect on jury pools is more subtle and also obscured by those eager jurors who claim never to have heard about the case, or are certain that what they have heard will in no way influence what they think. However, my personal experience in the Tim Anderson murder trial in 1992 clearly demonstrates the effect of media relations on potential jurors. I was in the courtroom the same day as *Orlando Sentinel* reporter Gerald Shields, listening to the juror's responses during *voir dire*: "12 of the 50 members in the jury pool said they saw media coverage, with one woman stating that a newspaper story made her more sympathetic toward Anderson."[17]

For all the reasons mentioned in this book, lawyers must be prepared to rise to the challenge of ethically representing their clients in both the courtroom and in the media.

The first step in developing media relations skills is to learn how the media operates and what their needs and objectives are. There are different mediums and important differences between them.

To illustrate certain media relations tactics, the *U.S. v. Clause Fuhler* case provides some examples. Dr. Clause Fuhler was a German eye surgeon dabbling in selling American-made weapons to foreign countries, including Iraq. He thought he was dealing with an American company; instead, he learned he had been negotiating with U.S. Justice Department agents. After months of long-distance negotiations, the U.S. agents lured Fuhler to Central Florida to complete the arms deal. He was then arrested for violating the U.S. Arms Export Act. Fuhler and his alleged co-conspirator were first represented by an assistant Federal Public Defender in Orlando. A very similar case was prosecuted in 1985, when the Orlando Federal Public Defender represented another foreign national accused of conspiring to sell arms to Iran.

The *Fuhler* case demonstrates the aggressive use of media relations by the Federal Prosecutor. From its first press release, the prosecution was prepared to depict Dr. Fuhler as an enemy of the United States, a greedy arms dealer.

Print

Before the advent of *CourtTV*, the print journalist would be the most likely to follow a complex case regularly. Unless the case is selected by *CourtTV*, this is still true. Newspapers have more space to tell the story. In the *Fuhler* case, the local newspaper assigned a reporter to cover the three-week trial. He sat in the courtroom every day and often wanted a comment from the lawyers.

Print works on a different deadline from the electronic media. Newspaper reporters come to work late, often after 10:00 a.m., and they work late, up to 8:00 p.m. They spend more time researching the issues, and they consider themselves smarter than TV and radio reporters.

When a case is developing that will require a more in-depth analysis, it is wise to speak first to a newspaper reporter. The reporter will also become more committed to the story if you do not release the story to the electronic media until after it has appeared in the newspaper. As a reporter once told me, "I have no use for press conferences. If it is going to be on the news the night before, then I don't know if I am even interested."[18]

Reporters who appear on television and radio, however, who see a story first in the paper, are going to be resentful and angry that you did not contact them first. And television does make a great impact. The best rule of thumb to apply is that unless you have something to gain by early release of the story to the print media, release your information all at once to everyone, without playing favorites.

In the twenty-first century, almost all television stations and many radio stations have Web sites. The site serves as a version of the print media; the stories on www.cbs radio.com or on www.nbcnews.com can, after all, be printed from a computer. This availability makes researching a case—or, for that matter, this book—practical as well as possible in a fraction of the time it took before the mid-1990s.

In the *Fuhler* case, when he was arrested, the Justice Department held two press conferences—one in Washington, D.C., and one in Orlando, Florida. In Washington, there was a small article in the *Washington Post*. Local TV and radio stations carried the story as well as the newspaper. The purpose of the government press conferences in the *Fuhler* case was twofold: they addressed the prosecution's position in the case and justified the Justice Department's budget for these kinds of sting operations.

Radio

Radio reporters are often electronic media professionals who sound great but do not have the TV look. Therefore, they may have an inferiority complex, an attitude. Sometimes they are former print journalists. Those are the best kind. If they are older, they will have mellowed. If they are young and aggressive, they are also quite testy. They feel like the poor boy on the block, and they are afraid of being left out. Most folks equate being on TV with stardom; radio plays second fiddle.

But radio stations are by the far the most accessible of the media and have large audiences. Radio also has the advantage of being able to conduct interviews over the telephone and, like *CNN* or *CourtTV*, provide frequent updates in high-profile cases.

In large markets there may still be one or two stations that will cover the news well, who have full-time news staff, not just DJs who read news off the wire services. Radio stations in most markets rely on "mini-networks," with reporters who go out and get the interviews that are available to various participating stations. These radio stations must be contacted at the same time as other media. In fact, when a reporter or a TV station calls, lawyers can maximize the coverage of their comments by then letting radio stations know that he or his high-profile client has a statement.

Radio may deliver the news twenty-four to forty-eight times per day. Therefore, they are always ready to cover a story. If a story runs in the newspaper in the morning, radio reporters will get the earliest edition possible—on their way to work at 4:00 a.m. They will report news right out of the newspaper. If a story is current on a particular day, lawyers might follow up with the radio news room as soon as they rise in the morning.

If a radio reporter knows that someone is available for a telephone interview concerning a case, he will call as early as 6:00 a.m., tape several comments and use them in several newscasts, using different sound bytes from an interview that was taped over the telephone. Later he may revert to a brief summary. I always make sure that radio reporters have my mobile and home telephone numbers. Interviews on a landline sound better. Also, drive-time radio newscasts have large listening audiences.

In the *Fuhler* case, the strong local AM news station assigned a reporter to cover the story. When he could not attend the trial, which was most of the time, I made sure he was able to talk to the defense lawyer by telephone. The accused client in this case was incarcerated.

TV

TV is sexy journalism. It is also the most difficult of the media to work with successfully. TV experiences often turn off lawyers who were not prepared, who didn't know what to expect. My experiences with TV when I was with the ACLU were at first terribly disappointing. I hated the way I looked. So I did something about it. I will never be a Katie Couric, but I have learned to minimize the negatives of the camera and feel comfortable and effective about what I have said.

Unlike radio, the TV media need more time to tape and edit their stories. Each market will have a number of local stations all vying for the highest ratings. Higher ratings translate into higher advertising revenues and more money in the news budget. When working with television stations, it is wise not to play favorites. Release all the information at the same time to everyone who might be interested. Then news directors at individual stations will decide if they want to cover the story and arrange an interview, perhaps with the lawyer or with the lawyer and his client. If more than two stations are interested, consider scheduling a press conference.

TV news airs in the early morning, sometimes repeating shortened versions of stories that were on the evening or late-night news the previous day. Noon news shows will concentrate both on feature stories and updates, more in-depth reporting on soft news and breaking news. However, late-breaking news will also be covered and followed up by an announcement that there will be more at 5:00, 5:30, or 6:00 p.m.

An ideal time to have an interview is 1:30 p.m. The noon show is a wrap, the reporters have had time for lunch—and reporters with a full stomach are easier to handle—and there is time enough to get the videotape back to the station for editing. If a lawyer is in court and cannot comment until after court ends, he may likely be caught on the courthouse steps, making a live appearance. But there are ways to prepare for that live comment.

Television anchors rarely go out and conduct interviews. Reporters must do it, and they have very busy, late-breaking schedules. So they will be grateful when you provide them a one-page synopsis on the case. If there is a "quotable" reference for them to use, they may well use it.

I use the same simplistic approach to journalism, the five Ws, to orient lawyers about the media, WHO, WHAT, WHEN, WHERE, WHY, and the one H, HOW.

Who?

"Who do you call?" Here is the scenario:

A lawyer in a criminal defense or personal injury case is either contacted by a reporter or decides that he or the client has something to say about the way the case is already being discussed in the media. An important tool is a media list. The media list should be updated bimonthly. Through updating the list, someone in the lawyer's office has the opportunity to update himself as a source. The local TV and radio stations, the newspapers, a city magazine and the wire services—for example, Reuters, Associated Press, and Bloomberg (for white-collar defense)—should be on the list. Telephone numbers and e-mail addresses that go directly to the newsroom are very different from the main number.

At the newspaper, there will be specific reporters who cover the court beat and specific issues. In addition, include the names of the city and state editors; for TV stations, have the name of the assignment editor for the radio stations, the name of the news director.

There's a defined hierarchy at every newspaper, TV, and radio station. I had one reporter tell me not to bother talking to the assignment editor at the *Daily News*. "He's just a clerk," he said disdainfully. Yet, in my experience, everyone plays an important role in getting the message to the decision makers. I show everyone the same respect, from assignment editors and reporters to news directors.

These are the names of "who to call" when a lawyer decides to conduct media relations in a high-profile case. Although, today "call" is often eclipsed by "email," so be sure to communicate electronically.

Who should keep this list and update it is also an issue. If indeed it is the case that there is no policy, you might consider developing some guidelines, for example, appointing a lawyer, paralegal, or support person to keep and update a media list.

What?

What does the reporter need and want from you? First and foremost, as much time as the lawyer can give to enable him or her to meet a deadline. Second, the reporter will need a quotation, an interpretation of the legal issue in layman's language, and finally to know how the lawyer and client feel—as opposed to what they think. If a lawyer prepares before the interview, he can do both at once.

Reporters love conflict. That is another characteristic lawyers and reporters have in common: both are involved in conflict. Don't be mealy-mouthed when making statements. Take a position, and speak strongly, firmly, and eloquently.

Lawyers must perform in the courtroom; repeat the same tactics with the media. In the *Fuhler* case, the defense lawyer made an issue of the dollars spent on the "sting operation" designed to entice a gullible foreign doctor into crossing the line to purchase weapons that were on a list of weapons it was forbidden to sell to certain countries.

Create a conflict that jurors and the general public can identify with.

When?

When do you make contact? The "when" of media relations has another name—timing—and it is crucial. Deadlines mean even more to the media than they do to lawyers. While lawyers can sometimes negotiate a trial date, reschedule a deposition, or ask for a continuance, the media do not tolerate delays well.

Lawyers, like PR professionals, need to use their knowledge of deadlines to determine who to call first for late-breaking news. If it is 6:30 p.m., the newspaper reporter will have time to write the story. If it is 4:00 p.m., there's still time to tape an interview for the evening news. Radio will be there and want to cover the story in the early a.m., drive time. This is one reason why you should give your home and mobile telephone numbers to reporters.

When a reporter calls, the receptionists, secretaries and lawyers must be sensitive to the deadline factor. This is not to say that a lawyer needs to respond immediately to a telephone call or to the camera outside the courtroom. There are strategies to allow the lawyer time to prepare himself to be quotable.

For example, as soon as a reporter has called, get back to him or her within fifteen minutes. Unless a lawyer is in court or in a judge's chamber, someone should be able to reach him. With today's technology of text messaging, a lawyer may see that a reporter has called even if he is in the courtroom. In this day of the Blackberry, cellular telephones and digital pagers, the lawyer with newsworthy clients or knowledge should always be equipped with communication gear. For the lowly paid public defenders or legal aid lawyer, this gear may not be as sophisticated, but the point is, get back to the reporter ASAP.

During your first conversation, find out the nature of the questions and ask the reporter, "What's your deadline?" and how he or she can be reached in the next few minutes. Explain that you want to get your files or a specific document to review before responding. Hang up. Then use that time to jot down a statement. Have someone make copies of documents or public records the reporter might find useful. Even if the questions posed do not call for the exact prepared response, lawyers are usually very capable about "thinking on their feet." Slightly rephrase the statement and say what looks best for the client. Chances are the reporter might change the question to fit the quotation.

Where?

Where will the story go after the first report? Lawyers can be involved in determining where the story will go from the time it is first reported. In many criminal cases, the lawyer for the accused may read about his future clients and the crimes they allegedly commit, before they become a client. During the initial meeting, ask the client, and do some research regarding what the media have reported so far about the crime or allegations about the client.

Today's online research options provide almost instant information. If a matter is high-profile or a client is going to generate media attention, sit down and speculate the best-case/worst-case scenario. Then prepare a statement to address either circumstance. If the lawyer for the accused becomes dissatisfied with the newspaper reports, then use the option to call a reporter at another media outlet.

Never seek a gag order. Gag orders apply to lawyers or those on a witness list. In criminal cases, police and prosecutors will have already released information to the media. In civil cases, corporations will find a way to get around the order. If a lawyer seeks a gag order, it looks as if he has something about his client he wants to hide.

If the news reports are biased, rewrite the story from your point of view and give the media a call. Volunteer to comment at the next newsworthy moment. Then stay in touch with the reporters. They will be eager to hear from lawyers in the case, and it will be a mutually beneficial relationship.

How?

How to develop relationships with reporters? The key word here is "carefully." I was going to say "cautiously," but most lawyers are already too shy of the media to recognize the value of savvy media relations. To develop a successful relationship with a reporter, lawyers need to know something about the profession and the people.

When I say relationship, I do not mean "friendship." I read a report once from a media law conference where Ellen Pollack, Deputy Law Director for the *Wall Street Journal*, said, "Reporters are not calling you because they want to be your friend. They want information."[19]

I have found that a large number of lawyers feel they or their clients have been "burned" by the media. But lawyers must rise to this challenge. Remember what happened to former President Nixon, who claimed to have suffered at the hands of the media; he said, "If we treat the press with a little more contempt, we'll probably get better treatment."[20]

Never be evasive with a reporter. The good ones are like bloodhounds—they can smell a fugitive hiding. I advise lawyers,

If the information you have to deliver is not good, tell the entire story up front. Don't leak it out day after day. Don't assume information. If you do not know, say you do not know. More than likely the reporter will move onto what you do know.

Do cultivate your relationships but never count on an outcome. You may develop a relationship to the point where you may expect respect and a return on what you have provided, but don't let the reporter know that you expect preferential treatment. It is a fine line to walk.[21]

Be a dependable and accurate source and be accessible, but prepared.

Why?

Why does a lawyer want to make the news?

Thousands of arrests occur and hundreds of accused felons are brought to trial in communities across America each year. The prosecutors and the police all conduct media relations, communicate with the people in each community and set the stage for an atmosphere sympathetic to their objectives.

Lawyers owe it to themselves, and ethically they owe it to the accused and accusing clients they represent, to improve their understanding of how to handle the media relations.

Media Know-How

In my seminars, I present a segment called Media Know-how 101 as a short course in the practical matters of dealing with the media. The challenge for lawyers is to practice these tips until they become second nature.

Placing the Story

There are two kinds of media relations: proactive and reactive. In the reactive arena, the potential for damage is much higher. When the reporter calls the lawyer regarding a case, an issue, or a client, it is wise never to respond at the first contact unless the questions have been anticipated and thoughtfully considered.

Lawyers are most familiar with reactive media relations. However, there are also opportunities for proactive efforts. Proactive media relations are initiated by the lawyer, an assistant, or a media relations representative.

Proactive media relations fall into two categories—news media and editorial boards. The second is rarely used but is an important place to turn with issues that significantly affect a case and a client. An editorial column can send a powerful message to elected officials, and many judges are indeed elected.

When an accused client is under media attack, it will be difficult to generate personal sympathy, but do not rule out media objectivity. A statement can be as simple as, "We are committed to maintaining our client's innocence under the laws that protect all of us." This statement focuses as much on the client as the lawyer's role in the case.

There will be times when a lawyer is sick and tired of talking about a case or a client. Recognize that in advance and prepare for it. Sometimes it helps to have on hand a few stock phrases.

The Sound Byte in Seconds

Seconds are exactly what the electronic media will give to those who comment. In this day of remote control and TiVo, television producers work with a truncated formula for news stories. The total time usually adds up to ninety seconds—that's a minute and a half—for a report on a high-profile client or case.

The news segment may break down like this: thirty seconds of facts and footage—a voice over, then a five-second introduction; then fifteen seconds; then the human perspective—a sound byte of approximately 15 seconds. Finally, thirty seconds for a wrap-up and speculation about what will happen next. In a story that reports a comment from both a lawyer and client, each may get ten–twelve seconds. By preparing a draft for a statement and rehearsing, a lawyer can increase control of how his statement or his client's is reported. A special features story may go a bit longer and continue the next day.

Looking Good and Sounding Better

As lawyers prepare for court appearances, they invest in the best wardrobe they can get. It is important to do the same thing for media appearances and photo opportunities. The first rule in dressing for TV is to avoid black and white. Pastels are a good choice for shirts or blouses—pinks, yellows, and blues. Stripes or prints should not be too "busy," or they may look alive and psychedelic and distract from what is said. For women, wearing a blouse that is higher around the neck softens the appearance and helps avoid the chicken-neck look. A grey or navy blue suit is also better than black. Avoid a blazer, which chops the body in half. Anyone can determine which side is his best side by looking at photographs or videotapes of himself. It is possible to angle the face to the camera for the best look.

When the interview is with print media only, worry about a camera only if a photographer comes along. Relax the voice. Don't take the crisp edge out of speaking, but drop down a tone or two. Women especially can sound shrill if they do not speak in full-rounded tones. It is easy to become nervous and let the throat close up. Microphones are very sensitive. Most times, the reporter or cameraman will ask for a voice level before taping. Use the voice intended for use during the interview. Don't change midstream. If a gesture is appropriate, minimize movement.

Training Your Support Staff

The most important skill the person who answers the telephone can have is to recognize the importance of getting the reporter's message to the lawyer as fast as possible and not sounding overeager, just professional. She should also be trained not to say "Oh yes, Channel 6 just called us before you did." Nor should she go to the other extreme and be short and rude or evasive about your whereabouts. Lawyers need to treat reporters as they would another lawyer, perhaps even with more respect.

In the public defender's office, it also be important to let the media know how to call in on an alternate "back" line. It might be completely frustrating on a busy day to get through on the main one.

The Rhetorical Question

A rhetorical question is one of the ways a lawyer can make a comment and state an opinion without committing himself one way or the other. For example, in the *Fuhler* case, his defense lawyer asked, to arouse sympathy for Dr. Fuhler, "How would an American tourist feel if they went to a foreign country to close a business deal and were suddenly arrested and thrown into jail without bail?"

Body Language and Facial Expressions

Minimize your facial expressions. TV exaggerates everything. Watch out for the bouncing chair. It is a classic lawyer faux pas. The large leather chair many lawyers use, the one that leans back so far he might disappear, is not supposed to be used as a moving prop. Sit in the chair, leaning slightly forward and place your hands on the desk for stability.

Quotable Quotation

Crafting a quotable quotation is a chance to put a persuasive argument into a succinct message that says something important for the client. Writing it is a good starting point, but speaking it out loud will be the true test of whether it sounds natural and powerful.

A rhetorical question can be quotable. Something that is not likely to be quoted is a lawyer quoting someone else. The media want something fresh, from the heart or from the gut. As I said earlier, they want to know the client feels more than what he thinks.

No to "No Comment"

"No comment" is a tired and dreary way for a lawyer to respond. In response, the media will announce that they tried to interview you. Actually, a lawyer cannot avoid being mentioned simply by sidestepping reporters' efforts to speak to them. If someone does not return a reporter's telephone call and he takes it personally or, if a lawyer or client refuses to see him or her, the news account could sound like this: "Counsel for the defendant refused repeated telephone calls." If the media are less angry, they might say, "Counsel could not be reached for comment."

On TV, the announcement may be, "We tried to talk to the lawyer, but he refused to talk to us." Even worse, the cameraperson may tape the reporter chasing after the lawyer or client with a microphone al la *60 Minutes*.

"No comment" is a complete negative. There is always a way to represent the client's position and give an opinion or react to an issue and be quoted and respected for what is printed or broadcast.

"Off the Record"

"Off the record" can either be an assurance by a reporter that what a source says will not be attributed to him, or it can be a request to a reporter when the source is deciding to share some information. In high-profile cases, the lawyer or publicist may wish to share information that is relevant to the case. For example, in Chapter 8, I discuss sharing a videotape of David Richmond, the abusive boyfriend Michele Roger killed. In the case, the accused was arguing self-defense and alleged that Richmond was a heavy cocaine user who often became violently abusive. The only image of Richmond that was public was an academic head shot of him wearing horn-rimmed glasses. The defense had a videotape of Richmond, a heavy metal rocker, performing. I went off the record with a TV reporter, released the tape, and it aired during a news segment of the family apologizing for disposing of Richmond's body but stressing he was abusive to Michele Roger.

The most important tactic to remember in using off-the-record is to be sure that you have a verbal contract with the reporter.

The "Off the record" issue was directly addressed by a 1991 Supreme Court ruling in the case *Cohen v. Cowles Media Company*, publisher of the *St. Paul Pioneer Press* and the *Star Tribune*.[22] The lower court ruled that Dan Cohen was to be paid both compensatory and punitive damages when the newspaper divulged him as a source when he had been promised confidentiality. While working on a political campaign, he released information about one candidate's arrest record to a reporter who agreed the information was provided off-the-record. The editors at the newspaper decided to reveal Cohen's identity because they questioned his motives. After he was reveled as the source in a published story, his company fired him. He sued the newspaper's parent company and won.

The Court ruled that Cohen had an unwritten contract with the newspaper and that verbal contract had been violated. After several reversals and appeals, the U.S. Supreme Court upheld the $200,000 in compensatory damages.

The Cohen case is taught in journalism classes today. It provides a road map for establishing a confidential exchange of information with a reporter. Indiana University Professor Jon P. Dilts, a lawyer and former journalist, includes the Cohen case in a textbook he coauthored, *Media Law*. [23] In the fifteen years since the Cohen decision, he says it remains "the only real leverage that someone has who wants to be a confidential source."[24] The way to go "off the record" is to establish a clear understanding, a verbal contract, that the media will not reveal its source of the information or evidence. This is done, not by saying, "This is off the record" and launching into all the details. First, establish that such an understanding exists. "What I am going to tell you is off the record. Do you agree?" Then wait for their answer. To be really cautious, after a reporter says "yes," repeat the agreement. "So what I will tell you will be kept in confidence. Do you promise?"

Ask the reporter how far he or she will go to protect you as a source. Will he go to jail? If you are dealing with a really sensitive matter, ask to hear an assurance from the reporter's editor.

Keep in mind that the reporter is fully entitled to try and find another source to confirm that the information provided was "off the record."

If a case involves alleged terrorism, no one may reveal the identity of undercover operatives and endanger their lives. In a post-9/11 world, this is not such a far-fetched possibility. In this type of case, the Cohen decision is not applicable.

Background Briefings

Background Briefing can provide all sorts of useful and persuasive information about the client and the case. Such a briefing in a complex case may help reporters keep the key facts and dates straight as they interview the lawyer or accused client. Develop a background briefing and keep it updated. Include information about the client's family, dates of allegations, filings, indictments—evidence that is public record. Use phonetic spellings for difficult names. Electronic media people will especially appreciate that. Everyone wants his name pronounced properly.

The Press Conference

There are two sides to the press conference that concern lawyers—the ethics and the mechanics. The ethics were addressed in Chapter 1, in my review of the seminal case *Gentile vs. The State Bar of Nevada*. Gentile adhered to the existing rules when he held a press conference commenting upon the character, credibility, reputation and criminal records of prospective witness and gave his opinion on the guilt or innocence of his accused client.

One of the issues—commenting on the guilt or innocence of your client—is clearly allowed. The press conference can be used to cut down on the number of interviews a lawyer wants to give about a particular development or issue.

Follow-up is an essential component in holding a successful press conference. Even if I've talked to someone and confirmed receipt of the press release, I call him or her again twenty–thirty minutes before the press conference. I may ask, "Who's coming?" and if they have any special requests or if they know exactly where we are; they can let us know if a certain reporter is coming or if the station is only sending a videographer without a reporter. Thick skin is a must in this business. Many times, busy editors will nearly hang up when they are consumed by a breaking story. I've had print reporters hang up the telephone after barking, "I'm on a deadline!" The key is never to take it personally; there is always someone else to hear your pitch or available to answer your question. If there's not, then there must be a story out there so overwhelming that, if possible, it's a good idea to reschedule your press conference for another day.

Staging a press conference means selecting a place, props, and people. It is always good to have more than one person available to interview. It will maximize the on-air time given to the case. If the accused is not in jail and the lawyer considers it appropriate, the client may attend. For a small press conference—with up to five media representatives—hold the press conference in a large conference room.

If available, place low-back straight chairs behind a table. The table is essential for microphones. Have the media escorted in by a secretary or assistant and let them get situated before you come into the room. Be seated behind the table. Ask if everyone is ready and if the microphones test okay. Then read a brief opening statement. If someone else has a statement, allow him or her time to speak before you take questions. Actually, the statements will probably wind up being used for background information. Most reporters will tape the statements and take footage from the period of time when they hear the first answer to a question. If there are printed copies of the statement available, do not give them out until the end. You can elect to have background sheets—instead of the statements—available. If names are difficult, spell them out phonetically, and make sure you pronounce them correctly on tape.

After the opening statements, the lawyer might announce there is a specified time frame for questions. Give everyone a chance to ask one question. Thank them for coming, and exit the room. Avoid having one or more reporters approach after the press conference to ask additional questions unless you are prepared to give individual interviews to everyone. Avoid the appearance of favoritism.

Lawyers must recognize that the battle for public opinion is real and may well have an effect on the outcome of a case. There are specific skills that lawyers can master to dramatically improve their media relations know-how. This is not to say that every question can be anticipated in any interview. To underestimate the independence of a reporter is to play the fool. However, any lawyer can increase his control over the news report by increasing his knowledge and practicing his skills.

One of the challenges that lawyers face in high-profile cases is the heinous crime allegedly committed by the client. It may be that what a lawyer can achieve in the public eye is not sympathy for his client—even though he or she may certainly deserve it—but respect and understanding for what you are doing on your client's behalf.

Common sense and a few key rules of procedure are a beginning. When a lawyer watches a TV interview, hears himself on the radio, or sees his comments in print, knowledgeable preparation will mean an articulate and ethical representation of the client.

The goals and purposes of media relations for the accused and accusers extend far beyond publicity. For the lawyer in private practice, the effect of increased publicity and a heightened profile in the community can result in more clients. I believe that a good lawyer owes it to the public to raise his profile. When someone is accused, the skills of the defense lawyer will affect the outcome of his case and, quite possibly, the rest of the accused person's life. Both the accused and the accuser need to know "who is the most capable lawyer in the marketplace for my case?"

Twelve

High-Profile Cases in the Twenty-First Century

When I created a public relations campaign for Ed Humphrey, a wrongfully suspected serial killer, in 1991, his lawyer and I were considered pioneers. Through public relations, we successfully countered press coverage that reflected one-sided accusations provided to the media by investigators and prosecutors. The relationship between the media and those who investigate and prosecute accused people is not going to change.

The media–prosecution arrangement is summed up in a 1985 movie, "The Mean Season," starring Kurt Russell as Malcolm Anderson, a fictitious *Miami Journal* newspaper reporter, and Andy Garcia as prosecutor Ray Martinez. When a murderer decides to give clues directly to the reporter, the prosecution wants access and strikes a deal with the reporter. The dialogue goes something like this: Reporter Anderson: "You give us everything twenty-four hours before you give it to anyone else." Prosecutor Martinez: "We all have relationships to maintain. Sixteen." Anderson: "Ten." Martinez: "Deal."

Public fascination with high-profile cases and media coverage are factors that every lawyer must consider when responding to, or initiating contact with, the media. Even as public habits for following the news change, lawyers must be aware that what the public hears and reads has an effect on the outcome of a case. This is true in criminal cases when information about the suspects begins the day they come in for questioning or are arrested as well as for victims who become plaintiffs in civil suits.

The way that people get their news is steadily changing. In a feature article in the *Los Angeles Times* published in *The New Yorker* magazine, author Ken Auletta examines the struggle over the bottom line between business managers and editors. He notes that "The Carnegie Corporation recently reported that the average age of newspaper readers is fifty-three. Baby boomers 'read newspapers one-third less than their parents and the Gen Xers read newspapers another one-third less than the Boomers.'"[1] A growing number of young adults, who will soon dominate jury pools, get their information from Internet sites. Still, what appears on the Internet is that which was first reported in traditional news media accounts, usually compiled from information released by the police and prosecutors.

Films and television shows have educated several generations about the criminal and civil justice system. The newest shows to cover crimes focus on investigations. Because of shows like *CSI*, potential jurors in criminal cases may soon decide they have a certain expertise in evaluating evidence at trials.

In 2006, more than fifteen years after Humphrey gave his prison interview, another suspect gave a jailhouse statement the day before he was indicted. This high-profile case and media reports of a suspect, a New York City bouncer, began with the murder of a young college student.

In the early morning hours of February 27, 2006, friends of Imette St. Guillen left her alone at a Soho Bar, where they had been drinking heavily. The next day, her bound body was found in a remote area of Kings County, where the Brooklyn District Attorney Charles Hynes probably prosecutes more cases per year than any other county in America.

Soon after the story broke, the *Daily News* gives the young woman a nickname, the mummy victim, because her head was wrapped in tape. By March 5, police had a suspect, the bar's forty-one-year-old bouncer, and his name, Darryl Littlejohn, is repeatedly mentioned in the news. On March 8, a mugshot taken of him in 2003 is all over the television airwaves and in the next day's newspapers.

On March 8, he's identified in a headline as an "Ex-Con" and the "only suspect." One day, there is a redeeming headline, "DNA Test Fails to Link Ex-Con. But Probers Insist Other 'Good Evidence.'"[2] By the time of the indictment press conference, Littlejohn's blood and DNA are linked to the murder, and the forensic evidence is reported all over New York.

By March 22, over 70 news articles had been published in New York's *Daily News*, only one of the five major daily newspapers in the city covering the case. Reports about the murder, investigation and, finally, the press conference announcing the indictment are on at least one television or radio show every few hours.

The day before the indictment, Littlejohn gives an "exclusive" to the local CBS news station that is repeatedly aired on television and WCBS radio on March 21, and available on the CBS news Web site. He also talks to the daily newspapers in telephone interviews. Littlejohn says he is "sorry" for the family, but he is innocent.

The media also covers the fact that a defense lawyer has allowed his suspect client to make a statement. Littlejohn's lawyer, Kevin O'Donnell, gives interviews and explains that he allowed his client to speak to the media. "It was important to me to let the public ... especially the potential jury pool in Brooklyn ... know what kind of a person he really is," O'Donnell said, "... to put a voice and a personality on someone as eloquent and intelligent as him."

Because he allowed this initial statement, O'Donnell will now have to make important decisions regarding media access to his client. News accounts about Littlejohn's interview include one in *The Boston* that analyzes how truthful he appeared in his media début.

The Boston media follow the case closely since that's where the victim grew up and her family still lives. The Boston CBS affiliate brings in an expert psychologist, Joseph Tecce, to analyze Littlejohn's interview and reports, "According to data, Littlejohn only blinks twenty-one times a minute in the interview, when it should be up around forty." "Most people blink more when they talk," said Professor Tecce. "This man (Littlejohn) blinks more when he's listening. His blinking more when listening suggests that he doesn't like the fact that the other guy is calling the shots."

"He's not feeling the full expression of emotions that he should be if he's innocent and accused of being guilty," added the expert in nonverbal communication. "He shouldn't be nervous. He should be upset."[3] National news programs are already looking at producing a segment of the murder case of Imette St. Guillen, to air later, of course, when the trial of the accused is looming. Timing is everything, and the interest in this case will peak again before and during any trial of the accused. All this publicity will be lapped up by potential jurors in the trial.

O'Donnell has initiated a dialogue with media about this case that he must strategically maintain and manage in the months to come. The media coverage of the investigation and indictment is an excellent example of how police and prosecutors understand the power of the press.

The majority of the media coverage was constructed from information released not by lawyers, but by the New York City police. Although St. Guillen's body was found in Kings County, where the courthouse is located in Brooklyn, the crime began in Soho, the trendy area of Manhattan below Houston Street. However, by the day of Littlejohn's indictment press conference, the district attorney, a lawyer, does not have to consider the ethics of pretrial publicity because the police conducted the media relations.

There are several types of rules and regulations regarding pretrial publicity: state bar rules, federal rules and rules published by professional legal organizations. The rules generally include the caveat that lawyers must consider whether the information they release is "likely to have a substantial likelihood of prejudicing a criminal proceeding." What that "substantial likelihood" means is addressed by the American Bar Association. Its standards regarding pretrial release of information are very specific on what information is "ordinarily likely to have a substantial likelihood of prejudicing a criminal proceeding":

1. the prior criminal record (including arrests, indictments, or other charges of crime) of a suspect or defendant;

2. the character or reputation of a suspect or defendant;

3. the opinion of the lawyer on the guilt of the defendant, the merits of the case or the merits of the evidence in the case.

Between March 5 and March 22, the media coverage in the investigation of Littlejohn goes well beyond these ABA rules on "extrajudicial statements by attorneys in criminal cases;" yet no rules are technically violated because the information was not released by lawyers. By the time of the indictment, information like that regarding Littlejohn's prior criminal record and the DNA evidence is in the public domain. The *Daily News* lists eight items regarding "circumstantial and forensic evidence [that] stack up against accused killer Darryl Littlejohn," and cite the source as "police and prosecutors."[4]

A few months before the Littlejohn case, New York City was rocked by the horrific child abuse case that left a six-year-old Brooklyn girl dead. The teachers of Nixmary Brown had tried to notify child welfare authorities. The city agency responsible for investigating child abuse was aware of the dangerous situation in her home yet failed to properly investigate and protect her. When she died after being beaten by her step-father and ignored by her mother, the case against the parents was undisputable.

Brooklyn District Attorney Charles Hynes was aggressive in his media relations, not to build a case against the accused parents, but to lobby the state legislature and city to make administrative changes that will protect other children in abusive homes. In this example, the commitment of a civic-minded and media-savvy prosecutor and can make a community a safer place for children.

As lawyers become more willing to respond to media opportunities and even to allow their accused clients to defend themselves as their accusers aggressively continue to employ media relations, there is one type of case that puts up a stringent and biased media barrier. Regardless of how the government conducts media relations to accuse terrorist suspects, both lawyers and those accused will be prohibited from responding. The type of gag order that Russell Yates defied (see Chapter 10) or that Bruce Cutler was punished for violating pales in comparison with the media restrictions of the government that affect any case involving accusations of terrorism.

These restrictions bar media contact in cases where terrorism is alleged. Initially put in place under Attorney General Janet Reno in 1997 to prevent prisoner terrorists with knowledge of classified information from giving that information to the media, these measures were broadened and became much better known after 9/11. According to law professor James McLaughlin, Special Administrative Measures (SAMs) "can be invoked by the government almost at will to prevent reporters and the public at large from having any contact with accused terrorists, even after they're convicted."[5]

When the government prosecuted John Walker Lindh in 2002, infamously labeled the "American Taliban," his lawyer faced an uphill battle on many levels. The Lindh case will be forever linked to the aftermath of the 9/11 terrorist attacks in New York City and Washington, D.C. Lindh is currently serving twenty years and is in a minimum security prison in San Bernardino County, California. He was initially charged with eleven criminal counts, including terrorism charges such as supporting Al Qaeda. All terrorism charges were later dropped and he agreed to a plea bargain on one charge: he provided assistance to the Taliban government in Afghanistan, which violated American economic sanctions. For this crime, he received a twenty-year prison sentence.

In November, 2001 Lindh was found in Afghanistan, where he was a volunteer soldier in the Taliban forces who were fighting against the Northern Alliance, a group of notorious warlords. He had been shot, imprisoned in a freezing basement filled with water, and surrounded by other Taliban soldiers, many of whom were executed.

Lindh was raised a Catholic, but converted to Islam when he was sixteen years old and living in Marin County, California. The following year, he went to Yemen to study Arabic, part of his goal in becoming a Muslim scholar and memorizing the Koran. Although he returned home for a short time in 1999, he returned to a school in Yemen. In 2000, he went to Pakistan and was recruited to join the Afghanistan army.

When the United States invaded Afghanistan in October 2001, with the goal of finding and capturing Osama bin Laden, Lindh was caught in the middle of a new war; he and hundreds of others were captured by a warlord on November 25. On November 30, 2001, when a *CNN* stringer found him in terrible physical shape with a bullet in his leg, he recruited a U.S. Army medic to help him. Then, against Lindh's request not to interview him, the stringer did an on-camera interview.

The media had a field day with this interview. When he was videotaped, Lindh was under the influence of morphine, and although he merely confirmed his purpose and the time he had been in Afghanistan, he also included the fact that he had met bin Laden. This alone was blown so far out of context that Lindh was named a terrorist. American military soon took him into custody.

Lindh's father, a lawyer who loves and supports his son, knew immediately he needed legal counsel. He reached one of the nation's top criminal defense lawyers, James Brosnahan, who had also seen the *CNN* excerpt of John Walker Lindh's "interview."

Once Brosnahan received the call, he says he told the senior Lindh, "I'll have to think about it."[6] After meeting with Lindh and consulting with his law partners about a case that was going to be intensely controversial in a post-9/11 America, Brosnahan agreed to take John Walker Lindh on as a client.

From the start, the government's treatment, investigation and ultimate prosecution of Lindh violated every principle of fairness established in the U.S. Constitution and the Geneva Convention agreements regarding the treatment of prisoners. Mr. Brosnahan was prevented from seeing his client for fifty-three days, nearly two months after he first requested to meet with him on December 3, informing the government he wanted to fly to Afghanistan, where his client was being held. Media reports later revealed that Lindh was isolated in an unheated, large metal drum, strapped to a table with a bullet in his leg, left there as "evidence."

During that time, the American news media lambasted John Walker Lindh. There were also reports—completely unfounded—that linked the death of a CIA agent, Mike Spann, working at the site where Lindh was captured, to Lindh.

Lindh's father describes the media coverage: "It wasn't just the television media that caused this prejudice; it was the print media as well." Publications as diverse as the tabloid *National Enquirer* to the *New York Times* called his son a traitor and implied he had caused the death of Spann.[7]

In addition, the media broadcast the damning comments of well-known politicians, who after initially showing some sympathy to the misguided American Taliban, began to label him a member of Al Qaeda. "I would venture to say that never before in the history of this country has any criminal defendant been subjected to anything approaching the kind of prejudicial statements made by officials in John's case," says Lindh.[8]

James Brosnahan puts it this way: "Government officials and congressmen had built up such an angry chorus of prejudice—a superbowl of prejudice."[9]

When Brosnahan finally met his young client in the Northern Virginia jail where he was held until his trial, he discovered a gentle and likeable young man. Mr. Brosnahan might have considered letting the public meet this young idealistic client, who had been tortured by American troops, except for SAMs restrictions. Without the option of correcting the inaccurate and prejudiced public profile that had dominated the coverage of Lindh's after he was found in Afghanistan, Brosnahan became his client's advocate. In order to handle the approximate seventy-five calls per day that he received from the media about John Walker Lindh, his law firm, Morrison and Foster hired a PR professional who had handled media for California

Bar Associations. She fielded the calls, and when there was something about the case that was allowable to report, Brosnahan supplied her with information to disseminate.

Brosnahan is no stranger to the media and he is not adverse to press conferences or to client's giving an interview when appropriate. He believes that every case and every client is different: "I've had six cases with national press coverage; I adhere to an ethical rule that I ask about every interview: "Will an appearance help the client."[10] Because of the SAMs, no matter how much it might have helped Lindh to address his accusers publicly, it was not an option to consider.

Brosnahan's criticisms of Attorney General John Ashcroft during the Lindh case are those of one lawyer chastising another for improper conduct. He says, "Ashcroft made one of the most unprofessional efforts I've ever seen a lawyer undertake. He called John a terrorist and made false statements."[11] In fact during a press conference outside the Arlington, Virginia, courthouse where the arraignment of Lindh was held, Brosnahan publicly asked Ashcroft "to adhere to prosecutorial conduct and follow the rules."[12]

Clearly, the SAMs regulations give federal prosecutors an unfair advantage in high-profile cases when terrorism is alleged. It also allows them to prevent an accused person from reporting incidents of torture and abuse in return for a plea bargain.

However, the John Walker Lindh case is far from over. In January 2006, his father, Frank, an eloquent and effective spokesman for his son, gave an impassioned speech before the Commonwealth Club in San Francisco. (A complete copy of the speech is available at www.alternet.org).[13]

Frank Lindh has become the voice of his wrongfully accused son. In August 2002, Brosnahan sought a reduction of the sentence for the younger Lindh, through a request for commutation. He maintains that his client is not a "hater" and was never a terrorist or supporter of terrorism.[14]

Lawyers who were responsive to the media in the early years, even before Dominic Gentile, like Albert Krieger and Barry Cohen, are attempting to mobilize their colleagues into working for new restrictions on prosecutors who issue "storyboard indictments." It is telling that when the State Bar of Nevada argued before the Supreme Court that lawyers like Gentile violated the professional rules by calling a press conference to defend an accused client, it was joined by the U.S. Justice Department in an amicus brief.[15]

Albert Krieger wants the judiciary to recognize the unfairness of allowing a prosecutor's indictment novella into the jury room yet restricting the defense to less than a one-page theory of their case. However, despite Krieger's admirable goal to effect changes that temper the publicity tactics of police or district attorneys, I doubt that will ever happen in our free society. The Littlejohn case is a topical example of how media relations by the accused and accusers are significant factors in the American judicial system.

Lawyers today must recognize and use media relations strategies for their clients in high-profile cases, not only at the earliest possible juncture, but months and years after an unjust conviction and sentence. It's not about courting the media for the sake of publicity; it's about recognizing the influence of the media on what happens in the courtrooms of America each and every day.

Notes

Introduction

1. Margaret Cronin Fisk, "10 Years of Life in the Law; At the Top, Joe Jamail," *National Law Journal*, September 26, 1988, p. 24.

2. Johnnie L. Cochran Jr., email to the author, November 15, 2004.

3. *Bates v. Arizona State Bar*, 76 U.S. 316, 1977. See www.firstamendmentcenter. com for an in-depth summary of Bates.

4. Lenard Saffir, *Power Public Relations*, "Murder Trial" (NTC Business Books, Lincolnwood, IL, 1994).

5. Willard Techmeier, see Chapter 11.

Chapter 1

1. Stephen Gillers, *Regulations of Lawyers: Problems of Law and Ethics*, 7th ed. (Aspen Law & Business, New York, 2005).

2. Stephen Gillers, telephone interview with the author, March 20, 2006.

3. *Bates v. Arizona State Bar*, 76 U.S. 316, 1977.

4. *Gentile v. Nevada*, 51 Commerce Clearing House, Supreme Court Bulletin, pp. B3446–3500.

5. Dominic Gentile, telephone interview with the author, April 3, 2006, 6:30 p.m., EST.

6. www.justia.us/us/501/1030/case.html, April 3, 2006.

7. Ibid.

8. Bruce Vielmetti, "Many Legal Eyes Are Trained on 'Revered Defense Lawyer Series: Tampa Law,'" *St. Petersburg Times*, November 13, 1989, 1.1.

9. Bruce Vielmetti, "Lawyers Learning to Plead in Court of Public Opinion," *St. Petersburg Times*, June 18, 1989, 6B.

10. Ibid.

11. Albert Krieger, telephone interview with the author, March 22, 2006.

12. Ibid.

13. Ibid.

14. "Committee on Public Information," http://www.soucewatch.org, accessed January 30, 2006.

15. John Hanc, "Rallying the Public: A Look Back at Government Effort to 'Spin War,'" *Newsday*, December 5, 2001, B-3.

16. Mark Memmott, "Most Think Propaganda Campaign in Iraq Wrong," *USA Today*, December 22, 2005, http://www.usatoday.com/news/nation/2005-12-22-poll-propaganda_x.htm/ February 22, 2006.

17. Ibid.

18. Stephen Duncombe and Andrew Mattson, "City Lore: Armed and Adorable," *The New York Times*, February 12, 2006.

19. Douglas Linder, "The Trial of Bruno Hauptmann," http://jurist.law.pitt.edu/trials26.htm, accessed February 22, 2006.

20. www.cnn.com, June 19, 2005; posted: 5:09 p.m., EDT (21:09 GMT).

21. Dominic Gentile, telephone interview with the author, April 3, 2006, 6:30 p.m., EST.

22. Ibid.

Chapter 2

1. Eric Franz, personal interview with the author, January 11, 2005.

2. www.news24.com, TV station in South Africa, reported the *Crowe* lawsuit on July 5, 2005, and cited the South African Press Association wire service.

3. Ibid.

4. Eric Franz, personal interview with the author, January 11, 2005.

5. Gerald Shields, "More Parties in Court Find Image Counts; Specialists Said Spinning Defendant's Images to the Media is a Critical Tool in the Court of Public Opinion," *Orlando Sentinel*, June 21, 1996.

6. "Russell Crowe's Statement: Blame Bad Customer Service," Citing "Drudge," www.defamer.com, accessed January 16, 2006.

7. Leigh Sales, "Russell Crowe Spruiks Apology," www.abc.net.au/pm/content/2005/s1388767.htm, accessed January 16, 2006.

8. Russ and Malloy, "Crowe Bust Blamed for KO of 'Man,'" *New York Daily News*, June 14, 2005.

9. Christopher Tennant, Editor, and Andrew Goldstein, Staff Writer, www.RadarOnline.com/fresh-intelligence, posted June 24, 2005.

10. Ibid.

11. "Scarborough Country," MSNBC.com, posted June 28, 2005.

12. Ibid.

13. Ibid.

14. Christopher Tennant, Editor, and Andrew Goldstein, Staff Writer, www.RadarOnline.com/fresh-intelligence, accessed January 15, 2006.

15. William Sherman, "Suit vs. Crowe to Fly," *New York Daily News*, July 5, 2005, p. 3.

16. Cindy Adams, "Crowe Calls Ordeal Just an Accident," *New York Post*, June 20, 2005, p. 6.

17. Nicole Lampert, "Crowe's L6m Phone Call," www.dailymail.co.uk, accessed January 15, 2006.

18. Annabel Crabb, "Crowe's Costly Phone Call," www.Age.com, accessed August 14, 2005.

19. William Sherman and Nicole Bode, "Att'y Denies Deal in Crowe's Hotel Phone-Fling Case," *New York Daily News*, August 15, 2005.

20. Ibid.

21. Josh Grossberg, "Crowe Settles Flying Phone Flap," August 25, 2005.

22. George Rush, "Crowe & Clerk in 6-Figure Deal," *New York Daily News*, August 25, 2005.

23. Eric Franz, personal interview with the author, January 11, 2005.

24. CNN.com, accessed May 31, 2005.

25. Karen Freifeld, "A Very Bad Thing? In Latest Brush with Law, Slater Is Charged for Allegedly Grabbing Woman's Buttocks," Newsday.com, May 31, 2005, A-02.

26. Andrew Jacobs, "Actor Rejects Plea in Harassment Case," *The New York Times*, Metro Briefings, July 15, 2005.

27. Lisa Sweetingham, "Actor Christian Slater Turns Down Plea Deal on Charges He Groped Woman," www.CourtTV.com, accessed July 14, 2005.

28. Sam Knight, "Christian Slater Fights Grope Charges," *London Times*, July 14, 2005.

29. See note 27.

30. www.robertblake.com.

31. Terry McCarthy, "Seen This Show Before?" *Time*, April 29, 2002.

32. "Robert Blake Talks," *48 Hours*, www.cbsnews.com, accessed January 26, 2006.

33. "Blake's Lawyer Resigns," Associated Press, www.courttv.com, accessed January 26, 2006.

34. Barbara Walter, Interview with Robert Blake, *20/20*, Web site, accessed January 26, 2006.

35. Ibid.

36. "Prosecutor: Blake Jurors Incredibly Stupid," www.courttv.com, accessed March 24, 2005.

37. CourtTV.com.

38. "Wife's Family Sues Blake, Bodyguard," www.courttv.com, accessed April 3, 2002.

Chapter 3

1. Ms. Hanover starred in the *Vagina Monologues*, May 30–June 14, 2000.

2. Michael Wolff, "Girls! Girls! Girls!" *New York Magazine*, May 22, 2000.

3. E. R. Shipp, " Rudy vs. the Media: Too Late, Mr. Mayor," *New York Daily News*, May 27, 2001, p. 45, and Frank Lombardi and Michael R. Blood, " Rudy Suit a Paper Tiger Not Eager to Sue the Post for 'Love Nest' Story," *New York Daily News*, July 18, 2001, p. 22.

4. Michael Wolff, "Identity Politics," *New York Magazine*, June 11, 2001.

5. Tom Watkins, "Giuliani Tears into News Media over Divorce Scrutiny," www.cnn.com, posted May 23, 2001.

6. Dahlia Lithwick, "For $6.8 Million, Giuliani Got Off Cheap," www.slate.com, posted July 12, 2002.

7. Ibid.

8. Jim Haggerty, *In the Court of Public Opinion* (John Wiley & Sons, Inc., New York, 2003).

9. Jane Carey, telephone interview with the author, January 13, 2006.

10. Ibid.

11. Phil Fernandez, "Lake County Boy Sues His Parents for 'Divorce,'" *Orlando Sentinel*, April 9, 1992, A-1.

12. "Foster Child Wants Divorce from Parents," *Daily Commercial* and *Ocala Star-Banner*, April 9, 1992.

13. Kyra Fluker, "Boy Sues His Parents for Divorce," *Daily Commercial*, April 9, 1992, B-2.

14. Phil Fernandez, "Lake County Boy Sues His Parents for 'Divorce,'" *Orlando Sentinel*, April 9, 1992, A-1.

15. Bob Levenson, telephone interview with the author, January 13, 2006.

16. Ibid.

17. Ibid.

18. Bob Levenson, *Orlando Sentinel*, September 22, 1992.

19. Bob Levenson, telephone interview with the author, January 13, 2006.

20. Corey Jo Lancaster, "Joy for Kimberly; Fear for Gregory; Kids Lose Right to Divorce Parents in Gregory K appeal, *Orlando Sentinel*, August 19, 1993, A-1.

21. Bob Levenson, telephone interview with the author, January 13, 2006.

22. Ibid.

23. Jane Carey, telephone interview with the author, January 2006.

24. Dominic Gentile, telephone interview with the author, April 3, 2006, 6:30 p.m., EST.

25. *People Weekly*, New York, October 12, 1992, Vol. 38, Issue 15; pp. 57–59.

26. Corey Jo Lancaster, "Joy for Kimberly; Fear for Gregory; Kids Lose Right to Divorce Parents in Gregory K Appeal," *Orlando Sentinel*, August 19, 1993, A-1.

27. Jane Carey, telephone interview with the author, January 2006.

28. Personal Recollection.

29. Gary Taylor and Doris Bloodsworth, "Lake Mary Mom, Son Charged in Sex-Abuse Case of Foster Kids," *Orlando Sentinel*, March 9, 2002, A-1; Gary Taylor, "Investigators Find 36 More Kids Who Lived at Foster Home," *Orlando Sentinel*, March 13, 2002, D-1.

30. Rene Stutzman, "Abuse Saga Started with Loving Mom; Social Workers Hailed Foster Mother Marie Jasmin as 'Nurturing' and Dedicated to Children," *Orlando Sentinel*, March 17 and 21, 2002.

31. Rene Stutzman, "Home Hid Pattern of Abuse, DCF Says," *Orlando Sentinel*, March 21, 2002, A-1.

32. Rene Stutzman and Gary Taylor, "Teen Accused of Abuse Goes Free, There Wasn't Enough Evidence to Hold Jacques Jasmin in the Foster Care Case," *Orlando Sentinel*, April 11, 2002, A-1.

33. Rene Stutzman, "Foster Mom Calls Allegations Against Her, Son 'False'; Marie Jasmin Asked to Care for Her Disabled Daughter Who Was Taken from Her When She Was Charged," *Orlando Sentinel*, March 23, 2002, A-1.

34. Ibid.

35. Rene Stutzman, "Audit Exposes Flaws in Foster Care," *Orlando Sentinel*, March 31, 2002.

36. Marie Jasmin, telephone interview with the author, January 2006.

37. www.courttv.com

38. *Cameras in Courtrooms*: Hearing Before the S. Comm. on the Judiciary, 109th Cong. (2005) (testimony of Henry Schleiff), available at http://judiciary.senate.gov/testimony.cfm.

39. Ibid.

Chapter 4

1. "A Chronology," *The Modesto Bee*, www.modbee.com/reports/peterson/trial/v-print/story, accessed February 12, 2006.

2. Jill Underwood, "Scot Peterson Is Innocent," *Time*, www.time.com, posted April 20, 2003.

3. Associated Press Report, MSNBC.com, November 13, 2004.

4. Garth Stapley, "Tales from a Trial," *The Modesto Bee*, November 6, 2005.

5. Jeff Jardine, "Unrelenting Media Gave Peterson Trial 'Celebrity,'" *The Modesto Bee*, November 6, 2005.

6 Ibid.

7. Bill Hewitt, Vickie Bane, Johnny Dodd, Howard Breuer, Frank Swertlow and Nicole Egan, "Scot Peterson: His Life," *People Magazine*, September 5, 2005, pp. 60–66.

8. http://www.tookie.com.

9. Dominic Gentile, telephone interview with the author, April 3, 2006, 6:30 p.m., EST.

10. Ibid.

11. Joseph DuRocher, personal interview with the author, April 25, 2002.

12. Ibid.

13. Ibid.

14. My proposal was submitted November 10, 1994, and approved November 19, 1994.

15. Gerald Shields, "Public to Pay for PR Expert to Help Defense in Murder Case Having Taxpayers Subsidize the Specialist Is a First in Orange County—and Maybe the Nation," *Orlando Sentinel*, January 11, 1996, A-1.

16. Ibid.

17. Joseph DuRocher, personal interview with the author, April 25, 2002.

18. *Florida Trend*, April 1996.

19. I interviewed Tim Anderson in the Orange County Jail on five occasions during the months preceding his trial.

20. Gerald Shields, "Boxer Faces the Fight of His Life," *Orlando Sentinel*, February 11, 1006, A-1.

21. Gerald Shields, "Grand Jury Indicts Ex-Bower in Slaying of Promoter Parker; Tim Anderson Had Accused Rick 'Elvis' Parker of Poisoning Him During a Fight in 1992," *Orlando Sentinel*, May 25, 1995, D-3.

22. Gerald Shields, "Boxer Faces the Fight of His Life," *Orlando Sentinel*, February 11, 1996, A-1.

23. Ibid.

24. WESH-TV, Channel 2, NBC.

25. File letter.

26. Gerald Shields, "More Parties in Court Find Image Counts; Specialists Said Spinning Defendant's Images to the Media Is a Critical Tool in the Court of Public Opinion," *Orlando Sentinel*, June 21, 1996.

27. Gerald Shields, "Jury Misled at Ex-Boxer's Murder Trial? If Jurors Had Known Tim Anderson Would Get Life Without Parole, the Verdict May Have Been Different, a Juror Says," *Orlando Sentinel*, July 26, 1996, C-1.

28. Gerald Shields, "More Parties in Court Find Image Counts; Specialists Said Spinning Defendant's Images to the Media Is a Critical Tool in the Court of Public Opinion," *Orlando Sentinel*, June 21, 1996.

29. Ibid.

30. Joseph DuRocher, personal interview with the author, April 25, 2002.

Chapter 5

1. Dr. Thomas O'Conner, telephone interview with the author, February 13, 2006.

2. Ibid.

3. David L. Hudson, Jr., "'Son of Sam' Laws: Overview," www.firstamendmentcenter.com, accessed February 26, 2006.

4. Ibid.

5. David L. Hudson, Jr., telephone interview with the author, February 13, 2006.

6. *Seres v. Lerner*, "Nevada High Court Strikes Down 'Son of Sam' Law," www.jimmylerner.com, February 26, 2006.

7. KariSable.com, accessed January 11, 2006.

8. Roger Roy, "Gainesville Police May Be Closing In," *Orlando Sentinel*, August 30, 1990, A-1.

9. Marisa J. Porto, Radonna Long and John A. Nagy, "Suspect's Bond: $1 Million, Brevard Teen Named in UF Slaying Probe," *Florida Today*, September 1, 1990.

10. Jim Leusner, "'It's Such a Horrible Way to Die': History Will Treat This as a Successful Investigation," *Orlando Sentinel*, August 25, 1991, A-1.

11. Donald A. Lykkebak, telephone interview with the author, February 9, 2006.

12. WESH, WFTV and WKMG.

13. Jim Leusner, "Tape Shows Humphrey 'As He Is Today,'" *Orlando Sentinel*, August 28, 1991, A-1.

14. Ibid.

15. I saved one example in my files: Gary Kane, Cox News Services, "Gainesville Killings Suspect Tries to Soften His Image," *Birmingham Post-Herald*, September 5, 1991, A-9.

16. "Makeover of a Monster," *A Current Affair*, aired in November 1991.

17. Lenard Saffir, *Power Public Relations*, 1992 (NTC Business Books, Lincoln wood, IL), pp. 144–145.

18. Sister Helen Prejan, *The Death of Innocents: A Eyewitness Account of Wrongful Executions* (Vintage Books, New York, 2005).

19. Donald A. Lykkebak, telephone interview with the author, February 9, 2006.

20. George Humphrey, telephone interview with the author, March 13, 2006, 8:30 p.m., EST.

Chapter 6

1. Stephen Bainbridge, "Run Away, Jury," www.tscdaily.com, accessed March 1, 2006.

2. Ibid.

3. *CBS Early Morning Show*, June 26, 2002.

4. www.cbsnews.com/stories/2002/06/26/national/printable513464.shtml.

5. "Larry King Live," December 20, 2003.

6. Gary Sussman, "www.entertainmentweekly.com" recapped the Barbara Walters interview on November 6, 2003.

7. Lenard Saffir, telephone interview with the author, March 3, 2006.

8. Chris Smith, "Can This Man Save Martha," *New York Magazine*, December 15, 2003.

9. Ibid.

10. Ibid.

11. www.savemartha.com; www.marthtalks.com.

12. Alison Gendar and Greg B. Smith, "Martha Juror's Regret," *Daily News* April 14, 2004.

13. Ibid.

14. The Associated Press; Text of Martha Stewart's Statement outside the Courthouse, www.boston.com, accessed February 16, 2006.

15. Ibid.

16. Krysten Crawford, "Martha, Out and About," CNN/Money.com, March 4, 2005, 3:15 p.m. EST.

17. U.S. Securities and Exchange Commission Press Release, 2003-34.

18. Ben White and Carrie Johnson, "Top Enron Officials' Trial Begins Today: Firms' Collapse Sparked Crackdown," *Washington Post*, January 30, 2006.

19. *PR Newswire*, November 9, 2003.

20. John Helyar, "The Man Who Saved Richard Scrushy," *Fortune*, July 25, 2005.

21. www.Business Week.com, accessed January 20, 2006.

22. Greg Farrell, "Former HealthSouth CEO Scrushy Turns Televangelist," *USA Today*, September 26, 2004.

23. John Helyar, "The Insatiable King Richard," *Fortune*, July 7, 2003.

24. John Helyar, "The Man Who Saved Richard Scrushy," *Fortune*, July 25, 2005.

25. "Scrushy Denies Role in Fraud," *Birmingham News*, October 13, 2003.

26. Ibid.

27. Associated Press, January 19, 2006.

28. Brian Grow, *Business Week Online*, January 20, 2006.

29. Ibid.

30. Jay Reeves, "Writer Claims HealthSouth CEO Scrushy Bought Favorable Press Coverage during Fraud Trial," Associated Press, January 19, 2006.

31. John Helyar, "The Insatiable King Richard," *Fortune*, July 7, 2003.

32. Richard.Edleman, "Enough Already," www.Richard.Edleman.com, Blog, accessed January 20, 2006.

33. Dan Ackman, "Richard Scrushy, Still Uncharged, Is Unfrozen," www.Forbes.com, accessed February 17, 2006.

34. John Helyar, "The Man Who Saved Richard Scrushy," *Fortune*, July 25, 2005.

35. Ben White and Carrie Johnson, "Top Enron Officials' Trial Begins Today: Firms' Collapse Sparked Crackdown," *Washington Post*, January 30, 2006, A-3.

36. John Helyar, "The Man Who Saved Richard Scrushy," *Fortune*, July 25, 2005.

37. Scott Pelley, *60 Minutes*, March 13, 2005.

38. Alexei Barrionuevo, *New York Times*, April 24, 2006, C-1.

39. Greg Farrell, *USA Today*, June 28, 2005.

Chapter 7

1. See www.nacdl.org/public.nsf/gideonannniversary/news05.

2. Editorial, *New York Times*, March 21, 2003.

3. Bill Rankin, *Atlanta Journal-Constitution*, March 24, 2003.

4. Editorial, *New York Times*, March 21, 2003.

5. "Cop Shoots Squeegee Man Critically Hurt in BX Face-Off" was the headline, *Daily News*, June 15, 2006.

6. "Off-Duty Officer Shoots Man on Freeway," *New York Times*, June 15, 2006.

7. Steve Dunleavy, "Hero Officer vs. a Lowlife, You Choose," *New York Post*, June 16, 1998.

8. Blaine Harden, "Off-Duty N.Y. Officer Accused in Shooting Wounding of Squeegee Man Reflects Official Tolerance of Brutality, Minority Groups Charge," *Washington Post*, June 16, 1998, A-2.

9. www.pbs.org/brothermen/higgins.html.

10. *El Diario* ran a prominent article on the Reid case on June 19, 1998, Juan Soto Bouzas, "Tormento del hombre baleado por policia."

11. Michael Cooper, "Squeegee Man Gives Account of Shooting by Police Officer," *The New York Times,* June 19, 1998, B-1.

12. Dan Morrison and Graham Rayman, "Witness Describes Squeegee Shooting," *Newsday*, June 19, 1998.

13. Ibid.

14. Alice McQuilian, "Squeegee Man to Kin: Why?" *Daily News*, June 19, 1998.

15. Patrick O'Shaughnesy, "Squeegee Man Goes Home," *Daily News*, June 28, 1998.

16. Ibid.

17. Bryan Virasami, "Squeegee Man Tells His Side," *Newsday*, June 19, 1998.

18. Adam Miller and Tom Topousis, "Suffering Squeegee Man: I've Been 'Living a Nightmare' Since the Shooting," *New York Post*, June 29, 1998.

19. Michael Cooper, "Officer Acquitted in Squeegee Man's Shooting," *New York Times*, July 9, 1991, B-1

20. Anthony Ramirez, "Metro Briefing," *New York Times*, June 16, 2000.

Chapter 8

1. Paul Holmes, *PR Week*, August 4, 2003.

2. Documents, www.courttv.com, accessed January 29, 2006.

3. Editorial, *Orlando Sentinel*, February 28, 1990.

4. Anita Chabria, *PR Week*, October 20, 2003.

5. "Judge Dismisses Kobe Bryant Case," www.courttv.com, accessed January 15, 2006. September 1, 2004.

6. Anita Chabria, *PR Week*, October 20, 2003.

7. Paul Holmes, *PR Week*, August 4, 2003.

8. Anita Chabria, *PR Week*, October 20, 2003

9. Anita Chabria, *PR Week*, October 20, 2003.

10. Paul Holmes, *PR Week*, August 4, 2003.

11. Mark O'Mara, telephone interview with the author, March 29, 2006.

Chapter 9

1. Candace Rondeaux, "No Prison Time in Fatal Hit-Run," *St. Petersburg Times*, November 5, 2005, A-1.

2. Barry Cohen, telephone interview with the author, March 2006, 9:45 a.m., EST.

3. Bruce Vielmetti, *St. Petersburg Times*, June 18, 1989, 6B.

4. Ibid.

5. Mark Journey, "Doctor Arrested in Boating Accident That Killed 4 Teens," *St. Petersburg Times*, August 9, 1989, 1-A.

6. Bruce Vielmetti, *St. Petersberg Times*, Jun 18, 1989, 6B.

7. Thomas French, Christopher Goffard, and Jamie Thompson, "Choreography: Part Two Series: The Hard Road: Inside the Jennifer Porter Case," *St. Petersburg Times*, November 14, 2005, p. 1.

8. Ibid.

9. Ibid.

10. Judy Hill, telephone interview with the author, March 15, 2006, 6:15 p.m., EST.

11. Ibid.

12. Barry Cohen, telephone interview with the author, March 21, 2006, 8:45 a.m., EST.

13. Dr. Barbara Engle, telephone interview with the author, March 8, 2006, 6:00 p.m., EST.

14. Ibid.

15. Thomas French, Christopher Goffard, and Jamie Thompson, "Choreography: Part Three of the Series: The Hard Road: Inside the Jennifer Porter Case," *St. Petersburg Times*, November 16, 2005, p. 1.

16. Bill Maxwell, "Do We Really Know What We Would Do?" *St. Petersburg Times*, May 1, 2004, p. 1.

17. Thomas French, Christopher Goffard, and Jamie Thompson, "Choreography: Part One of the Series: The Hard Road: Inside the Jennifer Porter Case," *St. Petersburg Times*, November 13, 2005, p. 1.

18. Ibid. Thomas French, Christopher Goffard, Jamie Thompson, "Choreography: Part Five of the Series: The Hard Road: Inside the Jennifer Porter Case," *St. Petersburg Times*, November 18, 2005, p. 1.

19. Ibid.

20. *Orlando Sentinel*, September 23, 1993, B-1.

21. Beth Taylor, *Orlando Sentinel*, August 23, 1995.

22. *Sanford Herald*, August 23, 1994.

23. Beth Taylor, *Orlando Sentinel*, August 9, 1994, C-3.

24. Ibid.

25. Ibid.

26. Gary Taylor, "Woman Who Killed Boyfriend to Go Free, Michele Roger of Oviedo Was Granted Clemency in a Last Ditch Bid. Claimed She Was the Victim of Abuse," *Orlando Sentinel*, January 5, 1999, D-1.

27. Mary Brooks, "Boy's Mom: Dentist Still Unpunished for Slapping Her Son Should Have Led to a Charge of Battery against Dr. Guy, a Longwood Woman Says," *Orlando Sentinel*, May 8, 1996, B-3.

28. Fred Barnes, telephone interview with the author, March 6, 2006.

29. Moria Baily, "Dentists Wooing Patients with Marketing Magic," *Orlando Sentinel*, June 25, 1987 E-1.

30. Mary Brooks, "Dentist Says Slapping Accusations Exaggerated," *Orlando Sentinel*, May 11, 1996, C-3.

Chapter 10

1. http://www.cnn.com/EVENTS/year_in_review/us/smith.html.

2. www.teleplex.net/shi/smith/photos/photos.html, photo caption, photo by Mike Bonner, *Spartanburg Herald Journal*, July 20, 1995.

3. Timothy Roshe, "Andrea Yates: More to the Story," *Time*, March 18, 2002.

4. Ed Bradley, Interview with Russell Yates, *60 Minutes*, CBS, December 9, 2001.

5. "Judge Belinda Hill, The Gag Order," http://www.yateskids.com, accessed January 15, 2006.

6. Brian Wice, telephone interview with the author, March 17, 2006.

7. Ibid.

8. George Parnham, telephone interview with the author, July 28, 2006, 2:15 p.m., EDT.

9. S.K. Bardwell, Mike Glenn, Ruthrendon, Miriam Garcia, and Lisa Teachey, "Mom Details Drownings of 5 Kids / Eldest Fled, Was Dragged Back to Tub," *Houston Chronicle*, June 22, 2001.

10. Ibid.

11. George Parnham, telephone interview with the author, July 28, 2006, 2:15 p.m., EDT.

12. Terri Langford, "Rusty Yates' Actions Puzzle Acquaintance," www.houstonchronicle.com, posted March 18, 2006.

13. Ed Mallett, telephone interview with the author, March 24, 2006, 2:45 p.m., EST.

14. Ibid.

15. Carol Christian, "Lawyers Seek Equal Public Commentary in Yates Case," www.houstonchronicle.com, December 19, 2001.

16. Lisa Teachey, "Yates' Words Are Limited by Gag Order/Briefing Permitted to Tell of Fund," *Houston Chronicle*, August 8, 2001, p. 29.

17. Brian Wice, telephone interview with the author, March 17, 2006.

18. Ibid.

19. "Mother Says She Thought about Killing for Months," *Dallas Morning News*, June 23, 2001.

20. Author, "Final Witness: Yates Was Psychotic 'She Wasn't Feeling Anything,'" *The Dallas Morning News*, March 12, 2002.

21. Lee Hancock, "Yates May Be Declared Competent, Brother Says/Mother Accused in Kids' Drownings Responding to Psychiatric Treatment," *The Dallas Morning News*, August 31, 2001.

22. www.houston chronicle.com.

23. "Yates' Attorneys Won't Seek Release / Woman to remain in Prison after Court Overturns Convictions," www.cnn.com, posted January 6, 2005.

24. George Parnham, Personal interview with the author, July 28, 2006, 2:15 p.m., EDT.

25. Brian Wice, telephone interview with the author, March 17, 2006.

26. "Newspaper: Mother Describes for Police How She Killed Her Kids," www.courttv.com, posted June 22, 2001, 10:00 a.m., EST.

27. Ibid.

28. http://www.yatescase.org.

29. Jennifer Bard, "Test of a Just Society: We Have 2nd Chance to Do Right by Yates," *Houston Chronicle*, July 16, 2006.

30. Brian Wice, telephone interview with the author, July 28, 2006, 12:30 p.m., EDT.

31. CNN.com Wednesday, July 26, 2006; Posted and viewed, 4:56 p.m. EDT.

32. George Parnham, telephone interview with the author, July 28, 2006, 2:15 p.m., EDT.

33. Editorial opinion, "Time to Talk," *Houston Chronicle*, March 22, 2006, B-8.

34. Editorial opinion, "District Attorney," *Houston Chronicle*, October 18, 2004, B-8.

35. NBC, *Today Show*, Interview with Matt Lauer, July 21, 2006, 7:30 a.m., EDT.

36. Ibid.

Chapter 11

1. Ed Hinshaw, NBC, WTMJ-TV, Tuesday, March 24, 1992.

2. Willard Techmeier, telephone interview with the author, April 5, 2006, 5:45 p.m., EST.

3. Andy Newman, "Multimillion-Dollar Settlement of Ferry-Crash Lawsuit Evaporates," *The New York Times*, March 21, 2006.

4. Ibid.

5. Ibid.

6. www.amazon.com.

7. www.usinfo.state.com.

8. www.mediatrust.org.

9. www.ncsu.edu/news/homepage/guide.htm.

10. Missouri Library.

11. Leonard Saffir, *Power Public Relations*, NTC Business Books, 1996.

12. Ibid. "From Lawsuits to Murder Trials: PR and the Scales of Justice," pp. 133–147.

13. Ibid, p. 142.

14. James F. Haggerty, Esq. "*In the Court of Public Opinion*," p. 98.

15. Douglas Martin, "Barbara Gamarekian, 78, Times Reporter, Is Dead," *New York Times*, February 3, 2004.

16. www.mediawatch.com.

17. Gerald Shields, "More Parties in Court Find Image Counts; Specialists Said Spinning Defendant's Images to the Media Is a Critical Tool in the Court of Public Opinion," *Orlando Sentinel*, June 21, 1996.

18. Bob Levenson, discussion with the author about a planned press conference before a case was filed in 1995.

19. Ellen Pollack, Deputy Law Director, *Wall Street Journal*, quoted at a conference on media law.

20. Tom Wicker, *On Press*, Viking, New York, 1978

21. This advice, as are most of the recommendations in this Chapter 11, is taken from my seminar notes. I also acknowledge the input of my friend and colleague, Jerry Klein, a former reporter and assignment editor in radio and TV who currently works in the University of Central Florida, Department of Media Services.

22. http://caselaw.lp.findlaw.com/scripts/getcase.pl?court=US&vol=501&invol=663.

23. Ralph L. Holsinger and John Paul Dilts, *Media Law*, 4th ed. (McGraw-Hill Companies, Inc., New York, 1997).

24. John Dilts, telephone interview with the author, March 30, 2006, 10:00 a.m., EST.

Chapter 12

1. Ken Auletta, *New Yorker Magazine*, New York, October 10, 2005, p. 60.

2. Tamer El-Ghobashy, William Sherman and Alison Gendar, "DNA Test Fails to Link Ex-Con. But Probers Insist Other 'Good Evidence,'" *Daily News*, March 9, 2006, p. 5.

3. *CBS4 Boston*, March 23, 2006.

4. Nancie L. Katz, Jonathan Lemire and Corky Siemasko, "He Can't Look Family in the Eye," *Daily News*, March 24, 2006, A-1.

5. "Speak No Evil, Hear No Evil," *The News Media & the Law*, Fall 2003 (Vol. 27, No. 4, p. 7 cover story).

6. James Brosnahan, telephone interview with the author, March 7, 2006, 6:10 p.m., EST.

7. Frank Lindh, Commonwealth Club, San Francisco, www. alternet.org., accessed January 2006.

8. Ibid.

9. James Brosnahan, telephone interview with the author, March 7, 2006, 6:10 p.m., EST.

10. Ibid.

11. Ibid.

12. Ibid.

13. See note 7.

14. Ibid.

15. ww.justia.us/us/501/1030/case.html.

Index

About the Author

MARGARET "MARTI" A. MACKENZIE is a pioneer in managing media relations for lawyers and their accused clients. In 1987, she founded Professional Profiles Inc., a public relations firm that specializes in court-related work, especially high-profile criminal trials and civil lawsuits. A history of the firm can be found on her Web site www.lawyerpr.com.

The granddaughter of a former journalist and public relations man, she has been an advocate for the unjustly accused ever since her stint as an executive director of the ACLU in Mississippi in the late 1970s and early 1980s.

Mackenzie has taught her media relations seminar, "Lawyers & the Media: Skill for the New Century," for Continuing Legal Education credit to bar associations, private law firms and at conventions of federal and state public defenders. She has spoken about the value of effective media relations in capital murder cases at death penalty conferences. She is the only media specialist in the nation to have been hired by a public defender to assist in a capital murder case, her fee paid by the county government. She has spoken before numerous professional groups, including the Florida Women's Lawyers Association, Criminal Defense Lawyers of America and the Association for Journalism and Mass Communication on topics of managing controversy and media relations skills.

Mackenzie has also conducted media training for university deans and vice-presidents on controversial issues management and how to deal with ambush interviews by the media. She has written articles on the importance of media relations and marketing for the legal professional in industry publications including the *Journal of the National Association for Law Firm Marketing Professionals*. Early in her career, she won awards for Best Public Relations Campaigns for the American Arbitration Association and for her work with criminal defense lawyers from the Central Florida Press Club. Marti Mackenzie is a master of lawyer PR and media relations on the courthouse steps and behind the scenes of high-profile cases.